Teacher's Edition
Level A

Kaleidoscope

An Intervention Program

Units 1–3

Columbus, OH • Chicago, IL • Redmond, WA

The **McGraw·Hill** Companies

Contributing Author

Michael Milone
Assessment Specialist

Program Reviewers

Carol Ball
Oregon, OH

Charlene Demidovich
Lakeland, FL

Janice Webb
Pensacola, FL

Trisha Callella
Los Alamitos, CA

Samantha Fuhrey
Oxford, GA

Tanya Yosanovich
Los Alamitos, CA

Linda Carle
Vinton, VA

Marguerite Sequin
Hartford, CT

Amy Demos
Los Alamitos, CA

Lisa Thaxton
Lewis Center, OH

Acknowledgments

Grateful acknowledgment is given to publishers and copyright owners for permissions granted to reprint selections from their publications. All possible care has been taken to trace ownership and secure permission for each selection included. In case of any errors or omissions, the Publisher will be pleased to make suitable acknowledgments in future editions.

www.sra4kids.com

 SRA

Send all inquiries to:
SRA/McGraw-Hill
8787 Orion Place
Columbus, OH 43240-4027

Printed in the United States of America.

ISBN 0-07-584135-5

4 5 6 7 8 9 RRW 09 08 07 06 05

The McGraw-Hill Companies

Program Authors

Carl Bereiter

•

Joe Campione

•

Iva Carruthers

•

Jan Hirshberg

•

Anne McKeough

•

Michael Pressley

•

Marsha Roit

•

Marlene Scardamalia

•

Gerald H. Treadway, Jr.

Introduction

Purpose

Kaleidoscope is designed to help students who are performing two or more years below their designated grade levels develop the skills they need to read with fluency and understanding. In order to achieve this goal, *Kaleidoscope* provides teachers with instruction in decoding, fluency, comprehension, dictation and spelling, grammar and mechanics, and writing.

How Does It Work?

Based on the proven strengths and pedagogy of the *SRA/Open Court Reading* program, *Kaleidoscope* takes the essence of *SRA/Open Court Reading* and condenses and intensifies the instruction in order to deliver two years of reading instruction in one year. The majority of students should be back on track in their grade-level materials within the first year of use, assuming that students receive at least two hours of intensive reading instruction per day.

Students entering *Kaleidoscope* are given a diagnostic Placement Assessment. This assessment identifies students' greatest areas of concern and weakness. Using this as a guide, students are placed in the appropriate level (A–E) of the program. A corresponding Exit Assessment can be administered at any time during the year depending on students' progress.

Areas of Concentration

- Phonemic Awareness (Level A)
- Phonics, Decoding, and Fluency (Levels A–B)
- Word Study—roots, affixes, syllabication, word structure, and so on (Levels C–E)
- Vocabulary Development (Levels A–E)
- Comprehension Skills and Strategies (Levels A–E)
- Writing (Levels A–E)

In addition the supplementary *Kaleidoscope* workbooks contain basic lessons that are easily integrated with the daily lessons.

Program Structure

Kaleidoscope consists of five overlapping levels that are designed to meet the needs of all struggling readers. The level of difficulty of the reading and of the skills gradually increases over time. The levels overlap to ensure that students receive the review and support they need to succeed. The levels of the program are as follows:

Program Level	Reading Grade Level
Level A	0–2
Level B	1–3
Level C	2–4
Level D	3–5
Level E	4–6

There are six units at each level. Each unit consists of thirty daily lessons.

Program Components

Teacher's Editions

Teacher's Edition
Teacher's Edition Level E
Teacher's Edition Level D
Teacher's Edition Level C
Teacher's Edition
Teacher's Edition Level B
Teacher's Edition
Teacher's Edition Level A

Kaleidoscope
An Open Court Intervention Program
Units 1–3

Student Readers

Kaleidoscope

Additional materials:

Decodable Stories and Comprehension Skills
Language Arts
Home Connection
Transparencies
Placement Guide
Assessment Guide
Cumulative Folders
Sound/Spelling Wall Cards
Individual Sound/Spelling Cards
High-Frequency Word Cards
Sound/Spelling Card Stories (Levels A & B)
  (CD/Audiocassette)
Leveled Classroom Libraries
Reader Story Recordings
  (CD/Audiocassette)

Lesson Structure

LESSON

Phonemic Awareness

Increases students' understanding of individual sounds, word parts, syllables, and phonemes.

● Listening Game conducted

Word Study

Engages students in phonics, fluency, blending, and spelling activities.

● Word Play conducted (Units 1–3)
● Sight Words introduced
● Blending words and sentences introduced
● Writing activity assigned
● Oral Language activity conducted
● Word lines dictated

Building Fluency

Provides practice for students to read words and sentences.

● Decodable Story assistance provided

LESSON ❷

Before Reading

Prepares students to read the selection.

● Prior knowledge activated
● Background Information provided
● Selection Vocabulary discussed
● Selection previewed

During Reading

Introduces students to reading comprehension strategies that allows them to read and interact with the selection.

● Comprehension Strategies introduced
● Selection read to students
● Comprehension Strategies modeled
● Vocabulary skill introduced
● Writing activity assigned

LESSON ③

Phonemic Awareness

Expands students' ability to separate words into sounds.

- Segmentation activity conducted

Word Study

Engages students in phonics, fluency, blending, and spelling.

- Word Play conducted (Units 1–3)
- Blending words and sentences introduced
- Writing activity assigned
- Oral Language activity conducted
- Word lines dictated

Building Fluency

Allows students to apply, review, and reinforce their expanding knowledge of sound/spellings.

- Decodable Story assistance provided

LESSON ④

Rereading the Selection

Introduces students to comprehension skills that will give them a more complete understanding of the selection.

- Comprehension Skill introduced
- Selection reread to students (Units 1–3)
- Students reread selection (Units 4–6)
- Grammar skill introduced
- Writing activity assigned

After Reading

Encourages students to choose books and read independently.

- Independent Reading discussed

LESSON ⑤

Assessment

Provides students with an opportunity to exhibit what they have learned.

- Weekly assessment administered
- Students' progress assessed

Ending the Lesson

Increases students' understanding of the selection by providing selection review and wrap-up activities.

Introduction to Assessment

Students for whom *Kaleidoscope* has been designed have not yet become fluent readers. In order to help these students build confidence and provide teachers with useful information, the assessment components of *Kaleidoscope* vary from traditional assessments in several ways.

- The assessments include both multiple-choice and open-ended questions that review a range of literal and inferential skills.

- For the first three units in each level, teachers will read the questions aloud while students silently follow along. For the last three units, students will independently read the questions and answer choices.

- Teachers should spend extra time helping students understand the questions before students attempt to answer them.

- In certain circumstances, teachers should help students formulate open-ended responses or assist students in finding the part of a reading selection to which a question refers.

- When teachers review the answers with students, students should be given an opportunity to correct their mistakes. They will realize that making mistakes is an important part of learning.

- The last instructional day of the week is intended for assessment. The assessment process is enriched with instructional support from teachers, and students are encouraged to interact with the teacher and one another.

- The unit assessment, which reviews the skills that were featured in a given unit, is an ongoing process that takes place during the course of instruction rather than at the end of the unit.

- The performance items that are part of the unit assessment are completed by students with the support of their teacher and their classmates.

- The culminating activity at the end of each unit includes some assessment exercises for students to complete at that time. It also includes the opportunity for students to share the performance assessments they completed earlier in the unit.

By designing assessment activities that are integrated into instruction and that include a significant interaction component, students will be encouraged to assume greater responsibility for their learning. They also may feel less anxious about assessment and will be more willing to take the risks necessary to become capable readers.

At the end of each selection, the *Teacher's Edition* provides specific suggestions about how to conduct the assessments for that lesson. In some cases, it will also recommend how to begin engaging students in the unit assessment. It is important that students begin the unit assessment during the course of lesson instruction. This early start will give students the time and support they need to complete the unit assessments successfully. It will also reduce the amount of time required for the unit assessment, which takes place on the same day as the final lesson assessment. Moreover, when students complete the unit assessment in stages, they will have more opportunities during the time set aside for assessment to share their work with other students, be recognized for their accomplishments, and reinforce the efforts of their peers.

Getting Started

Getting Started gives you an opportunity to get to know your students and to evaluate what they know and what they need to know in order to be successful. Although each student placed in the *Kaleidoscope* program will have had some diagnostic testing, Getting Started will allow you to understand each student's personal strengths. By making no assumptions about what your new students know or do not know, both you and your students will have the best opportunity to build on previously learned skills and learn new ones.

Getting Started will give you and your students:

● time to get to know each other.
● time to assess areas of strength and need.
● time to set up your classroom to reap the most benefit from the *Kaleidoscope* program.
● time to ascertain which of your students will need extra help in remembering prior instruction and which never had such instruction.
● time to prepare for the challenges of meeting the needs of each student.

Getting Started is designed to take approximately five days. Taking the time at the beginning to get to know your students' prior knowledge and needs will save much time and effort as you progress through the program.

Some of your students may have had no phonics instruction. The review of the *Sound/Spelling Cards,* along with discussions of phonics and opportunities to hear students read, should make you aware of the phonics instruction these students have had and how intense their phonics instruction will need to be.

Once you start the regular course of instruction, all students will have an opportunity to learn the common sounds and spellings of the English language. This review will take the first half of the program and should assure success for all students.

Organizing Your Classroom

Phonics

Put the *Sound/Spelling Cards* on display in numerical order in a prominent place in the classroom where all students will be able to see them and use them for reference. Since you and your students will need to point out specific cards, they should be placed low enough to make this possible but high enough for all students to have an unobstructed view.

The *Sound/Spelling Cards* should remain on display at all times. They are an invaluable tool for students in both their reading and writing.

Reading Center

Provide as many books in addition to the *Kaleidoscope* library as possible for your classroom Reading Center. Encourage students to bring in books they have enjoyed and would like to share with their classmates.

Take time on a regular basis to listen to students as they read aloud their favorite stories and books. Listening to students read books they have selected for themselves will give you insight into their tastes in reading materials, their opinion of their reading ability, and their reading progress.

Writing Center

Set up a Writing Center. The center should contain common materials students can use to write and illustrate their work such as pencils, crayons, pens, white paper, colored paper, old magazines, scissors, and staplers.

Listening Center

The *Student Reader* selections are available on audiocassettes and CDs. Include additional audiobooks in the center. Provide one or two audiocassette recorders or CD players that work both with and without earphones. This way individual students may listen to selections without disturbing the rest of the class. You will also be able to play the selections for the whole class if you choose.

Getting Started: Daily Lessons

The following Getting Started lessons are presented in a different format than the remaining lessons in the program. You should present the Getting Started lessons in a relaxed, getting-to-know-you atmosphere. Both you and your students should view this time as a period of discovery.

Day **1**

Getting Acquainted

Have students introduce themselves to each other. After students have introduced themselves, clap out syllables of some of their names. Draw students' attention to the fact that longer names usually have more syllables. Let students know that all words have parts, or syllables. Some words have one syllable, such as the name *Ann*. Others may have many syllables, such as *E-liz-a-beth*. Give students a few minutes to compare the number of syllables in the first and last names of different students.

Reading

To activate students' background knowledge, have them discuss what they know about reading. List their comments on the board or on paper.

Choose one of your favorite stories to read aloud to the class. Select a book that will take a few days to read. During this reading, you will not be formally introducing reading comprehension strategies. However, as you are reading encourage students to stop and ask for clarification of any unfamiliar words or ideas and to ask questions about the story. Remind students that questions often start with *Who, What, Why, Where* or *How.* You may want to write these words on the board as a reminder.

Have students help each other clarify words or ideas that confused them. When you come to the end of today's reading, have students retell or summarize what you read. Discuss the idea of making a prediction, and encourage students to predict what will happen in the next part of the story. Have them give reasons for their prediction.

By hearing how students summarize, ask questions, predict, make connections, and clarify, you can evaluate how much students remember about strategies from past years.

Writing—Prewriting

A complete description of the writing process is in the appendix. Discussing the writing process will help you evaluate your students' understanding of writing. Based on your students' responses, proceed with the week's writing activities. Keep in mind that all activities will not be appropriate for all students.

The most important thing good writers do is think before they write. They think about what they know, what they want to write about, and whether they need to get more information about their topic. Have students talk about reading, problems they have had, favorite stories they have read, and so on. Make a list of possible writing ideas, and keep it for tomorrow. Tell students to begin thinking about these ideas and that tomorrow you will review them and add any more ideas they have.

Day 2

Getting Acquainted

Ask students to give their names again, and have the class clap out the number of syllables in different names. Pair students, and have them write one positive statement about their partners on a piece of paper. You may need to model this. For example, *Elizabeth has a great smile.* Or, *Laval has blue eyes.* The positive statements should be short. Not only will this help students remember something about a fellow student, but they will be encouraged to make positive comments often.

Phonemic Awareness
Clapping Syllables

Discuss with students that words are made up of parts called *syllables.* Longer words usually have more syllables than shorter words. Give students words of varying length, and have them clap out the syllables. Once students have clapped out the word, write the word on the board and the number of syllables next to it. This procedure will help students see that longer words usually have more syllables. Possible words to use include:

cal·en·dar (3)	ball (1)
day (1)	bas·ket·ball (3)
syl·la·ble (3)	dog (1)
word (1)	hip·po·pot·a·mus (5)

Additional suggestions for teaching syllabication are included in the appendix.

Oral Blending: Syllables and Word Parts

Becoming aware of syllables and word parts is important for two reasons. First, it helps students appreciate the difference between words and syllables. Second, because syllables are easier to distinguish than individual sounds, syllable and word part blending is the first step in teaching students to become aware of the discrete units that make up speech (phonemes).

Oral blending activities should be quick and snappy. Do not let the activities drag.

Have students play a listening game to help them think carefully about how words sound. Tell them you have a list of words. You will say each word in two parts. They must listen carefully to discover what each word is. Read each word, pronouncing each part distinctly and pausing cleanly at the breaks indicated (. . .). Then ask students to tell you what the word is.

> **Teacher:** Dino . . . saur. What's the word?
> **Students:** dinosaur

Continue with these words:

cinna . . . mon   televi . . . sion   remem . . . ber
Septem . . . ber   alpha . . . bet   cucum . . . ber

If you choose, continue the game with similar words.

Reading

Have students summarize the part of the story you read yesterday. Discuss students' predictions, and then continue reading the story.

Writing—Drafting

Discuss with students the purposes of the Writing Center. Show students the different materials in the center: pencils, crayons, markers, pens, white paper, colored paper, old magazines, scissors, staplers, and a dictionary and thesaurus as reference tools.

Review the ideas for writing that students generated yesterday, and ask if there are new ideas they would like to add to the list. Explain that after writers think about what they might want to write, they begin writing a first draft. Tell students they do not have to worry about the draft being neat or perfect. Encourage students to skip a line between each line they write. This will give them room to make changes later. They will have a chance to rewrite their story after they have read it and made any changes. If students are having problems spelling a word, they can leave a blank, they can spell it as best they can, they can check the **Sound/Spelling Cards,** or they can ask a fellow student. The point of writing in Getting Started is for you to get a sense of students' knowledge of the writing process and of their writing skills, including spelling, grammar, and mechanics.

Have students select a topic from the list or one of their choosing, and if you feel they are ready, have them begin writing.

At the end of the writing time, have students put their drafts in their writing folders and either put their folders in their desks or in a file box in the Writing Center.

Day 3

Getting Acquainted

Have students work with a different partner and write a positive comment about that student. Then have partners read their comments to each other. As students are working on their comments, circulate around the room and conference with student pairs.

Phonemic Awareness

Rhyming

Tell students they are going to play a rhyming game. Invite volunteers to demonstrate rhyming by giving pairs of rhyming words such as *day/say* or *light/right*. Introduce the game, The Ship is Loaded with _____. You may want to have students sit in a circle. Have a ball or something students can toss. Start the game by saying, "The ship is loaded with cheese." Then roll the ball to a student who must produce a rhyme for the last word, *cheese* (for example, "The ship is loaded with peas."). After the student makes the rhyme, he or she returns the ball to you. Repeat the same rhyme the student made ("The ship is loaded with peas."), and roll the ball to a different student who will repeat the sentence substituting a different rhyming word for *peas*. Continue in this way until students have run out of rhymes for *cheese,* and then begin again with a new "cargo."

Suggested Rhymes:

The ship is loaded with cheese. (peas, fleas, trees, bees, keys, . . .)

The ship is loaded with logs. (dogs, hogs, frogs, . . .)

The ship is loaded with mats. (cats, rats, bats, hats, . . .)

The ship is loaded with stars. (cars, bars, jars, . . .)

Oral Blending: Syllables and Word Parts

Continue the exercise from yesterday with the following words.

baby-sit . . . er   ham . . . burger   air . . . port   air . . . plane

Segmentation: Restoring Initial Phonemes

This is a fun way for students to be introduced to segmenting, or isolating the sounds in words. You may want to use a puppet to help you with this exercise. Say a word, and have the puppet repeat the word, omitting the initial phoneme. For example,

Teacher: zip
Puppet: ip
Teacher: No, zzzzzip. You forgot the /z/.

After demonstrating, ask students to tell the puppet the sound it left out, and acknowledge the correction.

Teacher: zap
Puppet: ap
Teacher: Help the puppet. What did I say? What did it leave out?
Class: zzzap, /z/
Teacher: That's right, the whole word is *zap.*

Continue with the following words:

sea	seal	meat	sip	mitt
pip	nap	fit	ripple	zipper

Reading

Students have already learned about the Writing Center. Introduce the Reading Center today. In this center students will find books, magazines, newspapers, and other reading materials. Encourage students to bring in favorite books and share them in the center. Let students know they can select a book from the Reading Center whenever they have free time.

Discuss with students their favorite books or stories. Encourage students to explain what they like most about each story. After a few students have told about a favorite book or story, ask one of them to tell the story to the class.

Continue reading the story. Encourage students to stop and ask for clarification of unfamiliar words and to ask questions about the story if it is unclear.

Writing—Revising

During writing today, remind students they can use the center if they need any materials. Have students continue writing the stories they began yesterday. Hold conferences with students, and look for examples of stories with interesting ideas, creative topics, extended sentences, and so on. Remember the following:

● You do not have to meet with every student every day.
● Conferences should be brief.
● Do not take ownership of students' work.
● Encourage students to identify what is good and what problems they are having.
● Leave students with a positive comment.

After conferencing with students, have them revise their stories by making the changes you discussed. You may want to model how to use carets and deletion marks to show additions and subtractions from a piece.

Day ④
Phonemic Awareness
Oral Blending: Initial Consonant Sounds

Tell students you will help them practice putting the beginning sound with the rest of a word to make a whole word. Pronounce the initial consonant of each of the sample words, pausing slightly before saying the rest of the word. Students should then pronounce the whole word. The second part of each word gives a strong cue for students. For example:

> ***Teacher:*** /m/ . . . otorcycle
> ***Students:*** motorcycle

Use these words:

/l/ . . . ibrary	/s/ . . . entipede	/s/ . . . andwich
/m/ . . . ascot	/f/ . . . urniture	/m/ . . . orning

Segmentation: Restoring Initial Phonemes

Continue the puppet activity from yesterday. Say the word, and have the puppet repeat the word, omitting the initial consonant sound. Students should then say the complete word and tell what sound was omitted. Use the following words:

lips	split	grand	scale	bath
ring	sound	clip	crate	disk

Phonics

Students have probably noticed the **Sound/Spelling Cards** posted at the front of the room. Quickly go through the alphabet with students as you point to the letters at the top of each card. If any of your students are familiar with these cards, have them share what they know. Point out:

● *Letters can be capital or lowercase.* Be sure to remind students that capitals are used at the beginning of special names, such as a person's name. Have some students give their first name and then tell the capital letter that is at the beginning of it.

● *These are called **Sound/Spelling Cards**. They will help us connect sounds and spellings.*

● Have students name the cards they remember and the sounds associated with them. For example, *The sound the ball makes when Betty bounces it is /b/ /b/ /b/ /b/.* Some students may have been taught actions to go with the sounds. If they have, encourage them to demonstrate these actions.

● *There are vowels and consonants. The vowels are written in red, and the consonants are written in black.*

● Have students discuss why vowels are special: they can have more than one sound—usually long or short; long vowels can be spelled more than one way; sometimes vowels are spelled in a strange way—with a consonant such as *ow*.

● *Every word part or syllable in English has to have a vowel in it.* Write the following words on the board: *dog, help, bas-ket-ball, hip-po-pot-a-mus.* Have students clap out the number of syllables. Point out that if there is one syllable there is one vowel sound, if there are five syllables there are five vowel sounds.

● If students do not notice, point out that the vowels are not only in red, but that there are special color boxes to help them remember the vowels. The green box is for short vowels, the yellow box is for long vowels, and the blue box is for the vowels that have a strange name—diphthongs.

● *There are blanks with some of the letters. These blanks remind us that a letter needs be there. If it is a green box, it will be a short vowel.*

● *The **Sound/Spelling Cards** can be used to help us in writing. If you do not know how to spell a sound in a word, you can check the card.*

Do not be concerned if students are unable to remember everything or do not understand everything. All these points will be discussed as you systematically review the **Sound/Spelling Cards** during the first **Student Reader** lesson. The point of the Getting Started lessons is to acquaint students with the cards as a tool to help them in reading and writing.

Reading

If you have not completed the book you are reading to students, have volunteers summarize the part of the story you have read so far and predict what they think will come next. Then continue reading.

Writing—Proofreading

Students can begin proofreading a piece when they feel that it has been sufficiently revised. Remember, students should not be held responsible for skills they have not yet learned. Have students proofread their papers using the following checklist.

- Read each sentence.
- Does each sentence begin with a capital letter and end with correct punctuation?
- Are words missing from the sentence?
- Do you notice any misspelled words?

Day 5

Phonemic Awareness

Oral Blending: Final Consonant Sounds

In a variation of yesterday's activity, separate the final consonant from the first part of the word. These examples are simple for students to blend since the words are easily recognized before the final consonant is pronounced. Use the following words:

superma . . . /n/	astronau . . . /t/	elephan . . . /t/
sailboa . . . /t/	tremendou . . . /s/	telepho . . . /n/

Segmentation: Replacing Final Consonants

This activity advances students' awareness of the sounds of words by calling on them to replace final consonants. Use the puppet, and remind students that the puppet always plays games with words.

Teacher: soon
Puppet: soo
Teacher: /n/ You forgot the /n/. *Soon.*
Teacher: grab
Puppet: gra
Teacher: /b/ You forgot the /b/. *Grab.*

Continue the activity using the following words:

soup	loop	leap	beep
bake	bike	like	lake

Phonics

Review the Sound/Spelling Cards

Take a few minutes to review the information about the *Sound/Spelling Cards* you discussed in the previous lesson. This might include:

- *Each card represents a sound. The letter or letters at the bottom are called spellings—the way we write the sounds.*
- *There are vowels and consonants.*
- *Consonants are written in black, and vowels are written in red.*
- *Vowels are special, since every word or syllable in English needs to have a vowel.*
- *Vowels can have more than one sound.*
- *Short vowels have a green background; long vowels have a yellow background.*
- *Blank lines help us remember that a letter needs to go on the line.*

Introduce Sounds and Spellings

This lesson is designed to help students understand the purpose of the cards and how to use them. Once students understand how some of the cards are organized and used, they understand how all the cards are used. Then it is a matter of learning the specific sounds and spellings. Today you will focus on the consonants *b, m, s, t, n* and short *a*. These are Card 2—Ball, Card 13—Monkey, Card 19—Sausages, Card 20—Timer, Card 14—Nose, and Card 1—Lamb.

Begin with Card 2—Ball. Ask students what they already know about this card. This is a consonant, and they can tell this because it is a black letter. If students do not know the name of the card, tell them. Have students who remember the story about the ball share the story with the class. (The **Sound/Spelling Card Stories** are provided in the appendix and are also available on the **Sound/Spelling Card Stories Audiocassette/CD**.) Another way to remember the sound is to think about the sound a ball makes when it is bouncing /b/ /b/ /b/. Point to the *b* at the bottom of the card, and tell students the spelling for the /b/ sound is *b*. (Please note that using the term *spelling* helps students connect what they are learning about sounds to writing, specifically spelling. Also, as students review other sounds throughout the phonics review, there are many vowel sounds and some consonant sounds that are represented in print or spelled using more than one letter.) Review with students the name of the card, the sound it makes (/b/), and the spelling *b*. Repeat this procedure with the Monkey, Nose, Sausages, and Timer cards.

Review Short a

Point to the short *a* card, and have students share what they know about it. They can tell it is a vowel because it is in red, and it is a short vowel because of the green background. Short *a* makes the /a/ sound, and it is the sound you hear in the middle of the word *lamb*. Tell students the sound a lamb makes when it calls its mother is /a/ /a/ /a/, and the spelling is *a*. If any student remembers the lamb story, have them share the story with the class. Review the name of the card, the sound /a/, and the spelling *a*.

Getting Started

Blending

Blending is a strategy readers use to decipher unfamiliar words. The goal of blending is to give students a strategy for attacking or figuring out unfamiliar words, not to blend every single word. Blend the words on the board or on an overhead transparency.

Sound-by-Sound Blending

at	mat	sat	bat
am	Sam	man	tan

- Write the spelling of the first sound in the word. Point to the spelling, and have students say the sound. For example, write *a*, and ask for the /a/ sound.
- Write the second spelling, *t,* and ask for the /t/ sound.
- Move your finger from left to right under each spelling, and make a blending motion. Have students read the first word, *at*.
- Have students read the word again.

Blending provides an opportunity to develop vocabulary and build oral language naturally. Once students have read the word, call on a student to the use the word in a sentence and then extend the sentence. Encourage students to add their extensions in different places in the sentence, not just at the end.

Now blend the word *mat*.

- Write the spelling of the /m/ sound. Point to the spelling, and have students say the /m/ sound.
- Write the second spelling, *a*, and ask for the /a/ sound.
- Move your finger from left to right under each spelling, and make a blending motion. Have students blend through the vowel.
- Write the spelling for the /t/ sound *(t)*, and have students give the /t/ sound.
- Make the blending motion, and have students read the word *(mat)*.

Have a student use the word in a sentence and then extend the sentence.

Continue blending the remainder of the words sound by sound.

Give students the following clues, and have them find the word on the board or overhead transparency. *You can use this to play ball (bat); Find a word that rhymes with* mat *(sat or at); This is a name (Sam); This word rhymes with* tan *(man).*

xviii   Getting Started

Dictation and Spelling

The purpose of Dictation and Spelling is to give students a spelling strategy—to break a word into its component sounds and to write the spellings for the sounds. There are two kinds of dictation—sounds-in-sequence dictation and whole-word dictation. The two types differ mainly in the amount of help they give students in spelling the words. It is important to understand that Dictation and Spelling is not a test. It teaches students a strategy for spelling.

Dictation: tap   sat   rat   led

Give each student a sheet of paper. This lesson focuses on sound-in-sequence dictation using the following procedure.

- Pronounce the first word from the above list. Use the word in a sentence, and say the word again. Have students say the word.
- Tell students to think about the sounds they hear in the word. Ask, *What's the first sound in the word?*
- Have students say the sound.
- Point to the *Sound/Spelling Card,* and have students check the card and give the spelling.
- Continue with the remaining sounds until the word is spelled.

Once students have written the dictated word, have them proofread what they have written. Write the word on the board, or have a student write the word on the board. Have students check the spelling on their own papers. If the word is misspelled, have students circle the word and write it correctly, either above the word or next to it.

Dictate the remaining words in the same manner. Circulate around the room as students are writing the dictated words.

Reading

Invite more students to relate their favorite stories from books. Remind students to raise their hands and ask politely if they have questions about the story.

Finish reading to the class the book you chose, and then discuss it with the students. Make sure students ask for clarification if they need it. In your discussion, bring up topics such as character and setting to get an idea of how well students understand them.

Listening Center

Today introduce the Listening Center. If you have purchased the *Listening Library Audiocassettes* or *CDs,* tell students they will be available. In addition to listening to stories, students may record stories they create and share these stories with the class.

Writing—Publishing

Publishing is the process of bringing private writing to the reading public. Encourage students to share their stories with the class. Have them present their work in a way that makes it easy to read and understand.

As you proceed with the daily lessons, you may wish to extend the writing activities by guiding students through the writing process. A detailed description of the writing process is provided in the appendix.

Table of Contents

UNIT 1 Sharing Stories

UNIT 1 Sharing Stories

Table of Contents

UNIT 2 Kindness

Table of Contents

UNIT **3** Look Again

Overview

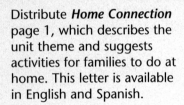
Unit Goals

Throughout the ***Kaleidoscope*** program, students will be introduced to a variety of reading and writing skills. In this unit students will

- develop phonemic awareness skills through oral blending and segmentation activities.
- learn to decode by being introduced to and reviewing the phonic elements: initial consonant sounds, /a/, /e/, /i/, /o/, /u/, /er/, /or/, /ar/.
- increase their proficiency in decoding and word–attack skills through practice with decodable text highlighting introduced phonic elements.
- build reading fluency through repeated reading of decodable text.
- expand their vocabulary through instruction and practice in using word structure.
- acquire an understanding of basic sentence structure by learning about simple sentences, end punctuation, and capitalization.
- improve reading comprehension by working with the comprehension strategies Making Connections, Asking Questions, Predicting, Visualizing, Monitoring and Clarifying, Monitoring and Adjusting Reading Speed, and Summarizing; and the comprehension skills Sequence, Author's Purpose, Reality and Fantasy, Cause and Effect, Main Idea and Details, and Drawing Conclusions.
- engage in daily writing activities related to the phonics and reading lessons.

Theme

Much of what we all know is passed on to us through sharing stories. The history of our families, the neighborhood culture, and our cultural heritage are all things that we learn about through listening to, telling, and reading stories. From the very youngest age, children are immersed in stories. Through listening to and participating in the telling of stories, they begin the process of understanding the world and their part in the world.

In this unit students will talk about stories, hear stories read to them, and tell their own stories.

Introducing the Unit

- Tell students they will be talking and reading about stories in this unit.
- Invite students to tell about stories they have read or heard that they particularly liked and why they liked them.
- Encourage students to bring to class stories they have read and enjoyed. Remind students to ask permission at home before they bring books to school.
- If students mention books they enjoyed but do not have, try to get copies from the school or local library.

Selection	Overview of Selection	Link to Theme
A From Rocks to Books	This piece of nonfiction describes what people wrote on before the invention of paper and how the invention of paper makes sharing stories much easier.	After the invention of paper, people could use books as a way to share ideas and stories.
B A Story for Pam	This humorous tale is about a little girl who keeps changing the bedtime story that her dad is telling her.	Many parents share stories with their children at bedtime.
C An Elephant Story	This selection tells of a boy and a girl who make up a silly story.	Sharing stories can be a way of sharing adventures.
D Keeping Secrets	This piece describes how people use codes to write secret messages.	Using codes is a way to share secret stories with others.
E Stories in the Sky	This piece of realistic fiction tells of a family who uses "sky pictures" to share stories.	People can use many different resources to tell stories.
F Kim Writes a Letter	Kim writes a letter to her Grandma and Grandpa to tell them about her new dog.	Many people love to share stories through letter writing.

CLASSROOM LIBRARY

Postcards to Paula

by Tracey E. Dils. SRA/McGraw-Hill, 1997.

Dawn writes postcards to Paula during her vacation at the lake.

Who Is on This Page?

by Jeff Putnam. SRA/McGraw-Hill, 1997.

A boy shares his family's photo album and the stories about each photo.

I Took My Frog to the Library

by Eric A. Kimmel. Viking Penguin, 1990.

The library is turned upside down when Bridgett brings her unusual pets to the library.

SELECTION A • **From Rocks to Books**

HOME CONNECTIONS

Distribute *Home Connection* page 3, which describes this week's classwork and suggests activities for families to do at home. This letter is available in English and Spanish.

Support Materials

LESSON 1
- Sound/Spelling Cards 1, 8, 16, 19, 20
- Decodable Stories and Comprehension Skills, p. 1
- Home Connection, p. 3
- High-Frequency Word Cards
- Sound/Spelling Card Stories Audiocassette/CD

LESSON 2
- Student Reader, pp. 2–3
- Language Arts, p. T2

LESSON 3
- Sound/Spelling Cards 8, 9, 16, 19, 20
- Decodable Stories and Comprehension Skills, p. 2
- High-Frequency Word Cards
- Sound/Spelling Card Stories Audiocassette/CD

LESSON 4
- Student Reader, pp. 2–3
- Transparencies 1, 2, 3
- Decodable Stories and Comprehension Skills, p. 75
- Language Arts, p. T1
- Listening Library Audiocassette/CD

LESSON 5
- Assessment Guide
- Student Reader, pp. 2–3

Teacher Focus	Student Participation
• Conduct Listening Game. • Conduct Word Play. • Introduce Sight Words, blending procedure, and Set 1 blending words and sentences. • Provide riddle clues. • Dictate word lines. • Assist students with decodable text. • Assign writing activity.	• Take part in Listening Game. • Take part in Word Play. • Read Sight Words. • Blend words and sentences. • Solve riddles. • Write dictated words and sentences. • Read a decodable story. • Complete writing activity.
• Activate Prior Knowledge and provide background information. • Introduce and discuss selection vocabulary. • Preview selection. • Introduce Comprehension Strategies—Asking Questions and Making Connections. • Read the selection to students. • Introduce vocabulary skill. • Assign writing activity.	• Contribute to class discussion. • Read and discuss vocabulary words. Complete selection vocabulary activity. • Browse the selection. • Follow along as selection is read. • Complete vocabulary skill activity. • Complete writing activity.
• Conduct Clapping Syllables in Names game. • Conduct Word Play. • Review blending procedure; introduce Set 2 blending words and sentences. • Provide riddle clues. • Dictate word lines. • Assist students with decodable text. • Assign writing activity.	• Participate in Clapping Syllables in Names game. • Take part in Word Play. • Blend words and sentences. • Solve riddles. • Write dictated words and sentences. • Read a decodable story. • Complete writing activity.
• Introduce Comprehension Skill—Sequence. • Reread and discuss the selection with students. • Discuss Independent Reading. • Assign writing activity. • Introduce grammar skill.	• Follow along as selection is read again. • Discuss the selection. • Select a book to take home and read. • Complete writing activity. • Complete grammar skill activity.
• Administer weekly assessments. • Assess students' progress.	• Complete lesson assessment.

Unit 1 • LESSON

1

OBJECTIVES

- Blend and break apart sounds in words.
- Read sight words.
- Participate in Word Play activity.
- Develop fluency by reading aloud.
- Apply decoding skills by reading *Unit 1, Decodable Story 1*.
- Develop writing skills by writing words and identifying sound/spellings.

MATERIALS

Sound/Spelling Cards:
1—Lamb
8—Hound
16—Popcorn
19—Sausages
20—Timer
Decodable Stories and Comprehension Skills, p. 1
Home Connection, p. 3
High-Frequency Word Cards
Sound/Spelling Card Stories Audiocassette/CD

Phonemic Awareness

The goal of phonemic awareness activities is to help students understand that spoken words are made up of smaller sounds—word parts, syllables, and phonemes. Learning this concept is important to reading success because of the systematic relationship between speech sounds and written letters. If students cannot hear and manipulate the individual sounds in spoken words, they usually have difficulty deciphering that relationship. Phonemic awareness is also important to students' spelling success. Students who understand that sounds and letters are related usually are able to attach the sounds to letters and spell words.

Oral blending and segmentation are complementary processes in developing phonemic awareness and in learning to read and write. Just as learning to blend smaller units of sound into words is essential to decoding, learning to segment, or break apart, words into smaller units of sound is essential to spelling.

Oral Blending

Tell students that they are already good at listening; they obviously understand words they hear. Then explain that to be really good readers and writers, they need to learn to listen even more closely—they need to be able to hear the separate sounds that make up words. Tell them that when they can hear the separate sounds, they can read and spell most words.

Listening Game: Word Parts and Syllables

Tell students that to help them hear sounds in words, you are going to play a listening game with them. You will say some words that they know, but you will say them in two parts. To discover what each word is, they must listen very carefully and put the two parts together. Use the following example:

Teacher: *Dino . . . saur. What's the word?*

Students: *dinosaur*

Read each of the following words, pronouncing each part distinctly and pausing clearly at the breaks indicated (. . .). Then ask students to tell you what the word is.

cinna . . . mon	alpha . . . bet
Septem . . . ber	ham . . . burger
whis . . . per	remem . . . ber
air . . . plane	cucum . . . ber
televi . . . sion	air . . . port

Pacing Phonemic Awareness
Phonemic awareness activities should be quick and snappy. Do not let these activities drag, and do not expect mastery before moving on to the day's next activity. Students' ability to master phonemic awareness varies greatly and is normal. Many students who do not catch on at first will learn how to respond by observing their classmates.

SELECTION A • **From Rocks to Books**

Word Study

In this section of the lesson, students work on phonics, fluency, blending, and spelling. Increasing students' ability to work smoothly with printed words is one of the primary goals of the *Kaleidoscope* program.

Word Play

This section of each lesson in Units 1–3 will contain activities to help students review and reinforce what they have learned in previous Word Study lessons. For today's lesson, have students sing "The Alphabet Song" to determine whether each student knows the names of all the alphabet letters. As you sing the song, point to the letters on the letter side of the *Sound/Spelling Cards.*

Sight Words

Many high-frequency or sight words are phonetically irregular. They don't follow the rules, and students need to learn to recognize them "on sight." Some sight words are phonetically regular, but they contain sound/spellings that students have not yet learned and so are not yet decodable.

This week's sight words:

| a | on | the |

Use the following procedure for teaching sight words:

- Write this week's sight words on the board.
- Read the words to students, then have them read the words.
- Pronounce any words with which students have difficulty.
- Have students use each sight word in a sentence.

Phonics—Blending: Set 1

/a/ spelled *a*	/h/ spelled *h_*	/p/ spelled *p*
/s/ spelled *s*	/t/ spelled *t*	

This section of the phonics lesson provides practice in building sounds and spellings into words. The purpose of blending is to help students develop a strategy for reading unfamiliar words.

- Point out each *Sound/Spelling Card* to be used. Ask students what they know about these cards. For example, they may identify which card is for a vowel and which cards are for consonants.

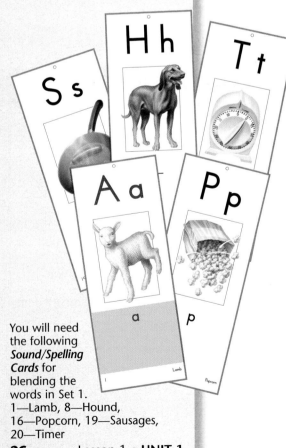

You will need the following *Sound/Spelling Cards* for blending the words in Set 1.
1—Lamb, 8—Hound, 16—Popcorn, 19—Sausages, 20—Timer

- Touch each card and tell students the name of the card, the sound, and the spelling. (For detailed information on how to introduce **Sound/Spelling Cards**, see Getting Started.)

Blending Exercise

The words in the lines provide practice with the Set 1 sound/spellings. Write the following words and sentences on the board.

Line 1:	at	hat	Pat
Line 2:	sat	hats	pats
Sentence 1:	Pat taps a hat.		
Sentence 2:	Pat sat on the hat.		

About the Words and Sentences

Teach the blending exercise using the sound-by-sound procedure below, without varying from it. That way, students will become accustomed to the routine they will use to blend words.

- Blend the words sound by sound. Write the first spelling, *a*, and ask students to give the sound. Then write the second spelling, *t*, and have students give the sound. Have students blend the two sounds together to read the word *at* as you move your hand in a blending motion from left to right beneath the word.

- For the second word, write the spelling *h_* and ask students to give the sound. Write the spelling *a* and ask students to give the sound. Have students blend through the vowel, saying /ha/. Write the final spelling, *t*, and ask students to give the sound. Using a blending motion from left to right, have students say all three sounds and blend the word *hat*.

- Continue in this way for the remaining words and the sentences.

- Then have a student use each word in a sentence. Extend the sentence by asking questions such as *where, when, why,* or *how*. Encourage students to extend sentences by adding information at the beginning and not just at the end of the sentence.

- Be sure to discuss the meanings of any unfamiliar words.

TEACHER TIP

Sound/Spelling Cards Remind students of any special features on the cards. For example, the letters on Card 1 *(Aa)* are red, and the card has a green background. This means the card is for a vowel sound/spelling. For the *Hh* card, have students note the blank after the *h*. Explain that the blank is a signal that *h_* says /h/ only at the beginning of a word or a syllable. Another letter must follow *h_* for it to say /h/.

SELECTION A • From Rocks to Books

About the Words and Sentences

- On Line 1, point out the word *Pat* and explain that the capital letter means that this is someone's name.

- On Line 2, point out the word *pats*. Ask if this is someone's name. If necessary, point out that the word is not a name because it does not begin with a capital letter. Ask students what the word *pats* means.

- Remind students that the plural form of many words is made by adding *s* to the word. Have them blend *hat* and *hats* and use each word in a sentence.

- Before reading a sentence, point to and read the underlined sight words. Have students reread the sentences to build fluency and comprehension.

Oral Language

Provide "riddle" clues and have students find and read the word that answers the riddle. Here are some possible clues:

What is the opposite of *stood up?* *(sat)*

What rhymes with *sat* but starts with /p/? *(Pat)*

What do you wear on your head? *(hat)*

Dictation

Dictation gives students an opportunity to spell words by using the sound/spellings that they have learned. For this dictation exercise, have students use writing paper. Dictate the words and sentence for them to write. Use the following sounds-in-sequence procedure:

- Say the first word in the Dictation word lines. Use the word in a sentence, then say the word again. Have students say the word.

- Have students say the first sound. Then have them write the spelling. Have students say the next sound, and then write its spelling. Encourage them to check the **Sound/Spelling Cards.**

- Complete the spelling of the remainder of the words in the same manner.

- After each word line, write (or have a student write) the words on the board. Have students proofread their words. Tell them to circle any incorrect words and to correct them.

- Next, dictate the sentence. Dictate one word at a time, following the sounds-in-sequence dictation procedure. Remind students to start the sentence with a capital letter and to use correct end punctuation.

- Write (or have a student write) the sentence on the board. Have students proofread their work and correct any incorrect words.

WRITING

Have students write the words from Line 2. Tell them to circle the spelling for /s/ in each word.

Line 1:	at hat
Line 2:	tap pats
Sentence:	Pat taps the hat.

Building Fluency

Decodable Story: Unit 1, Story 1

- This story reviews the sound/spelling /a/ spelled *a*; /h/ spelled *h_*; /p/ spelled *p*; /s/ spelled *s*; /t/ spelled *t*.
- Have students silently read ***Decodable Stories and Comprehension Skills*** page 1.
- Call on volunteers to read each paragraph aloud.
- For those students who need help, divide sentences according to natural phrases. Mark these phrases with diagonal slash marks on their worksheets.
- After students have read the story aloud, ask them questions and have them point to and read the answers in the story.
- Have students reread the story aloud with a partner. Rereading builds automaticity and fluency.
- Over the next few days, listen to each student reread the story.

Develop Fluency Some students may find it difficult to read with fluency because they do not recognize the importance of grouping words into natural meaning units, such as phrases, as they read. Model fluent reading frequently for students, showing them how pausing in the right places and adding expression can make a passage easier to understand.

 QUICK CHECK

As a quick review of today's sound/spellings, say some sentences, and ask students to suggest words to fill the blanks. Sentences you might read aloud include:

Sam _____ on the sofa. *(sat)*
A black cat is _____ the door. *(at)*
The wind blew the _____ off my head. *(hat)*

OBJECTIVES

- Discuss vocabulary words and their meanings.
- Develop reading skills as the story is read to them.
- Gain knowledge of the comprehension strategies Asking Questions and Making Connections.
- Build vocabulary by classifying objects into groups.
- Develop writing skills by writing a prediction.

MATERIALS

Student Reader, pp. 2–3
Language Arts, p. T2

Before Reading

Build Background

Activate Prior Knowledge

- Remind students that this unit is about stories. Explain that people have enjoyed hearing and telling stories for a long, long time. In countries all over the world, stories have been passed down from generation to generation over many, many years.
- Ask students if they know of any such stories. Do they know any stories about princes and princesses, about monsters or dragons, about great battles, or about heroes and heroines?
- Explain to students that we know many of these stories because, even before paper and books were invented, people discovered that by writing their stories, they could save them forever and share them with more people. Ask them if they know what people wrote their stories on before the invention of paper.

Background Information

Use the following information to help students understand the story you are about to read.

- Tell students that the selection you are about to read is a kind of writing called *nonfiction*. Ask if anyone knows what nonfiction is. If no one does, explain that nonfiction writing gives information and is about real people, places, events, and things.
- Tell students that there are several kinds of nonfiction writing and that they will read and learn about several of them.

Selection Vocabulary

Write the following vocabulary words on the board. Before reading the selection, introduce and discuss the following words and their meanings.

marks: lines or spots made on a surface

happened: to have taken place

Then have students read the words, stopping to blend any words that they have trouble reading. Demonstrate how to decode multisyllabic words by breaking the words into syllables and blending the syllables. Then have students try. If they still have trouble, refer them to the **Sound/Spelling Cards.** If the word is not decodable, give students the pronunciation.

As students study vocabulary, they will use a variety of skills to determine the meaning of a word. These skills include context clues, word structure, and apposition. In this unit, students will be learning about context clues.

Write the following example on the board: *The pictures and marks on the rock were hard to see.* Explain to students that they are going to use the context, or other words in the sentence, to help them decipher the meaning of the word *marks.* Guide students until they can give a reasonable definition of the word.

Vocabulary Activity: Write the word *marks* on the board. Have volunteers come to the board and make "marks" on the board, such as letters, lines, dots, circles, or pictures.

Preview and Prepare

Before you read, use modeling and prompts such as:

● *Let's browse this selection before I read it. Since it's nonfiction, we can look at the entire selection without spoiling any surprise.*

● *First, let's read the title, "From Rocks to Books." That's interesting, isn't it? Based on the title and what we said about writing down stories, what do you think this selection will be about? Let's read and find out.*

WRITING

After browsing the selection, have students write a word or phrase that describes what they think the selection will be about.

During Reading

Read Aloud

In this section of the lesson, you will read aloud the anthology selections in Units 1–3. Reading aloud to students will introduce them to both print and book conventions and to the behaviors and strategies good readers use to get meaning from what they read. The goal is to ensure that after three units of instruction, students have acquired the skills to read, with fluency and comprehension, the many different kinds of literature they encounter in **Kaleidoscope** and in trade books.

For this lesson, read the entire selection aloud. If you feel your students are ready to read the selection orally, have them do so. As you read, stop at the points that are marked with numbers in magenta circles on the reduced student pages, and model for them how to use the indicated strategy. Encourage students to stop at any point in their reading if they don't understand something or want to talk about the meaning of a passage or word.

Comprehension Strategies

During the reading of "From Rocks to Books" on pages 2–3, you will model the following reading comprehension strategies:

Asking Questions: As they read, good readers ask themselves questions to see if they are making sense of what they are reading.

Making Connections: Good readers improve their understanding of a selection by making connections between what they already know and what they are reading.

2

First Read

Text Comprehension *Strategies*

As you read the selection, use modeling and prompts such as:

❶ Making Connections

Good readers relate past experiences to what they read to make the selection more interesting and easier to understand. I remember when I was a kid, I liked to use a stick to draw pictures in the mud. Sometimes I would write secret messages for my friends to find when the mud dried out. So I understand how people started making marks in the mud when they wanted to tell somebody something.

❷ Asking Questions

Asking yourself questions is a good way to be sure you understand what you're reading. I have some questions here. Plant leaves don't last very long. They dry up and crumble. If people wrote on leaves, wouldn't what they wrote get lost? Couldn't they find something better to write on? Let's read on and find out. I see. People finally found out how to make paper.

❸ Making Connections

What would we do if people hadn't found out how to make paper and books? I can't get through the day without reading. It's one of the most important things in my life. How about you? Are you glad that we have books?

HOMEWORK TIP

Have students bring in their favorite book from home. Set aside class time for students to share their stories.

From Rocks to Books

by Elizabeth Paré

Long ago there was no paper. There were no books. Some people made pictures on rocks. Others made <u>marks</u> ❶ on wet mud.

But rocks and mud are hard to pick up. What else did people write on? For a long time people wrote on plant leaves. ❷ They rolled them up to make books.

2

VOCABULARY

Tell students that grouping words into categories can help them understand the meaning of a word. For a lesson on classification, use *Language Arts* page T2.

Much more time went by. Then people found out how to make paper. Now they could make lots of books. These books tell us what <u>happened</u> long, long ago.

You don't have to read rocks or hard mud or leaves. You can read books. Aren't you glad?

3

GRAMMAR

Introduce the different types of sentences to students. Tell them that a statement gives information, a question asks something, and an exclamation expresses strong feelings. For a lesson on types of sentences, use **Language Arts** page T1.

Text Comprehension

Sequence

Explain to students that events in a reading selection usually happen in a certain order or a *sequence.* Sequence can mean that the author tells what happens from the first to the last event, from one day to the next day, or in some other kind of order. The author may use words such as *first, then, next,* and *finally* to help readers follow the order of events. If authors don't use these words, readers need to pay close attention to what they are reading to figure out the sequence of events.

- Reread the selection. Tell students to listen for the order in which events take place.
- When you have finished reading, call on volunteers to tell what people first used to write on, then what they used next, and so on. Use **Transparency** 1 to record their responses.
- Review the events with students. Have them respond, using the words *first, then, next,* and *last.*
- For additional practice with Sequence, have students complete **Decodable Stories and Comprehension Skills** page 75.

Discussing the Selection

After you have read the selection, discuss it with students. Use prompts such as:

- *What did you like most about "From Rocks to Books"? What didn't you like about it?*
- *How does this story relate to the unit theme, Sharing Stories?*

 ## QUICK CHECK

As a quick review, ask students to retell the events in the selection in the correct order.

OBJECTIVES

- Clap out syllables in names.
- Blend and break apart sounds in words.
- Participate in Word Play activity.
- Develop fluency by reading aloud.
- Apply decoding skills by reading **Unit 1, Decodable Story 2.**
- Develop writing skills by writing words and identifying sound/spellings.

MATERIALS

Sound/Spelling Cards:
8—Hound
9—Pig
16—Popcorn
19—Sausages
20—Timer
Decodable Stories and Comprehension Skills, p. 2
High-Frequency Word Cards
Sound/Spelling Card Stories Audiocassette/CD

Segmentation Remember to move quickly through these activities. Do not hold the class back waiting on all students to catch on. Return to the same activity often. Frequent repetition is very beneficial and allows students additional opportunities to catch on.

SELECTION A • **From Rocks to Books**

Phonemic Awareness

Segmentation: Clapping Syllables in Names

Tell students that it is their turn to break words into parts.

- Choose a student's name that has more than one syllable. Starting with multisyllabic names will help students to understand quickly the kind of units they are listening for. Say, for example, "Let's clap out Taylor's name: Tay…lor." Then ask, "How many times did we clap?"

- Repeat with other students' names. For each name, have students count the claps. Alternate a few one-syllable names with multisyllabic names. Continue until students are consistently identifying the correct number of claps.

- Tell students that the word parts they are counting are called *syllables*. Explain that in the name *Taylor, Tay* is the first syllable and *lor* is the second syllable. Tell students that they will learn more about syllables later.

Word Study

Word Play

Throughout the program, this section of a lesson will contain activities to help students review and reinforce what they have learned in previous Word Study lessons. For this lesson, have students sing "The Alphabet Song" once again. After singing, have them point to the letters on the *Sound/Spelling Cards* that represent sounds they have learned so far.

Phonics—Blending: Set 2

/h/ spelled *h_*	/i/ spelled *i*	/p/ spelled *p*
/s/ spelled *s*	/t/ spelled *t*	

- Review the previously introduced *Sound/Spelling Cards*.
- Display and discuss the new *Sound/Spelling Card* (9—Pig). Have students notice that this is a card for a vowel.

Blending Exercise

- Write the following words and sentences on the board.
- Have students blend the words and sentences using the sound-by-sound procedure described on page 2H.

Line 1:	it	hit	pit
Line 2:	hip	sit	tip
Line 3:	hits	sip	sits
Sentence 1:	It hit Pat <u>on the</u> hip.		
Sentence 2:	Pat tips <u>a</u> hat.		

- Before reading each sentence, point to and read the underlined sight words.
- Discuss with students that each sentence begins with a capital letter and ends with a punctuation mark.
- Have students reread the sentences to build fluency and comprehension.

TEACHER TIP

Sound/Spelling Card Stories Review today's sounds by using the *Sound/Spelling Card Stories.* Listening to the stories will help students understand how they can use the pictures on the *Sound/Spelling Cards* to remember the sounds associated with them. The stories are provided in the appendix and are also available on the *Sound/Spelling Card Stories Audiocassette/CD.*

You will need the following *Sound/Spelling Cards* for blending the words in Set 2. 8—Hound, 9—Pig, 16—Popcorn, 19—Sausages, 20—Timer

Unit 1 • LESSON

3

About the Words and Sentences

- The words on the lines provide practice with the Set 2 sound/spellings.
- Have students blend *sit* and *sits* and use each word in a sentence. Repeat with *hit* and *hits*.
- For Sentence 1, point out the name, *Pat*. Explain that because it is someone's name, this word is capitalized even though it does not come at the beginning of the sentence.

Oral Language

Point to a word line and invite a student to choose a word on the line, and then give a riddle or clue for it, such as *It's a deep hole (pit)* or *It's part of the body (hip)*.

Dictation

For the dictation exercise, have students use writing paper. Dictate the words and sentence for them to write.

Use the following sounds-in-sequence procedure:

- Say the first word in the dictation word line. Use the word in a sentence, and then say the word again. Have students say the word.
- Have students say the first sound. Then have them write the spelling. Have students say the next sound, and then write its spelling.
- Complete the spelling of the remainder of the words in the same manner.
- After each word line, write (or have a student write) the words on the board. Have students proofread their words. Tell them to circle any incorrect words and to correct them.
- Next dictate the sentence. Dictate one word at a time, following the sounds-in-sequence dictation procedure. Remind students to start the sentence with a capital letter and to use correct end punctuation.
- Write (or have a student write) the sentence on the board. Have students proofread their work and correct any incorrect words.

WRITING

Have students write the words from Line 3. Tell them to circle the spelling for /i/ in each word.

Line 1:	it sit hit
Line 2:	sip tip hip
Sentence:	It hit the tip.

Building Fluency

Decodable Story: Unit 1, Story 2

- This story reviews the sound/spellings /i/ spelled *i*; /h/ spelled *h_*; /p/ spelled *p*; /s/ spelled *s*; /t/ spelled *t*.
- Have students silently read **Decodable Stories and Comprehension Skills** page 2.
- Call on volunteers to read each paragraph aloud.
- For those students who need help, divide sentences according to natural phrases. Mark these phrases with diagonal slash marks on their worksheets.
- After students have read the story aloud, ask them questions and have them point to and read the answers in the story.
- Have students reread the story aloud with a partner.

HOMEWORK TIP

To help students build fluency, have them take home the **Decodable Stories and Comprehension Skills** stories to read with their families.

Unit 1 • LESSON

4

OBJECTIVES

- Develop reading skills as the story is read to them.
- Gain knowledge of the comprehension skill Sequence.
- Develop vocabulary by listening to and discussing the selection.
- Develop writing skills by writing sequence words.
- Identify sentence types.

MATERIALS

Student Reader, pp. 2–3
Transparencies 1, 2, 3
Decodable Stories and Comprehension Skills, p. 75
Language Arts, p. T1
Listening Library Audiocassette/CD

Rereading the Selection

Comprehension Skills

Revisiting or rereading a selection allows students to learn and apply skills that give them a more complete understanding of a selection. For today's lesson, reread the selection to students. During the second reading, students will apply the following comprehension skill:

Sequence: Good readers understand that sequence follows the writer's line of thought. Students will identify the order in which the events of the story take place.

After Reading

Independent Reading

- Have students choose books from the **Classroom Library** or other available books to take home and read.
- Encourage students to read on their own at least one book each week.
- Spend some time discussing the students' independent reading with them.
- Copy **Transparency** 3 and post it on the bulletin board. Encourage students to record on it the titles of the books they are reading.

Have students listen to the selection recording on the **Listening Library Audiocassette/CD** for a proficient, fluent model of oral reading.

WRITING

Have students write three words that an author might use to sequence a story, such as *first, next, then, finally,* or *last.*

SELECTION A • **From Rocks to Books**

Assessment

Formal

At the end of each lesson, students will have an opportunity to exhibit what they have learned. The Lesson Assessments are found in the *Assessment Guide.* They include both multiple-choice and extended response items that measure students' understanding of the selection as well as the reading and language arts skills featured in a lesson. Students should have the lesson selection available when they complete the assessment.

For this lesson, have students complete the assessment Unit 1: From Rocks to Books. For all the items in this assessment, you should read both the question and answer choices out loud while students follow along silently. Spend a moment with students explaining how to fill in the circle beside the answer they think is correct for the multiple choice items. You may find it helpful to walk around the room while students are completing the assessment to provide them with any help they need to understand the questions.

Informal

During the lesson, engage students in a discussion of the selection. Talk about the different things on which people write. Have students name everyday things that have writing, from cereal boxes to roadside signs. This discussion will build students' confidence and help them understand that writing and reading are important parts of our lives.

Ending the Lesson

Read "From Rocks to Books" out loud slowly while students follow along silently. Encourage them to point to the words in the story as you read them. Pause periodically and point to a word in a student's book, a word you have just read. Ask a volunteer to read the word.

OBJECTIVES

- Complete lesson assessment.
- Promote student engagement.
- Build student confidence.
- Demonstrate the importance of reading in everyday life.

MATERIALS

Assessment Guide
Student Reader, pp. 2–3

SELECTION B • **A Story for Pam**

Support Materials

LESSON 6

- Sound/Spelling Cards 4, 13, 14, 26
- Decodable Stories and Comprehension Skills, p. 3
- Home Connection, p. 5
- High-Frequency Word Cards
- Sound/Spelling Card Stories Audiocassette/CD

HOME CONNECTIONS

Distribute *Home Connection* page 5, which describes this week's classwork and suggests activities for families to do at home. This letter is available in English and Spanish.

LESSON 7

- Student Reader, pp. 4–7
- Language Arts, p. T4
- Transparency 4

LESSON 8

- Sound/Spelling Cards 2, 6, 11, 12
- Decodable Stories and Comprehension Skills, p. 4
- High-Frequency Word Cards
- Sound/Spelling Card Stories Audiocassette/CD

LESSON 9

- Transparencies 3, 5
- Decodable Stories and Comprehension Skills, p. 76
- Student Reader, pp. 4–7
- Language Arts, p. T3
- Listening Library Audiocassette/CD

LESSON 10

- Assessment Guide
- Student Reader, pp. 4–7

Teacher Focus

- Conduct Listening Game.
- Conduct Word Play.
- Introduce Sight Words, blending procedure, and Set 1 blending words and sentences.
- Provide riddle clues.
- Dictate word lines.
- Assist students with decodable text.
- Assign writing activity.

- Activate Prior Knowledge and provide background information.
- Introduce and discuss selection vocabulary.
- Preview selection.
- Introduce Comprehension Strategies—Predicting and Making Connections.
- Read the selection to students.
- Introduce vocabulary skill.
- Assign writing activity.

- Conduct Clapping Syllables in Names game.
- Conduct Listening for Vowel Sounds game.
- Conduct Word Play.
- Review blending procedure; introduce Set 2 blending words and sentences.
- Provide riddle clues.
- Dictate word lines.
- Assist students with decodable text.
- Assign writing activity.

- Introduce Comprehension Skill—Author's Purpose.
- Reread and discuss the selection with students.
- Discuss Independent Reading.
- Assign writing activity.
- Introduce grammar skill.

- Administer weekly assessments.
- Assess students' progress.

Student Participation

- Take part in Listening Game.
- Take part in Word Play.
- Read Sight Words.
- Blend words and sentences.
- Solve riddles.
- Write dictated words and sentences.
- Read a decodable story.
- Complete writing activity.

- Contribute to class discussion.
- Read and discuss vocabulary words. Complete selection vocabulary activity.
- Browse the selection.
- Follow along as selection is read.
- Complete vocabulary skill activity.
- Complete writing activity.

- Participate in Clapping Syllables in Names game.
- Participate in Listening for Vowel Sounds game.
- Take part in Word Play.
- Blend words and sentences.
- Solve riddles.
- Write dictated words and sentences.
- Read a decodable story.
- Complete writing activity.

- Follow along as the selection is read again.
- Discuss the selection.
- Select a book to take home and read.
- Complete writing activity.
- Complete grammar skill activity.

- Complete lesson assessment.

Unit 1 • LESSON

6

OBJECTIVES

- Blend and break apart sounds in words.
- Read sight words.
- Participate in Word Play activity.
- Develop fluency by reading aloud.
- Apply decoding skills by reading **Unit 1, Decodable Story 3.**
- Develop writing skills by writing a caption.

MATERIALS

Sound/Spelling Cards:
4—Dinosaur
13—Monkey
14—Nose
26—Zipper
Decodable Stories and Comprehension Skills, p. 3
Home Connection, p. 5
High-Frequency Word Cards
Sound/Spelling Card Stories Audiocassette/CD

Phonemic Awareness

The goal of phonemic awareness activities is to help students understand that spoken words are made up of smaller sounds—word parts, syllables, and phonemes. Learning this concept is important to reading success because of the systematic relationship between speech sounds and written letters. If students cannot hear and manipulate the individual sounds in spoken words, they usually have difficulty deciphering that relationship. Phonemic awareness is also important to students' spelling success. Students who understand that sounds and letters are related usually are able to attach the sounds to letters and spell words.

Oral blending and segmentation are complementary processes in developing phonemic awareness and in learning to read and write. Just as learning to blend smaller units of sound into words is essential to decoding, learning to segment, or break apart, words into smaller units of sound is essential to spelling.

Oral Blending

Tell students that they are already good at listening; they obviously understand words they hear. Then explain that to be really good readers and writers, they need to learn to listen even more closely—they need to be able to hear the separate sounds that make up words. Tell them that when they can hear the separate sounds, they can read and spell most words.

Listening Game: Word Parts and Syllables

Tell students that they're going to play the Word Parts game again. Remind them that you will say some words that they know, but you will say them in two parts. To discover what each word is, they must listen very carefully and put the two parts together. Use the following example:

> **Teacher:** *Di . . . nosaur. What's the word?*
>
> **Students:** *dinosaur*
>
> Continue with the following words, pronouncing each part distinctly and pausing clearly at the breaks indicated (. . .). Alternate between having all students respond together and calling on individuals.
>
> re . . . member   ba . . . nana
>
> le . . . mon   pur . . . ple
>
> tel . . . evision   car . . . toon

TEACHER TIP

Listening for Word Parts The words used in this activity are somewhat harder for students to guess from just the first part of the word. Say each part of the word clearly, and tell students to listen very carefully.

<small>SELECTION B •</small> **A Story for Pam**

Word Study

In this section of the lesson, students work on phonics, fluency, blending, and spelling. Increasing students' ability to work smoothly with printed words is one of the primary goals of the *Kaleidoscope* program.

Word Play

This activity reinforces the idea that changing the spellings in words also changes the way the words sound and their meanings. Write the letters *a, h, i, p, s, t* on the board. Tell students to write the word *hit.* Then tell them to replace only one letter in the word to make a new word. Call on volunteers to read the new words they make. (Possible words include *hat, hip, sit, pit.*) Have them continue to make new words by changing only one letter at a time.

Sight Words

Many high-frequency or sight words are phonetically irregular. They do not follow the rules, and students need to learn to recognize them "on sight." Some sight words are phonetically regular, but they contain sound/spellings that students have not yet learned and so are not yet decodable.

This week's sight words:

is	**like**	**to**

You will need the following **Sound/Spelling Cards** for blending the words in Set 1. 4—Dinosaur, 13—Monkey, 14—Nose, 26—Zipper

Use the following procedure for teaching sight words:

- Write this week's sight words on the board.
- Read the words to students, then have them read the words.
- Pronounce any words with which students have difficulty.
- Have students use each sight word in a sentence.

Phonics—Blending: Set 1

/d/ spelled *d* | /m/ spelled *m* | /n/ spelled *n* | /z/ spelled *z*

This section of the phonics lesson provides practice in building sounds and spellings into words. The purpose of blending is to help students develop a strategy for reading unfamiliar words.

- Display and discuss each new **Sound/Spelling Card** to be used. Before discussing Card 14—Nose, use tape to cover the *kn_* sound/spelling. Make sure students know that the *n* sound/spelling is the focus of this set.

● Touch each card and tell students the name of the card, the sound, and the spelling. (For detailed information on how to introduce **Sound/Spelling Cards,** see Getting Started.)

Blending Exercise

● The words in the lines provide practice with the Set 1 sound/spellings. Write the following words and sentences on the board.

Line 1:	am	ham	Sam	Pam
Line 2:	an	man	tan	had
Line 3:	dip	zip	nip	did
Line 4:	zap	nap	mist	mast
Sentence 1:	Tim and Dan like to spin.			
Sentence 2:	Hit it to dad.			
Sentence 3:	Is the pin on the mat?			

Teach the blending exercise using the sound-by-sound procedure below:

● Blend the words sound by sound. Write the first spelling, *a,* and ask students to give the sound. Then write the second spelling, *m,* and have students give the sound. Have students blend the two sounds together to read the word *am* as you move your hand in a blending motion from left to right beneath the word.

● For the second word, write the spelling *h_* and ask students to give the sound. Write the spelling *a* and ask students to give the sound. Have students blend through the vowel, saying /ha/. Write the final spelling, *m,* and ask students to give the sound. Using a blending motion from left to right, have students say all three sounds and blend the word *ham.*

● Continue in this way for the remaining words and the sentences.

● Then have students use each word in a sentence. Extend the sentence by asking questions such as *where, when, why,* or *how.*

● Be sure to discuss the meanings of any unfamiliar words.

6

SELECTION B • **A Story for Pam**

About the Words and Sentences

- The boldfaced words are from the selection.
- Ask students to identify words that are names in Line 1 *(Sam, Pam)*.
- On Line 4, point out the words *mist* and *mast,* and ask students what each word means. If necessary, tell them that *mist* is a fine, soft rain, and a *mast* is a pole, usually one on a ship that holds a sail. Ask students to identify the one sound/spelling that is different in the words *(the vowel sound)*. Reinforce the understanding that changes in sound/spellings also mean changes in the meanings of words.
- Before reading a sentence, point to and read the underlined sight words. Have students reread the sentences to build fluency and comprehension.
- Have them find and read the sentence that is a question.

Oral Language

Provide riddle clues and have students find and read the word that answers the riddle. Here are some possible clues:

What rhymes with *map* but starts with /n/? *(nap)*

Which word names something to eat? *(ham)*

Which word means "to go somewhere fast"? *(zip)*

Dictation

Dictation gives students an opportunity to spell words by using the sound/spellings that they have learned. For this dictation exercise, have students use writing paper. Dictate the words and sentence for them to write. Use the following sounds-in-sequence procedure:

- Say the first word in each word line. Use the word in a sentence, then say the word again. Have students say the word.
- Have students say the first sound. Then have them write the spelling. Have students say the next sound, and then write its spelling. Encourage them to check the **Sound/Spelling Cards.**
- Complete the spelling of the remainder of the words in the same manner.
- After each word line, write (or have a student write) the words on the board. Have students proofread their words. Tell them to circle any incorrect words and to correct them.
- Next, dictate the sentence. Dictate one word at a time, following the sounds-in-sequence procedure. Remind students to start the sentence with a capital letter and to use correct end punctuation.
- Write (or have a student write) the sentence on the board. Have students proofread their work and correct any incorrect words.

WRITING

Have students select a word from the word lines and create an illustration and a short caption using the word. Ask students to share their drawings and captions with the class.

Line 1:	at	hat	tin
Line 2:	dim	him	zap
Sentence:	Taz and Dad like the sand.		

Building Fluency

Decodable Story: Unit 1, Story 3

- This story reviews the sound/spellings /d/ spelled *d*; /m/ spelled *m*; /n/ spelled *n*; /z/ spelled *z*.

- Have students silently read **Decodable Stories and Comprehension Skills** page 3.

- Call on volunteers to read each paragraph aloud.

- For those students who need help, divide sentences according to natural phrases. Mark these phrases with diagonal slash marks on their worksheets.

- After students have read the story aloud, ask them questions and have them point to and read the answers in the story.

- Have students reread the story aloud with a partner. Rereading builds automaticity and fluency.

- Over the next few days, listen to each student reread the story.

Develop Fluency Model fluent reading frequently for students, showing them how pausing in the right places and adding expression can make a passage easier to understand.

✓ QUICK CHECK

As a quick review of today's sound/spellings, say some sentences, and ask students to suggest words to fill the blanks. Sentences you might read aloud include:

My baby sister takes a _____ in the afternoon. *(nap)*
My puppy likes to _____ my fingers. *(nip)*
The _____ is wearing a brown hat. *(man)*

OBJECTIVES

- Discuss vocabulary words and their meanings.
- Develop reading skills as the story is read to them.
- Gain knowledge of the comprehension strategies Predicting and Making Connections.
- Build vocabulary by identifying rhyming words.
- Develop writing skills by changing and writing parts of a story.

MATERIALS

Student Reader, pp. 4–7
Language Arts, p. T4
Transparency 4

Before Reading

Build Background

Activate Prior Knowledge

- Remind students that this unit is about stories. Then tell them that the story you are about to read involves a bedtime story.
- Ask students to talk about bedtime stories that they know. Call on one or two students to tell their favorite bedtime stories.

Background Information

Use the following information to help students understand the story you are about to read.

- Ask students to tell what they remember about *nonfiction.* If necessary, remind them that nonfiction gives information and is about real people, places, events, and things. Next, ask them if they know what *fiction* is. If they can't answer, explain that the word *fiction* means "not real" or "made up." Tell them that many of the selections they will read over the year will be fiction.
- Tell them that the story you are going to read in this lesson is a kind of writing called *realistic fiction.* Explain that this means that although the story is made up, it does not contain anything that is impossible, such as talking animals, or could not happen in the real world, such as time travel. Tell students that, over the year, they will read and learn about other kinds of fiction.

Selection Vocabulary

Write the following vocabulary words on the board. Before reading the selection, introduce and discuss the following words and their meanings:

laughed: made sounds that show amusement or joy

finish: to complete

Then have students read the words, stopping to blend any words that they have trouble reading. Demonstrate how to decode multisyllabic words by breaking the words into syllables and blending the syllables. Then have students try. If they still have trouble, refer them to the ***Sound/Spelling Cards.*** If the word is not decodable, give students the pronunciation.

As students study vocabulary, they will use a variety of skills to determine the meaning of a word. These skills include context clues, word structure, and apposition. In this unit, students will be learning about context clues.

Write the following example on the board: *I completed my homework at 8:00 p.m. What time did you finish your homework?* Explain to students that they are going to use the context, or other words in the sentences, to help them decipher the meaning of the word *finish.* Guide students until they can give a reasonable definition of the word.

Vocabulary Activity: Have students look through magazines or newspapers and cut out pictures or cartoons that make them laugh. Ask them to share their examples with the class.

Preview and Prepare

Before you read, use modeling and prompts such as:

● *Let's browse this story before I read it. Because it's fiction, we should only read the first few sentences so that the ending will be a surprise.*

● *First, let's read the story's title. What can you tell about the story from the title? Who's Pam? Who's telling her a story? Let's read and find out.*

During Reading

Read Aloud

For this lesson, read the entire selection aloud. As you read, stop at the points that are marked with numbers in magenta circles on the reduced student pages, and model for them how to use the indicated strategy. Encourage students to stop at any point in their reading if they don't understand something or want to talk about the meaning of a passage or word.

Comprehension Strategies

During the reading of "A Story for Pam" on pages 4–7, you will model the following reading comprehension strategies:

Making Connections: Good readers improve their understanding of a selection by making connections between what they already know and what they are reading.

Predicting: Good readers know when to pause during reading to think about what is going on and to use their own knowledge and information from what they read to decide what will happen next. Good readers also return to their predictions to see whether the reading confirms them.

TEACHER TIP

Comprehension Strategies Encourage students to ask any questions they have about things in the story that they do not understand. Remind them that good readers often stop to clarify things that are not clear.

Text Comprehension *Strategies*

As you read the selection, use modeling and prompts such as:

❶ Making Connections

Good readers relate past experiences to what they read to make the selection more interesting and easier to understand. I remember that my dad used to read me stories before bedtime to help me have good dreams at night. He was a great reader! He made funny voices for all the story characters. I loved story time, and I'm sure Pam does, too.

❷ Making Predictions

Good readers make predictions constantly about what's going to happen next in a story, and then they confirm or change their predictions as they read. This keeps them interested in what is happening in the story and helps them to understand it better. I know that Pam has already changed Dad's story once. I predict that she is going to change the story again. She seems to like doing this. What do you think she'll do? Let's read on to find out.

❸ Confirming Predictions

See! My prediction came true! Pam does change the story again.

A Story for Pam

by Meish Goldish
illustrated by Gerardo Suzán

"Time for bed," Dad said. Pam looked up.

❶ "Oh, Dad," she said. "Please tell me a story."

Dad sat down. "All right," he said.

4

VOCABULARY

Tell students that rhyming words are words that have the same ending sounds. For a lesson on rhyming words, use *Language Arts* page T4.

"Once there was a pet cat named Sam."

"No!" cried Pam. "It was a pet hen named Deb."

Dad laughed.

"All right," he said. "Once there was a pet hen named Deb. She was a red hen."

"No, Dad," said Pam. "She was a blue hen."

5

Text Comprehension *Skills*

Author's Purpose

Explain to students that authors have a purpose for writing. Sometimes the purpose is to give information, to entertain readers—to make them laugh or to enjoy a good story, or to persuade.

- For these pages, have students tell what they think the author's purpose for "A Story for Pam" is. *(to entertain)*

- Have students find examples in the story to support their answer.

- Use **Transparency** 5 to record their responses.

GRAMMAR

Introduce the different types of end punctuation marks to students. Tell them that a statement ends with a period, a question ends with a question mark, and an exclamation ends with an exclamation point. For a lesson on end marks, use *Language Arts* page T3.

First Read

Text Comprehension *Strategies*

❹ **Making Connections**

This story reminds me of how much I enjoyed listening to my dad tell me bedtime stories. I always laughed at his stories, just like Dad is laughing at Pam's story.

❺ **Making Predictions**

Pam likes playing this game with her dad so much, I predict she'll end up telling the whole story herself. Share with the class any predictions you are making.

❻ **Confirming Predictions**

Well, this time my prediction is not confirmed. Pam doesn't end up telling the whole story herself. She wants Dad to continue telling the story. When you make a prediction, be sure to check whether or not your prediction came true.

HOMEWORK TIP

Ask students to make up and tell a bedtime story to a family member. Remind them that the purpose of their story should be to inform, to entertain, or to persuade.

❹ Dad laughed again.
"All right," he said. "Deb was a blue hen. One day she flew out of the barn."
"No, Dad," said Pam. "Deb flew into
❺ the sky."

6

WRITING

Ask students to make up their own version of Pam's story. Have them write the type of animal, the animal's name, and the color of the animal for their story. Have students share their version of the story with the class.

Dad laughed again.

He said, "Pam, why don't you <u>finish</u> telling the story?"

"Oh, no!" Pam said. "You tell a story much better than I do!"

That *really* made Dad laugh!

7

Text Comprehension

Author's Purpose

Remind students that authors have a purpose for writing. Continue to discuss the author's purpose for "A Story for Pam."

- For these pages, have students find additional examples in the story to support the author's purpose.
- Continue recording their responses on **Transparency** 5.
- For additional practice with Author's Purpose, have students complete **Decodable Stories and Comprehension Skills** page 76.

Discussing the Selection

After you have read the story, discuss it with students. Use prompts such as:

- *What do you think might have happened to give the author the idea for this story?*
- *Have you read any other story that is like "A Story for Pam"?*
- *Did the ending of the story surprise you? How?*
- *How does this story relate to the unit theme, Sharing Stories?*

 QUICK CHECK

Quickly review with students the different comprehension strategies and skills that they've used so far.

SELECTION B • **A Story for Pam**

OBJECTIVES

- Clap out syllables in names and words.
- Listen for /ā/ in words.
- Blend and break apart sounds in words.
- Participate in Word Play activity.
- Develop fluency by reading aloud.
- Apply decoding skills by reading **Unit 1, Decodable Story 4.**
- Develop writing skills by writing rhyming words.

MATERIALS

Sound/Spelling Cards:
2—Ball
6—Fan
11—Camera
12—Lion
Decodable Stories and Comprehension Skills, p. 4
High-Frequency Word Cards
Sound/Spelling Card Stories
  Audiocassette/CD

Phonemic Awareness

Segmentation: Clapping Syllables in Names and Words

Tell students that it is their turn to break words into parts. Remind students that the word parts they are counting are called *syllables.* Tell them that they will learn more about syllables later.

- Proceed as in Lesson 3, choosing students' names that have not been clapped out.
- Say the word *principal.* Have students repeat the word, then clap out the syllables. Ask them how many times they clapped.
- Continue with the following words:

rocket	package	horse	newspaper
perfume	spaghetti	applesauce	calcium
ambulance	settlement	bottle	camp

- Have students work with partners to figure out the number of syllables in each partner's first and last names. Encourage them to tell the number of syllables in each name and in both names together.

Listening for Vowel Sounds

Listening for /ā/

Point to each long-vowel **Sound/Spelling Card** and tell students that these red letters, vowels, are special because they can say their names. Say the sound of each long vowel as you point to the card. Then have students say the sound of each long vowel.

- Write the letters *Aa* on the board and tell students that you will read a list of words aloud. Explain that you want them to listen carefully. If you say a word that has the sound of long *a*, such as *acorn,* they are to clap their hands and say /ā/. If the word does not have that sound, they are to say and do nothing.
- Say the following words:

day	**say**	so	**place**
bake	**mate**	cute	clue
case	rude	mood	**bay**
choose	**table**	tooth	**clay**
cap	**cape**	hop	hope

Word Study

Word Play

This activity reinforces the idea that changing the spellings in words also changes the way the words sound and their meanings. Write the letters *a, d, i, m, n, p, t* on the board. Tell students to write the word *nip*. Then tell them to replace only one letter in the word to make a new word. Call on volunteers to read the new words they make. (Possible words include *dip, tip*.) Have them continue to make new words by changing only one letter at a time.

Phonics—Blending: Set 2

/b/ spelled *b*	/f/ spelled *f*
/k/ spelled *k*	/l/ spelled *l*

● Review the previously introduced **Sound/Spelling Cards.**
● Display and discuss the new **Sound/Spelling Cards.**

Blending Exercise

● Write the following words and sentences on the board.
● Have students blend the words and sentences using the sound-by-sound procedure described on page 2H.

Line 1:	bad	bit	bib	bill
Line 2:	kin	kiss	kidnap	kid
Line 3:	fad	fat	flip	fill
Line 4:	lap	last	skip	sniff
Sentence 1:	Is the film in the lab?			
Sentence 2:	Bill and Kit like to bat.			

You will need the following **Sound/Spelling Cards** for blending the words in Set 2.
2—Ball, 6—Fan, 11—Camera, 12—Lion

● Before reading each sentence, point to and read the underlined sight words.
● Discuss with students that each sentence begins with a capital letter and ends with a punctuation mark.
● Have students reread the sentences to encourage fluency and comprehension.

TEACHER TIP

Double Consonants On Line 1, point out the word *bill.* Explain to students that the double consonants, *ll,* represent only one sound, /l/. Point out the other words on the lines that have double consonants (*kiss, fill, sniff*), and have students say the sounds as you touch the letters.

SELECTION B • **A Story for Pam**

About the Words and Sentences

- The words on the lines provide practice with the Set 2 sound/spellings.
- For Line 1, point out the word *bill*. Then have them find the same word in one of the sentences. Ask how the word in the sentence differs from the word on the line.
- For Line 2, ask students to identify the two-syllable word. *(kidnap)*
- For the sentences, have students identify the sentence that is a question.

WRITING

Have students identify and write the two words from the word lines that rhyme with *hill* (bill, fill). Discuss as a class other words that rhyme with *hill,* such as *pill, sill,* and *dill.*

Line 1: bat   last   lad
Line 2: fin   kid   fast
Sentence: The man in the bank is kind.

Oral Language

Say some incomplete sentences and have students point to and read words on the lines to complete each one. Here are some possible sentences.

I spilled the coffee in my _____. *(lap)*
My baby sister wears a _____ when she eats. *(bib)*
Friday is the _____ day of this month. *(last)*

Dictation

For the dictation exercise, have students use writing paper. Dictate the words and sentence for them to write.

Use the following sounds-in-sequence procedure:

- Say the first word in each word line. Use the word in a sentence, and then say the word again. Have students say the word.
- Have students say the first sound. Then have them write the spelling. Have students say the remaining sounds sound-by-sound, and then write the spelling for each sound.
- Complete the spelling of the remainder of the words in the same manner.
- After each word line, write (or have a student write) the words on the board. Have students proofread their words. Tell them to circle any incorrect words and to correct them.
- Next dictate the sentence. Dictate one word at a time, following the sounds-in-sequence procedure. Remind students to start the sentence with a capital letter and to use correct end punctuation.
- Write (or have a student write) the sentence on the board. Have students proofread their work and correct any incorrect words.

Building Fluency

Decodable Story: Unit 1, Story 4

- This story reviews the sound/spellings /b/ spelled *b;* /f/ spelled *f;* /k/ spelled *k;* /l/ spelled *l.*
- Have students silently read ***Decodable Stories and Comprehension Skills*** page 4.
- Call on volunteers to read each paragraph aloud.
- For those students who need help, divide sentences according to natural phrases. Mark these phrases with diagonal slash marks on their worksheets.
- After students have read the story aloud, ask them questions and have them point to and read the answers in the story.
- Have students reread the story aloud with a partner.

Sound/Spelling Card Stories Review today's sounds by using the *Sound/Spelling Card Stories.* Listening to the stories will help students understand how they can use the pictures on the *Sound/Spelling Cards* to remember the sounds associated with them. The stories are provided in the appendix and are also available on the *Sound/Spelling Card Stories Audiocassette/CD.*

To help students build fluency, have them take home the *Decodable Stories and Comprehension Skills* stories to read with their families.

SELECTION B • **A Story for Pam**

OBJECTIVES

- Develop reading skills as the story is read to them.
- Gain knowledge of the comprehension skill Author's Purpose.
- Develop vocabulary by listening to and discussing the selection.
- Develop writing skills by writing the author's purpose.
- Identify end marks.

MATERIALS

Student Reader, pp. 4–7
Decodable Stories and Comprehension Skills, p. 76
Language Arts, p. T3
Transparencies 3, 5
Listening Library Audiocassette/CD

Rereading the Selection

Comprehension Skills

Revisiting or rereading a selection allows students to learn and apply skills that give them a more complete understanding of a selection. For today's lesson, reread the selection to students. During the second reading of this selection, students will apply the following comprehension skill:

Author's Purpose: Good readers recognize that authors have a reason for writing—to entertain, to inform, to persuade, and so on—and they use this knowledge to help them better understand a selection.

After Reading

Independent Reading

- Have students choose books from the **Classroom Library** or other available books to take home and read.
- Encourage students to read at least one book each week on their own.
- Set aside a few minutes each day for students to talk to each other about what they are reading and to recommend books to each other.
- Continue to post the copy of **Transparency** 3 on the bulletin board. Encourage students to record the titles of the books they are reading.

TEACHER TIP

Have students listen to the selection recording on the *Listening Library Audiocassette/CD* for a proficient, fluent model of oral reading.

WRITING

Remind students that an author can write to inform, to entertain, or to persuade. Ask students to write the author's purpose for "A Story for Pam."

SELECTION B • **A Story for Pam**

Assessment

Formal

At the conclusion of the lesson, have students complete the assessment Unit 1: A Story for Pam. The Lesson Assessments are found in the *Assessment Guide.*

For all the items in this assessment, you should read both the question and answer choices out loud while students follow along silently. You may find it helpful to walk around the room while students are completing the assessment to provide them with any help they need to understand the questions.

After completing the lesson assessment, discuss the answers with students. Be sure they understand what they were supposed to do and encourage them to explain both their correct and incorrect answers. Be sure to explain that making mistakes is an important part of learning and that no one is always right. This discussion will encourage risk taking and will build students' self-confidence.

Informal

On a routine basis, ask students to name rhyming words for words in the story or words you use in everyday conversation. Write the rhymes on the board, pointing out how the endings of the words are spelled the same.

Ending the Lesson

Read "A Story for Pam" aloud to students. Have volunteers read short portions of the story out loud. The portions of the story should be only a few words, and students should be familiar with the text so they can read it with confidence.

OBJECTIVES

- Complete lesson assessment.
- Review rhyming words.
- Build student confidence.

MATERIALS

Assessment Guide
Student Reader, pp. 4–7

SELECTION C • **An Elephant Story**

Support Materials

LESSON 11
- Sound/Spelling Cards 5, 7, 10, 18, 23
- Decodable Stories and Comprehension Skills, p. 5
- Home Connection, p. 7
- High-Frequency Word Cards
- Sound/Spelling Card Stories Audiocassette/CD

LESSON 12
- Student Reader, pp. 8–11
- Language Arts, p. T6

LESSON 13
- Sound/Spelling Cards 15, 22, 24, 25, 26
- Decodable Stories and Comprehension Skills, p. 6
- High-Frequency Word Cards
- Sound/Spelling Card Stories Audiocassette/CD

LESSON 14
- Student Reader, pp. 8–11
- Transparencies 3, 6, 7
- Decodable Stories and Comprehension Skills, p. 77
- Listening Library Audiocassette/CD
- Language Arts, p. T5

LESSON 15
- Assessment Guide
- Student Reader, pp. 8–11

HOME CONNECTIONS

Distribute *Home Connection* page 7, which describes this week's classwork and suggests activities for families to do at home. This letter is available in English and Spanish.

Teacher Focus	Student Participation
• Conduct Listening Game. • Conduct Word Play. • Introduce Sight Words, blending procedure, and Set 1 blending words and sentences. • Conduct Oral Language activity. • Dictate word lines. • Assist students with decodable text. • Assign writing activity.	• Take part in Listening Game. • Take part in Word Play. • Read Sight Words. • Blend words and sentences. • Identify short-vowel sounds. • Write dictated words and sentences. • Read a decodable story. • Complete writing activity.
• Activate Prior Knowledge and provide background information. • Introduce and discuss selection vocabulary. • Preview selection. • Introduce Comprehension Strategies—Making Connections and Visualizing. • Read the selection to students. • Introduce vocabulary skill. • Assign writing activity.	• Contribute to class discussion. • Read and discuss vocabulary words. Complete selection vocabulary activity. • Browse the selection. • Follow along as selection is read. • Complete vocabulary skill activity. • Complete writing activity.
• Conduct Comparing Word Length game. • Conduct Listening for Vowel Sounds game. • Conduct Word Play. • Review blending procedure; introduce Set 2 blending words and sentences. • Provide riddle clues. • Dictate word lines. • Assist students with decodable text. • Assign writing activity skill.	• Participate in Comparing Word Length game. • Participate in Listening for Vowel Sounds game. • Take part in Word Play. • Blend words and sentences. • Solve riddles. • Write dictated words and sentences. • Read a decodable story. • Complete writing activity.
• Introduce Comprehension Skill—Reality and Fantasy. • Reread and discuss the selection with students. • Discuss Independent Reading. • Assign writing activity. • Introduce grammar skill.	• Follow along as selection is read again. • Discuss the selection. • Select a book to take home and read. • Complete writing activity. • Complete grammar skill activity.
• Administer weekly assessments. • Assess students' progress.	• Complete lesson assessment.

SELECTION C • **An Elephant Story**

OBJECTIVES

- Identify and blend initial consonant sounds in words.
- Blend and break apart sounds in words.
- Read sight words.
- Participate in Word Play activity.
- Develop fluency by reading aloud.
- Apply decoding skills by reading *Unit 1, Decodable Story 5.*
- Develop writing skills by writing words and identifying sound/spellings.

MATERIALS

Sound/Spelling Cards:
5—Hen
7—Gopher
10—Jump
18—Robot
23—Washer
Decodable Stories and Comprehension Skills, p. 5
Home Connection, p. 7
High-Frequency Word Cards
Sound/Spelling Card Stories Audiocassette/CD

Phonemic Awareness

The goal of phonemic awareness activities is to help students understand that spoken words are made up of smaller sounds—word parts, syllables, and phonemes. Learning this concept is important to reading success because of the systematic relationship between speech sounds and written letters. If students cannot hear and manipulate the individual sounds in spoken words, they usually have difficulty deciphering that relationship. Phonemic awareness is also important to students' spelling success. Students who understand that sounds and letters are related usually are able to attach the sounds to letters and spell words.

Oral blending and segmentation are complementary processes in developing phonemic awareness and in learning to read and write. Just as learning to blend smaller units of sound into words is essential to decoding, learning to segment, or break apart, words into smaller units of sound is essential to spelling.

Oral Blending

Tell students that they are already good at listening; they obviously understand words they hear. Then explain that to be really good readers and writers, they need to learn to listen even more closely—they need to be able to hear the separate sounds that make up words. Tell them that when they can hear the separate sounds, they can read and spell most words.

Listening Game: Initial Consonant Sounds

Initial consonant blending builds on the word part and syllable blending that students have been doing. It also prepares students for upcoming and more demanding consonant replacement activities.

Tell students that you are going to ask them to put together some sounds to make words. Explain that you will say the beginning sound, pause, then say the rest of the word. Then you will ask them to put the two parts together and say the word. Demonstrate with the following example.

Teacher: /s/ . . . ofa. What's the word?

Students: sofa

Continue with the following words, pronouncing each part distinctly. If some students are unfamiliar with a word, stop to give its meaning. Alternate between having all students respond together and calling on individuals. Use words that begin with continuant consonant sounds such as /s/, /m/, /f/, /r/, and /l/ that are easy for you to stretch out.

/s/ . . . ample	/m/ . . . argarine
/l/ . . . ong	/s/ . . . aucer
/m/ . . . ailbox	/l/ . . . ather
/f/ . . . eather	/r/ . . . ubber
/s/ . . . entimental	/f/ . . . actory

TEACHER TIP

Phonemes Slash marks denote phonemes. When a letter is enclosed by slash marks, you should pronounce the letter's sound, and not its name.

SELECTION C • **An Elephant Story**

Word Study

In this section of the lesson, students work on phonics, fluency, blending, and spelling. Increasing students' ability to work smoothly with printed words is one of the primary goals of the **Kaleidoscope** program.

Word Play

Say the following words sound by sound: *lamp* (/l/ /a/ /m/ /p/); *bad* (/b/ /a/ /d/); *fat* (/f/ /a/ /t/); *flap* (/f/ /l/ /a/ /p/); *blank* (/b/ /l/ /a/ /n/ /k/). Call on volunteers to identify and say each word. After you say all the words, ask students what sound was in every word that they heard. (/a/)

Sight Words

Many high-frequency or sight words are phonetically irregular. They do not follow the rules, and students need to learn to recognize them "on sight." Some sight words are phonetically regular, but they contain sound/spellings that students have not yet learned and so are not yet decodable.

This week's sight words:

are	here	there

Use the following procedure for teaching sight words:

- Write this week's sight words on the board.
- Read the words to students, and then have them read the words.
- Pronounce any words with which students have difficulty.
- Have students use each sight word in a sentence.

Phonics—Blending: Set 1

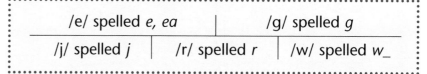

/e/ spelled e, ea		/g/ spelled g	
/j/ spelled j	/r/ spelled r	/w/ spelled w_	

This section of the phonics lesson provides practice in building sounds and spellings into words. The purpose of blending is to help students develop a strategy for reading unfamiliar words.

- Display and discuss each new **Sound/Spelling Card** to be used. Ask students what they know about these cards.

Sight Words Use the *High-Frequency Word Cards* to assess and review students' knowledge of sight words.

You will need the following *Sound/Spelling Cards* for blending the words in Set 1.
5—Hen, 7—Gopher, 10—Jump, 18—Robot, 23—Washer

- Point out that /e/ is usually spelled *e*, but it can also be spelled *ea*.
- Touch each card and tell students the name of the card, the sound, and the spelling. (For detailed information on how to introduce **Sound/Spelling Cards**, see Getting Started.)

Blending Exercise

- The words in the lines provide practice with the Set 1 sound/spellings. Write the following words and sentences on the board.

Line 1:	wed	Ned	head	jet
Line 2:	ran	ram	jab	Jan
Line 3:	win	wand	gap	bread
Line 4:	gill	will	Jill	Jeff
Sentence 1:	Ken and Meg <u>are</u> at the red windmill.			
Sentence 2:	<u>There</u> is a rat in the tent!			
Sentence 3:	Jeb is <u>here</u>.			

Teach the blending exercise using the sound-by-sound procedure below, without varying from it. That way, students will become accustomed to the routine they will use to blend words.

- Blend the words sound-by-sound. Write the first spelling, *w*, and ask students to give the sound. Then write the second spelling, *e,* and have students give the sound. Have students blend through the vowel, saying /we/. Write the final spelling, *d,* and ask students to give the sound. Using a blending motion from left to right beneath the word, have students say all three sounds and blend the word *wed.*
- Continue in this way for the remaining words and the sentences.
- Then have a student use each word in a sentence. Extend the sentence by asking questions such as *where, when, why,* or *how.* Encourage students to extend sentences by adding information at the beginning and not just at the end of the sentence.
- Be sure to discuss the meanings of any unfamiliar words.

WRITING

Have students identify and write the two words from the word lines that have /e/ spelled *ea (head, bread).* Tell students to circle the *ea* sound/spelling in each word.

SELECTION C • **An Elephant Story**

About the Words and Sentences

- Ask students to identify the names in the lines. *(Ned, Jan, Jill, Jeff)*

- Have students find words on the lines that have double consonants to represent single sounds. *(gill, will, Jill, Jeff)*

- On Line 4, have students say the words *gill* and *Jill,* listening for the difference in the initial sounds, /g/ and /j/.

- Before reading a sentence, point to and read the underlined sight words. Have students reread the sentences to encourage fluency and comprehension.

- For Sentence 2, have students identify the end punctuation mark. Ask them what the mark tells them about how the sentence should be read.

Oral Language

Remind students that every word must have a vowel sound. Randomly point to words from the lines, and have students identify the short-vowel sound in each word.

Dictation

Dictation gives students an opportunity to spell words by using the sound/spellings that they have learned. For this dictation exercise, have students use writing paper. Dictate the words and sentence for them to write. Use the following sounds-in-sequence procedure:

- Say the first word in the dictation word line. Use the word in a sentence, then say the word again. Have students say the word.

- Have students say the first sound. Then have them write the spelling. Have students say the remaining sounds sound-by-sound, and then write the spelling for each sound. Encourage them to check the *Sound/Spelling Cards.*

- Complete the spelling of the remainder of the words in the same manner.

- After each word line, write (or have a student write) the words on the board. Have students proofread their words. Tell them to circle any incorrect words and to correct them.

  - Next, dictate the sentence. Dictate one word at a time, following the sounds-in-sequence procedure. Remind students to start the sentence with a capital letter and to use correct end punctuation.

  - Write (or have a student write) the sentence on the board. Have students proofread their work and correct any incorrect words.

Line 1:	rag went gab
Line 2:	head egg jet
Sentence:	Jeff let the jam get wet.

Building Fluency

Decodable Story: Unit 1, Story 5

- This story reviews the sound/spellings /e/ spelled *e, ea;* /g/ spelled *g;* /j/ spelled *j;* /r/ spelled *r;* /w/ spelled *w_.*
- Have students silently read *Decodable Stories and Comprehension Skills* page 5.
- Call on volunteers to read each paragraph aloud.
- For those students who need help, divide sentences according to natural phrases. Mark these phrases with diagonal slash marks on their worksheets.
- After students have read the story aloud, ask them questions and have them point to and read the answers in the story.
- Have students reread the story aloud with a partner. Rereading builds automaticity and fluency.
- Over the next few days, listen to each student reread the story.

Sound/Spelling Card Stories Review today's sounds by using the *Sound/Spelling Card Stories.* Listening to the stories will help students understand how they can use the pictures on the *Sound/Spelling Cards* to remember the sounds associated with them. The stories are provided in the appendix and are also available on the *Sound/Spelling Card Stories Audiocassette/CD.*

 QUICK CHECK

As a quick review of today's sound/spellings, say some sentences, and ask students to suggest words to fill the blanks. Sentences you might read aloud include:

I flew across the country in a big _____. *(jet)*
The clown wore a _____ on his _____. *(wig, head)*
Sam _____ in a long race. *(ran)*

OBJECTIVES

- Discuss vocabulary words and their meanings.
- Develop reading skills as the story is read to them.
- Gain knowledge of the comprehension strategies Making Connections and Visualizing.
- Build vocabulary by identifying compound words.
- Develop writing skills by writing a caption.

MATERIALS

Student Reader, pp. 8–11
Language Arts, p. T6

SELECTION C • **An Elephant Story**

Before Reading

Build Background

Activate Prior Knowledge

- Remind students that this unit is about stories. Remind them of the silly bedtime story that Pam and her father told in "A Story for Pam," and then tell them that the story you are about to read to them involves another silly story.
- Ask students if they have ever made up a silly story. Call on a few volunteers to tell their silly story.

Background Information

Use the following information to help students understand the story you are about to read.

- Ask students to tell what they remember about *fiction* writing. If necessary, remind them that *fiction* means "not real," and a story that is fiction is made up. Explain that the story you are going to read is fiction.
- Ask them to describe an elephant and to talk about what elephants can and cannot do. For example, they can walk, but they can't wear running shoes; they can eat, but they can't cook; and so on. Tell them to keep this kind of information in mind as they listen to the story.

Selection Vocabulary

Write the following vocabulary words on the board. Before reading the selection, introduce and discuss the following words and their meanings:

silly: funny

exit: the way out

fancy: very decorated

Then have students read the words, stopping to blend any words that they have trouble reading. Demonstrate how to decode multisyllabic words by breaking the words into syllables and blending the syllables. Then have students try. If they still have trouble, refer them to the **Sound/Spelling Cards.** If the word is not decodable, give students the pronunciation.

As students study vocabulary, they will use a variety of skills to determine the meaning of a word. These skills include context clues, word structure, and apposition. In this unit, students will be learning about context clues. Write the following example on the board: *Rosa and Ned's silly story made me laugh.* Explain to students that they are going to use the context, or other words in the sentence, to help them decipher the meaning of the word *silly.* Guide students until they can give a reasonable definition of the word.

Vocabulary Activity: Write the word *fancy* on the board and have students give examples of objects that could be fancy, such as a dress, a hat, or a tablecloth.

Preview and Prepare

Before you read, use modeling and prompts such as:

● *Let's browse this story before I read it. Because it's fiction, we should only read the first few sentences so that the ending will be a surprise.*

● *First, let's read the story's title, "An Elephant Story." What does that tell you? Do you think an elephant is telling the story? Or is the story about an elephant? Let's read and find out.*

During Reading

Read Aloud

For this lesson, read the entire selection aloud. As you read, stop at the points that are marked with numbers in magenta circles on the reduced student pages, and model for them how to use the indicated strategy. Encourage students to stop at any point in their reading if they don't understand something or want to talk about the meaning of a passage or word.

Comprehension Strategies

During the reading of "An Elephant Story" on pages 8–11, you will model the following reading comprehension strategies:

Making Connections: Good readers improve their understanding of a selection by making connections between what they already know and what they are reading.

Visualizing: As they read, good readers often make pictures in their minds of the characters, events, and places in a story to help them better understand what they're reading.

TEACHER TIP

Comprehension Strategies Good readers constantly evaluate their understanding of what they read. Stop often to make sure students are doing this.

First Read

Text Comprehension *Strategies*

As you read the selection, use modeling and prompts such as:

❶ Making Connections

Good readers relate past experiences to what they read to make the selection more interesting and easier to understand. I've always liked silly stories. My brother and I made them up all the time. Some of them were really silly too! How about you? Do you ever make up silly stories?

❷ Visualizing

Good readers make mental pictures, or visualize as they read. By picturing in their minds the characters and what they're doing in the story, readers are better able to understand a story. I'm having fun visualizing the elephant. First I saw him trying to squeeze through a little door labeled "EXIT." Then I saw him on a slide at the park. What are you visualizing?

An Elephant Story

by Carolyn Gloeckner
illustrated by Tom Barrett

Rosa and Ned sat on the steps. "What can we do?" asked Ned.

"I know a silly story," Rosa said.

❶ "Tell me," Ned said.

8

WRITING

Have students think about how they are visualizing the elephant and then create an illustration of what they are visualizing. Tell students to write a short caption for their drawing. Ask students to share their illustrations and captions with the class.

VOCABULARY

Tell students that a *compound word* is a word that is made by joining two smaller words. For a lesson on compound words, use **Language Arts** page T6.

"You must help," Rosa said. "I will say something. Then you must say, 'So did the elephant.' Ready? Here's the story. I went through the <u>exit</u>."

"So did the elephant," Ned said.

"I got on my bike."

"So did the elephant."

"I went to the park."

"So did the elephant."

9

Second Read

Text Comprehension *skills*

Reality and Fantasy

Tell students that *fantasy* refers to something that is made up and that could not possibly happen in the real world. Then explain that authors can sometimes use a little fantasy in their realistic stories. They might have both realistic and made-up characters or realistic and made-up events or places.

- After you have reread these pages, have students tell what is realistic about Ned and Rosa. *(Answers will vary.)*

- Have students describe what is realistic and what is fantasy about the elephant in Ned's story. *(Possible answers: realistic—elephants are real; fantasy—elephants cannot ride bicycles.)*

- Use **Transparency** 6 to record their responses.

GRAMMAR

Remind students that capital letters are used every time we write sentences. For a lesson on capitalization, use **Language Arts** page T5.

First Read

Text Comprehension *Strategies*

❸ Making Connections

Oh, wow! I can certainly make connections here. My brother got me to say silly things all the time. Remember to be aware of how events in the story remind you of things that have happened to you. When you make these kinds of connections, share them with the class.

❹ Visualizing

This is easy for me to visualize. I see the kids laughing about their stories, then Ned getting the idea to go to the zoo, and then the two of them riding off down a nice, shady street on their bikes. What are you picturing in your mind?

HOMEWORK TIP

Remind students that the strategies and skills that they are learning can be used with all their reading. Ask them to practice using what they have learned as they read on their own.

"I got a fancy balloon."
Ned smiled. "So did the elephant."
"My balloon popped!"
❸ "So did the elephant!" Ned cried.
"I knew you would say that," Rosa laughed.

10

Rosa and Ned had fun telling their silly story.

Then Ned said, "You gave me an idea. Let's ride our bikes to the zoo."

And that's what they did. Without the elephant.

11

 Second Read

Text Comprehension

Reality and Fantasy

● After reading these pages, have students tell what is realistic and what is fantasy. *(Answers will vary.)*

● Continue to use **Transparency** 6 to record their responses.

● For additional practice with Reality and Fantasy, have students complete **Decodable Stories and Comprehension Skills** page 77.

Discussing the Selection

After you have read the story, discuss it with students. Use prompts such as:

● *Have you read any other story that is like "An Elephant Story"?*

● *Why do you think Ned and Rosa told this silly story?*

● *Did the ending of the story surprise you? How?*

● *How does this story relate to the unit theme, Sharing Stories?*

✓ QUICK CHECK

Quickly review with students the different comprehension strategies and skills that they've used so far.

SELECTION C • **An Elephant Story**

Phonemic Awareness

Comparing Word Length

The purpose of this activity is to help students understand that the spellings of words represent their sounds. More sounds usually means more letters.

● Choose two students' names that begin with the same sound, one long name and one short one (for example, Art and Anthony, Kim and Kathleen, Stan and Stephanie). On the board, write the names one above the other so that the difference in length is obvious.

● Tell students that one name is *Art* and one is *Anthony*. Ask them to clap and say each name, syllable by syllable, as you move your finger beneath the printed letters. Then, have them tell which written word they think says Anthony. Have students notice that the word with more letters has more sounds.

● Present students with other pairs of names that begin with the same sound.

● Next, expand the activity with the following pairs of words:

boy . . . basketball	dragonfly . . . dog
hippopotamus . . . hill	rag . . . rectangle
Mississippi . . . Mars	flea . . . family

Listening for Vowel Sounds

Listening for /ē/

Point to each long-vowel **Sound/Spelling Card** and remind students that these red letters, vowels, are special because they can say their names.

● Write the letters *Ee* on the board and tell students that you will read a list of words aloud. Explain that you want them to listen carefully. If you say a word that has the sound of long *e,* such as *even,* they are to clap their hands and say /ē/. If the word does not have that sound, they are to say and do nothing.

● Say the following words:

meet	new	**speak**	pie
toe	**key**	**see**	mow
she	**cheese**	table	**teeth**
we	sail	**sneeze**	rope

Word Study

Word Play

Write the letters *a, b, e, i, j, g, p, s, t, w* on the board. Tell students to write the word *wag.* Then tell them to replace only one letter in the word to make a new word. Call on volunteers to read the new words they make. (Possible words include *bag, jag, sag, tag, wig.*) Have them continue to make new words by changing only one letter at a time.

Phonics—Blending: Set 2

/o/ spelled o	/v/ spelled v	/ks/ spelled ■x
/y/ spelled y_		/z/ spelled _s

- Review the previously introduced **Sound/Spelling Cards.**
- Display and discuss each new **Sound/Spelling Card.** For example, for Card 26, point out and discuss the two spellings for the /z/ sound. Point to the blank before *s* and remind them that this means that the sound only comes at the end of a syllable or word.

Blending Exercise

- Write the following words and sentences on the board.
- Have students blend the words and sentences using the sound by sound procedure described on page 2H.

Line 1:	tax	six	text	fox
Line 2:	zest	vest	box	yip
Line 3:	yell	visit	yaks	yams
Line 4:	fizz	ox	jobs	odds
Sentence 1:	Here is a velvet box for his gift.			
Sentence 2:	Are Sal and Rex here yet?			
Sentence 3:	There are the pigs and hens.			

- Before reading a sentence, point to and read the underlined sight words.
- Discuss with students that each sentence begins with a capital letter and ends with a punctuation mark.
- Have students reread the sentences to encourage fluency and comprehension.

You will need the following **Sound/Spelling Cards** for blending the words in Set 2.
15—Fox, 22—Vacuum, 24—Exit, 25—Yak, 26—Zipper

13

SELECTION C • **An Elephant Story**

About the Words and Sentences

- The words on the lines provide practice with the Set 2 sound/spellings.
- For Line 1, ask students to identify the short vowel sound/spelling in each word.
- For Line 3, have students say the words *yaks* and *yams*. Ask them to identify the final sound in each word. Which word ends with /z/ spelled *s*? *(yams)* Which word ends with /s/ spelled *s*? *(yaks)*
- Have students find words in which a single sound is spelled with a double consonant. *(yell, fizz, odds)*
- For the sentences, have students identify all previously introduced sight words.

Oral Language

Give clues and have students find the words on the lines that the clues identify. Here are some possible clues:

It's something to wear. *(vest)*

It's a sound made by a puppy. *(yip)*

It's something to read. *(text)*

Dictation

For the dictation exercise, have students use writing paper. Dictate the words and sentence for them to write.

Use the following sounds-in-sequence procedure:

- Say the first word in the dictation word line. Use the word in a sentence, then say the word again. Have students say the word.
- Have students say the first sound. Then have them write the spelling. Have students say the remaining sounds sound-by-sound, and then write the spelling for each sound.
  - Complete the spelling of the remainder of the words in the same manner.
  - After each word line, write (or have a student write) the words on the board. Have students proofread their words. Tell them to circle any incorrect words and to correct them.
  - Next dictate the sentence. Dictate one word at a time, following the sounds-in-sequence procedure. Remind students to start the sentence with a capital letter and to use correct end punctuation.
- Write (or have a student write) the sentence on the board. Have students proofread their work and correct any incorrect words.

WRITING

Have students identify and write the words from the word lines that are animals *(fox, yaks, ox)*. Discuss these animals as a class.

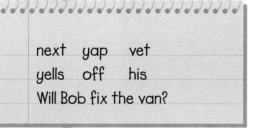

Line 1:   next   yap   vet
Line 2:   yells   off   his
Sentence: Will Bob fix the van?

Building Fluency

Decodable Story: Unit 1, Story 6

● This story reviews the sound/spellings /o/ spelled *o*; /v/ spelled *v*; /ks/ spelled ■*x*; /y/ spelled *y_*; /z/ spelled *_s*.

● Have students silently read **Decodable Stories and Comprehension Skills** page 6.

● Call on volunteers to read each paragraph aloud.

● For those students who need help, divide sentences according to natural phrases. Mark these phrases with diagonal slash marks on their worksheets.

● After students have read the story aloud, ask them questions and have them point to and read the answers in the story.

● Have students reread the story aloud with a partner.

To help students build fluency, have them take home the **Decodable Stories and Comprehension Skills** stories to read with their families.

SELECTION C • **An Elephant Story**

Rereading the Selection

Comprehension Skills

Revisiting or rereading a selection allows students to learn and apply skills that give them a more complete understanding of a selection. For today's lesson, reread the selection to students. During the second reading, students will apply the following comprehension skill:

Reality and Fantasy: Good readers are able to find clues in their reading to let them know if the characters, events, and places are real or if they are just the product of the author's imagination and could not possibly exist.

After Reading

Independent Reading

● Have students choose books from the **Classroom Library** or other available books to take home and read.

● Encourage students to read at least one book each week on their own.

● Set aside a few minutes each day for students to talk to each other about what they are reading and to recommend books to each other.

● Continue to post the copy of **Transparency** 3 on the bulletin board. Encourage students to record the titles of the books they are reading.

OBJECTIVES

• Develop reading skills as the story is read to them.
• Gain knowledge of the comprehension skill Reality and Fantasy.
• Develop vocabulary by listening to and discussing a selection.
• Develop writing skills by writing about the selection.
• Learn about capitalization rules.

MATERIALS

Student Reader, pp. 8–11
Language Arts, p. T5
Transparencies 3, 6, 7
Decodable Stories and Comprehension Skills, p. 77
Listening Library Audiocassette/CD

TEACHER TIP

Have students listen to the selection recording on the *Listening Library Audiocassette/CD* for a proficient, fluent model of oral reading.

WRITING

To reinforce the skill Reality and Fantasy, dictate the following sentence and have students fill in the blank by writing a short phrase about the selection. "We know part of 'An Elephant Story' is fantasy because an elephant cannot _____."

SELECTION C • **An Elephant Story**

Assessment

Formal

At the conclusion of the lesson, have students complete the assessment Unit 1: An Elephant Story. The Lesson Assessments are found in the *Assessment Guide.*

For all the items in this assessment, you should read both the question and answer choices out loud while students follow along silently. You may find it helpful to walk around the room while students are completing the assessment to provide them with any help they need to understand the questions.

In the Unit Assessment, students will answer reading and language arts questions about a new selection, "Story Time." Even though this assessment won't take place for several weeks, we recommend reading the story out loud several times in advance while students follow along silently. If you start this process now, students should be familiar with the story by the end of the unit.

Informal

Name some compound words with which students are familiar. Some examples include *football, raincoat,* and *bedtime.* Ask students to identify other compound words. If students struggle with this task, write half of a compound word on the board and have them identify the rest of the word.

Ending the Lesson

Ask students what they thought about "An Elephant Story." Try to determine if they understood the story. You may find it necessary to explain the story so all of the students understand its humor.

OBJECTIVES

- Complete lesson assessment.
- Preview the unit assessment selection.
- Review compound words.
- Solicit students' opinions about the lesson selection.

MATERIALS

Assessment Guide
Student Reader, pp. 8–11

SELECTION D • **Keeping Secrets**

Support Materials

LESSON 16
- Sound/Spelling Cards 11, 19
- Decodable Stories and Comprehension Skills, p. 7
- Home Connection, p. 9
- High-Frequency Word Cards
- Sound/Spelling Card Stories Audiocassette/CD

LESSON 17
- Student Reader, pp. 12–13
- Language Arts, p. T8
- Transparency 8

LESSON 18
- Sound/Spelling Card 10
- Decodable Stories and Comprehension Skills, p. 8
- High-Frequency Word Cards
- Sound/Spelling Card Stories Audiocassette/CD

LESSON 19
- Student Reader, pp. 12–13
- Transparencies 3, 9, 10
- Decodable Stories and Comprehension Skills, p. 78
- Listening Library Audiocassette/CD
- Language Arts, p. T7

LESSON 20
- Assessment Guide
- Student Reader pp. 12–13

HOME CONNECTIONS

Distribute *Home Connection* page 9, which describes this week's classwork and suggests activities for families to do at home. This letter is available in English and Spanish.

Teacher Focus	**Student Participation**
● Conduct Listening Game. ● Conduct Word Play. ● Introduce Sight Words, blending procedure, and Set 1 blending words and sentences. ● Conduct Oral Language activity. ● Dictate word lines. ● Assist students with decodable text. ● Assign writing activity.	● Take part in Listening Game. ● Take part in Word Play. ● Read Sight Words. ● Blend words and sentences. ● Create sentences. ● Write dictated words and sentences. ● Read a decodable story. ● Complete writing activity.
● Activate Prior Knowledge and provide background information. ● Introduce and discuss selection vocabulary. ● Preview selection. ● Introduce Comprehension Strategies—Monitoring and Clarifying and Monitoring and Adjusting Reading Speed. ● Read the selection to students. ● Introduce vocabulary skill. ● Assign writing activity.	● Contribute to class discussion. ● Read and discuss vocabulary words. Complete selection vocabulary activity. ● Browse the selection. ● Follow along as selection is read. ● Complete vocabulary skill activity. ● Complete writing activity.
● Conduct Repeating Word Parts game. ● Teach phonemic rhyme. ● Conduct Word Play. ● Review blending procedure; introduce Set 2 blending words and sentences. ● Conduct Oral Language activity. ● Dictate word lines. ● Assist students with decodable text. ● Assign writing activity.	● Participate in Repeating Word Parts game. ● Learn phonemic rhyme. ● Take part in Word Play. ● Blend words and sentences. ● Solve riddles. ● Write dictated words and sentences. ● Read a decodable story. ● Complete writing activity.
● Introduce Comprehension Skill—Cause and Effect. ● Reread and discuss the selection with students. ● Discuss Independent Reading. ● Assign writing activity. ● Introduce grammar skill.	● Follow along as selection is read again. ● Discuss the selection. ● Select a book to take home and read. ● Complete writing activity. ● Complete grammar skill activity.
● Administer weekly assessments. ● Assess students' progress.	● Complete lesson assessment.

16

OBJECTIVES

- Identify and blend initial consonant sounds in words.
- Read sight words.
- Blend and break apart sounds in words.
- Participate in Word Play activity.
- Develop fluency by reading aloud.
- Apply decoding skills by reading *Unit 1, Decodable Story 7.*
- Develop writing skills by writing words.

MATERIALS

Sound/Spelling Cards:
11—Camera
19—Sausages
Decodable Stories and Comprehension Skills, p. 7
Home Connection, p. 9
High-Frequency Word Cards
Sound/Spelling Card Stories Audiocassette/CD

Phonemic Awareness

The goal of phonemic awareness activities is to help students understand that spoken words are made up of smaller sounds—word parts, syllables, and phonemes. Learning this concept is important to reading success because of the systematic relationship between speech sounds and written letters. If students cannot hear and manipulate the individual sounds in spoken words, they usually have difficulty deciphering that relationship. Phonemic awareness is also important to students' spelling success. Students who understand that sounds and letters are related usually are able to attach the sounds to letters and spell words.

Oral blending and segmentation are complementary processes in developing phonemic awareness and in learning to read and write. Just as learning to blend smaller units of sound into words is essential to decoding, learning to segment, or break apart, words into smaller units of sound is essential to spelling.

Oral Blending

Tell students that they are already good at listening; they obviously understand words they hear. Then explain that to be really good readers and writers, they need to learn to listen even more closely—they need to be able to hear the separate sounds that make up words. Tell them that when they can hear the separate sounds, they can read and spell most words.

Listening Game: Initial Consonant Sounds

Initial consonant blending builds on the word part and syllable blending that students have been doing. It also prepares students for upcoming and more demanding consonant replacement activities.

Tell students that you are again going to ask them to put together some sounds to make words. Explain that you will say the beginning sound, pause, then say the rest of the word. Then you will ask them to put together and say the word. Demonstrate with the following example:

Teacher: /m/ . . . otorcycle. What's the word?

Students: motorcycle

Continue with the following words, pronouncing each part distinctly. If some students are unfamiliar with a word, stop to give its meaning. Alternate between having all students respond together and calling on individuals.

/l/ . . . ibrary	/m/ . . . emory
/s/ . . . uddenly	/l/ . . . etter
/r/ . . . anch	/f/ . . . urniture
/s/ . . . andwich	/m/ . . . usical
/f/ . . . ortune	/r/ . . . estaurant
/m/ . . . onument	/l/ . . . aboratory

TEACHER TIP

Listening Game Use your own words in addition to the words on this list. Be sure to use only words with single initial consonant sounds. (Do not use blends.) Using words that begin with continuant consonant sounds such as /l/, /m/, /r/, /f/, and /s/ will allow you to stretch out the initial sounds, making the words easier for students to identify.

SELECTION D • **Keeping Secrets**

Word Study

In this section of the lesson, students work on phonics, fluency, blending, and spelling. Increasing students' ability to work smoothly with printed words is one of the primary goals of the *Kaleidoscope* program.

Word Play

Teach students the I'm Thinking of Something game. Choose a previously taught sound/spelling. Look around the room until you see something that starts with the sound. Say, for example, "I'm thinking of something in the room that starts with /w/." Give a clue, such as the object's size or color, or direct students' attention to the correct part of the room. You might choose objects in pictures, posters, or large maps. Objects you might name include window, wall, water, watch, wagon. Continue by choosing objects that begin with other previously taught sound/spellings.

Sight Words

This week's sight words:

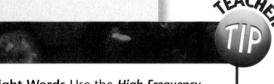

look   said   was

TEACHER TIP

Sight Words Use the *High-Frequency Word Cards* to assess and review students' knowledge of sight words.

Use the following procedure for teaching sight words:

● Write this week's sight words on the board.
● Read the words to students, and then have them read the words.
● Pronounce any words with which students have difficulty.
● Have students use each sight word in a sentence.

Phonics—Blending: Set 1

> /k/ spelled *c*, ■*ck* | /s/ spelled *ce, ci_*

● Review the previously introduced *Sound/Spelling Cards.*
● For Card 11, point out the various spellings for /k/. Tell students that in this lesson, they will focus only on the c and _ck spellings. Remind them that the green box before the _ck spelling stands for a short-vowel sound. A short-vowel spelling will always come before this spelling for /k/.
● For Card 19, point out the spellings ce and ci_. Tell students that these are the spellings for /s/ they will work with in this lesson.

You will need the following *Sound/Spelling Cards* for blending the words in Set 1. 11—Camera, 19—Sausages

Blending Exercise

● The words in the lines provide practice with the Set 1 sound/spellings. Write the following words and sentences on the board.

Line 1:	lick	lock	Nick	click
Line 2:	cell	cent	pencil	stencil
Line 3:	can	camp	Cal	cot
Sentence 1:	Greg said the black cap was in the backpack.			
Sentence 2:	Look at Rick dance!			

Teach the blending exercise using the procedure below, without varying from it. That way, students will become accustomed to the routine they will use to blend words.

● Blend the first line of words sound by sound. Write the first spelling, *l*, and ask students to give the sound. Then write the second spelling, *i*, and have students give the sound. Have students blend through the vowel, saying /li/. Write the final spelling, *ck*, and ask students to give the sound. Using a blending motion from left to right beneath the word, have students blend the word *lick*.

● Continue in this way for the remaining words on the first line.

● Begin Line 2 by doing whole-word blending. Write the word on the board. Have students say the sound as you point to each spelling. Then have students pronounce the word naturally—it is important for them to realize that blending sounds results in a word.

● Continue in this way for the remaining words and the sentences.

● If students have trouble reading a word, stop and do sound-by-sound blending.

● Then have a student use each word in a sentence. Extend the sentence by asking questions such as *where, when, why,* or *how.* Encourage students to extend sentences by adding information at the beginning and not just at the end of the sentence.

● Be sure to discuss the meanings of any unfamiliar words.

TEACHER TIP

As you read the words with the ending *-il*, pronounce the endings for students and tell them the vowel sound in the endings is called a schwa sound. Students should be able to sound out the words once you pronounce the endings for them.

16

SELECTION D • **Keeping Secrets**

About the Words and Sentences

- For Line 1, ask students what the word *Nick* would mean if it did not start with a capital letter. *(a small cut)*
- For Line 1, ask students to identify the words that rhyme. *(lick, Nick, click)*
- Before reading a sentence, point to and read the underlined sight words. Have students reread the sentences to build fluency and comprehension.
- For the sentences, have students find the sentence that is an exclamation.

Oral Language

Have students take turns coming to the board, touching a word, and using it in a sentence. Encourage them to extend their sentences by asking *when, where, how,* and *why* questions.

Dictation

Dictation gives students an opportunity to spell words by using the sound/spellings that they have learned. For this dictation exercise, have students use writing paper. Dictate the words and sentence for them to write. Use the following whole-word procedure:

- Say the first word in the Dictation word lines. Use the word in a sentence, then say the word again. Have students say the word.
- Tell students to think about how to segment the word into sounds. Then have them write the spelling for each sound. Encourage them to check the **Sound/Spelling Cards.**
- After each word line, write (or have a student write) the words on the board. Have students proofread their words. Tell them to circle any incorrect words and to correct them.
- Next, dictate the sentence. Dictate one word at a time, following the sounds-in-sequence or whole-word dictation procedure, depending on your students. Remind students to start the sentence with a capital letter and to use correct end punctuation.
- Write (or have a student write) the sentence on the board. Have students proofread their work and correct any incorrect words.

Line 1:	clock	cat	stick
Line 2:	cent	since	back
Sentence:	The dance was at six.		

- Point out that /e/ is usually spelled *e*, but it can also be spelled *ea*.

- Touch each card and tell students the name of the card, the sound, and the spelling. (For detailed information on how to introduce *Sound/Spelling Cards*, see Getting Started.)

Blending Exercise

- The words in the lines provide practice with the Set 1 sound/spellings. Write the following words and sentences on the board.

Line 1:	wed	Ned	head	jet
Line 2:	ran	ram	jab	Jan
Line 3:	win	wand	gap	bread
Line 4:	gill	will	Jill	Jeff
Sentence 1:	Ken and Meg <u>are</u> at the red windmill.			
Sentence 2:	<u>There</u> is a rat in the tent!			
Sentence 3:	Jeb is <u>here</u>.			

Teach the blending exercise using the sound-by-sound procedure below, without varying from it. That way, students will become accustomed to the routine they will use to blend words.

- Blend the words sound-by-sound. Write the first spelling, *w,* and ask students to give the sound. Then write the second spelling, *e,* and have students give the sound. Have students blend through the vowel, saying /we/. Write the final spelling, *d,* and ask students to give the sound. Using a blending motion from left to right beneath the word, have students say all three sounds and blend the word *wed.*

- Continue in this way for the remaining words and the sentences.

- Then have a student use each word in a sentence. Extend the sentence by asking questions such as *where, when, why,* or *how.* Encourage students to extend sentences by adding information at the beginning and not just at the end of the sentence.

- Be sure to discuss the meanings of any unfamiliar words.

WRITING

Have students identify and write the two words from the word lines that have /e/ spelled *ea (head, bread).* Tell students to circle the *ea* sound/spelling in each word.

SELECTION C • **An Elephant Story**

About the Words and Sentences

- Ask students to identify the names in the lines. *(Ned, Jan, Jill, Jeff)*

- Have students find words on the lines that have double consonants to represent single sounds. *(gill, will, Jill, Jeff)*

- On Line 4, have students say the words *gill* and *Jill,* listening for the difference in the initial sounds, /g/ and /j/.

- Before reading a sentence, point to and read the underlined sight words. Have students reread the sentences to encourage fluency and comprehension.

- For Sentence 2, have students identify the end punctuation mark. Ask them what the mark tells them about how the sentence should be read.

Oral Language

Remind students that every word must have a vowel sound. Randomly point to words from the lines, and have students identify the short-vowel sound in each word.

Dictation

Dictation gives students an opportunity to spell words by using the sound/spellings that they have learned. For this dictation exercise, have students use writing paper. Dictate the words and sentence for them to write. Use the following sounds-in-sequence procedure:

- Say the first word in the dictation word line. Use the word in a sentence, then say the word again. Have students say the word.

- Have students say the first sound. Then have them write the spelling. Have students say the remaining sounds sound-by-sound, and then write the spelling for each sound. Encourage them to check the **Sound/Spelling Cards.**

- Complete the spelling of the remainder of the words in the same manner.

- After each word line, write (or have a student write) the words on the board. Have students proofread their words. Tell them to circle any incorrect words and to correct them.

  - Next, dictate the sentence. Dictate one word at a time, following the sounds-in-sequence procedure. Remind students to start the sentence with a capital letter and to use correct end punctuation.

  - Write (or have a student write) the sentence on the board. Have students proofread their work and correct any incorrect words.

Line 1:	rag went gab
Line 2:	head egg jet
Sentence:	Jeff let the jam get wet.

Building Fluency

Decodable Story: Unit 1, Story 7

- This story reviews the sound/spellings /k/ spelled *c*, ▪*ck*; /s/ spelled *ce, ci_*.
- Have students silently read *Decodable Stories and Comprehension Skills* page 7.
- Call on volunteers to read each paragraph aloud.
- For those students who need help, divide sentences according to natural phrases. Mark these phrases with diagonal slash marks on their worksheets.
- After students have read the story aloud, ask them questions and have them point to and read the answers in the story.
- Have students reread the story aloud with a partner. Rereading builds automaticity and fluency.
- Over the next few days, listen to each student reread the story.

QUICK CHECK

As a quick review of today's sound/spellings, say some sentences, and ask students to suggest words to fill the blanks. Sentences you might read aloud include:

I plan to go to summer _____ this year. *(camp)*
I lost my yellow _____ before the math test. *(pencil)*
Did you _____ the door? *(lock)*

TEACHER TIP

Develop Fluency Model fluent reading frequently for students, showing them how pausing in the right places and adding expression can make a passage easier to understand.

SELECTION D • **Keeping Secrets**

OBJECTIVES

- Discuss vocabulary words and their meanings.
- Develop reading skills as the story is read to them.
- Gain knowledge of the comprehension strategies Monitoring and Clarifying and Monitoring and Adjusting Reading Speed.
- Build vocabulary by identifying homophones.
- Develop writing skills by writing a prediction.

MATERIALS

Student Reader, pp. 12–13
Language Arts, p. T8
Transparency 8

Before Reading

Build Background

Activate Prior Knowledge

- Ask students to recall and retell briefly "From Rocks to Books," "A Story for Pam," and "An Elephant Story."
- Ask them to tell how each selection relates to the unit theme, Sharing Stories.

Background Information

Use the following information to help students understand the selection you are about to read.

- Tell students that the selection you are going to read is nonfiction. Have them talk about the differences between nonfiction and fiction.
- Ask them to think about how people can write down important information and still keep it secret from people who shouldn't see it.

Selection Vocabulary

Write the following vocabulary words on the board. Before reading the selection, introduce and discuss the following words and their meanings:

message: information sent from one person or group to another

hazy: not clear; blurry

secrets: private information known by one or a few

codes: written symbols that have special meanings

Then have students read the words, stopping to blend any words that they have trouble reading. Demonstrate how to decode multisyllabic words by breaking the words into syllables and blending the syllables. Then have students try. If they still have trouble, refer them to the *Sound/Spelling Cards.* If the word is not decodable, give students the pronunciation.

As students study vocabulary, they will use a variety of skills to determine the meaning of a word. These skills include context clues, word structure, and apposition. In this unit, students will be learning about context clues. Write the following example on the board: *On a hazy day, we can see only a dim outline of the mountains.* Explain to students that they are going to use the context, or other words in the sentence, to help them decipher the meaning of the word *hazy.* Guide students until they can give a reasonable definition of the word.

Vocabulary Activity: Using the vocabulary words, create riddles for students to solve. You can use the following examples:

I rhyme with lazy. (hazy)

A letter or a note can be this. (message)

I write this type of information in my private diary. (secret)

Preview and Prepare

Before you read, use modeling and prompts such as:

- *Let's browse this story before I read it. Remember, it's nonfiction. We browse nonfiction by looking at the entire selection.*
- *The title of this selection is "Keeping Secrets." That sounds interesting. What might you learn from a selection with a title like this? See the table of letters and numbers? What does that look like to you? Let's read and find out what it is.*

WRITING

After browsing the selection, have students write a word or phrase that describes what they think the selection will be about.

During Reading

Read Aloud

For this lesson, read the entire selection aloud. As you read, stop at the points that are marked with numbers in magenta circles on the reduced student pages, and model for them how to use the indicated strategy. Encourage students to stop at any point in their reading if they don't understand something or want to talk about the meaning of a passage or word.

Comprehension Strategies

During the reading of "Keeping Secrets" on pages 12–13, you will model the following reading comprehension strategies:

Monitoring and Clarifying: Good readers pay attention to how well they understand what they are reading. They stop to clarify the meanings of new words and to think about unfamiliar or difficult passages.

Monitoring and Adjusting Reading Speed: If they notice that they are having trouble understanding what they read, good readers slow down. They also may reread passages.

17

First Read

Text Comprehension Strategies

As you read the selection, use modeling and prompts such as:

❶ Monitoring and Clarifying

Good readers pay attention to how well they understand what they read. They stop to clarify, or figure out, the meanings of words they don't know and of passages that confuse them. I'm not sure what this paragraph means, because I don't know what hazy *means here. Hazy to me means "foggy" or "rainy," but that doesn't make sense in this paragraph. I'll look it up in the dictionary. OK, the dictionary says that* hazy *also means "blurry." I'll read the sentence again with* blurry *in place of* hazy. *Now I understand. The smoke signals were blurry to others far away. Using a dictionary is a good way to clarify as you read.*

❷ Monitoring and Adjusting Reading Speed

I didn't understand this page at all. It has so much information. I'm going to reread it, but slower this time. Well, it's a code. By reading what Jim wrote to Eve and using the code to translate it, I know how to use the code to read the secret message. Can you read it? What does it say? (MAKE YOUR OWN CODE.) Great!

HOMEWORK TIP

Have students make their own codes and write a secret message for family members to read at home.

Keeping Secrets

by Edward Brimacombe
illustrated by Sally Schaedler

Once people could not write and they could not phone. But they found ways to tell the news. One way was to build a fire. The smoke was a <u>message</u>. Others ❶ far away could see it, but it was <u>hazy</u>.

Later people learned to write. But some things had to be <u>secrets</u>. So they used marks and numbers for letters. The marks and numbers were <u>codes</u>.

Jim has a message for Eve. He writes a note in their secret code.

12

VOCABULARY

Tell students that a *homophone* is a word that sounds the same as another word but has a different spelling and meaning. For a lesson on homophones, use *Language Arts* page T8.

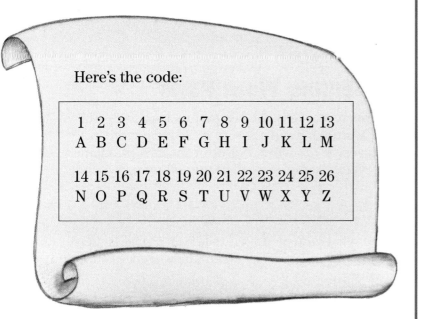

Here's the code:

1	2	3	4	5	6	7	8	9	10	11	12	13
A	B	C	D	E	F	G	H	I	J	K	L	M

14	15	16	17	18	19	20	21	22	23	24	25	26
N	O	P	Q	R	S	T	U	V	W	X	Y	Z

Each number stands for the letter below it. Jim writes:

13-5-5-20   13-5   1-20   20-8-5   12-1-11-5

The message is MEET ME AT THE LAKE.

Here's a secret message for you. Can you read it? It is in Jim's code.

13-1-11-5   25-15-21-18   15-23-14   3-15-4-5

13

Text Comprehension

Cause and Effect

Explain to students that often something happens that makes something else happen. For example, a flat tire on a school bus could cause students to miss their first class of the day. The flat tire is the *cause,* or why something happened. Students missing their first class is the *effect,* or what happened.

- Tell students that authors often use cause-and-effect relationships as a way to organize their writing.
- Ask them to identify the causes for these effects: People built fires and sent smoke signals. People wrote in codes.
- Use **Transparency** 9 to record their responses.
- For additional practice with Cause and Effect, have students complete **Decodable Stories and Comprehension Skills** page 78.

Discussing the Selection

After you have read the selection, discuss it with students. Use prompts such as:

- *What did you like about this selection?*
- *What did you learn from reading it?*
- *How does this selection relate to the unit theme, Sharing Stories?*

GRAMMAR

Tell students that every sentence must have two things: a *subject* (who or what the sentence is about) and a *predicate* (what the subject is or does). For a lesson on identifying subjects and predicates, use **Language Arts** page T7.

 QUICK CHECK

Quickly review with students the previous comprehension strategies and skills that they've used so far.

TEACHER TIP

Segmentation In order to make sure that every student is thinking on every turn, switch unpredictably from asking for a whole group response to asking for individual responses.

SELECTION D • **Keeping Secrets**

Phonemic Awareness

Segmentation: Repeating Word Parts

- In this activity, have students repeat only the last part of a syllable—the *rime.* As an example, look at students and say very clearly the word *zoo,* exaggerating the /z/. Then repeat the word, but omit the first phoneme—the *onset* (say /o͞o/). Give several examples, such as the following:

moo . . . /o͞o/	ray . . . /ā/
so . . . /ō/	see . . . /ē/

- When students understand what you are doing, tell them that it is their turn to repeat the last part of the syllable. Say *toe* and have students respond by saying /ō/. Continue with these words:

sigh	me	hue
low	no	pay
pie	we	go
fee	ray	boo

Willaby Wallaby Woo

- Teach students this rhyme, which involves students in phonemic play.

    Willaby Wallaby Woo

    An elephant sat on you!

    Willaby Wallaby We

    An elephant sat on me!

  - Change the rhyme, using students' names:

        Willaby Wallaby Wonya

        An elephant sat on Tonya!

        Willaby Wallaby Weve

        An elephant sat on Steve!

  - After demonstrating the rhyme with several names, ask students to supply classmates' names to complete the couplets.

Word Study

Word Play

Play the I'm Thinking of Something game again. Choose a previously taught sound/spelling. Look around the room until you see something that starts with the sound. Say, for example, "I'm thinking of something in the room that starts with /k/." Give a clue, such as the object's size or color, or direct students' attention to the correct part of the room. Objects you might name include cabinet, crayon, calendar, keyboard, kite. If you choose, turn the game over to students to find and give clues for other objects that begin with a previously taught sound/spelling.

Phonics—Blending: Set 2

> /j/ spelled *ge*, *gi_*

- Display and discuss the new **Sound/Spelling Card.** Point out the spellings for /j/. Ask students which spelling they have worked with *(j)*. Tell them that in this lesson they will work with the *ge* and *gi_* spellings.

Blending Exercise

- Write the following words and sentences on the board.
- Have students blend the words and sentences using the whole-word procedure described on page 12F.

Line 1:	gem	singe	hinge
Line 2:	logic	tragic	rigid
Sentence 1:	Look at the frigid frog!		
Sentence 2:	Jeff said the gem was red.		

- Before reading a sentence, point to and read the underlined sight words.
- Discuss with students that each sentence begins with a capital letter and ends with a punctuation mark.
- Have students reread the sentences to encourage fluency and comprehension.

Sound/Spelling Card Stories Review today's sounds by using the *Sound/Spelling Card Stories.* Listening to the stories will help students understand how they can use the pictures on the *Sound/Spelling Cards* to remember the sounds associated with them. The stories are provided in the appendix and are also available on the *Sound/Spelling Card Stories Audiocassette/CD.*

You will need the following *Sound/Spelling Card* for blending the words in Set 2. 10—Jump

SELECTION D • **Keeping Secrets**

About the Words and Sentences

- The words on the lines provide practice with the Set 2 sound/spellings.
- Have students find words on the lines that rhyme. *(singe, hinge)*
- For Line 2, have students count the syllables in each word.
- Discuss the meanings of any unfamiliar words.
- For the sentences, have students identify the sentence that is an exclamation and the sentence that is a statement.

WRITING

Have students write the words from Line 2 and circle the *gi_* sound/spelling for /j/ in each word.

Oral Language

Give clues and have students find words on the lines that the clues identify. Here are some possible clues:

It's another name for *jewel. (gem)*
It can be found on a door. *(hinge)*
It means "to burn slightly." *(singe)*

Dictation

For the dictation exercise, have students use writing paper. Dictate the words and sentence for them to write.

Use the following whole-word procedure:

- Say the first word in the dictation word line. Use the word in a sentence, then say the word again. Have students say the word.
- Tell students to think about how to segment the word into sounds. Then have them write the spelling for each sound.
- After each word line, write (or have a student write) the words on the board. Have students proofread their words. Tell them to circle any incorrect words and to correct them.

- Next dictate the sentence. Dictate one word at a time, following the sounds-in-sequence or whole-word dictation procedure, depending on your students. Remind students to start the sentence with a capital letter and use correct end punctuation.
- Write (or have a student write) the sentence on the board. Have students proofread their work and correct any incorrect words.

Line 1:	frigid rigid
Line 2:	gem hinge
Sentence:	The fringe on the dress is red.

Building Fluency

Decodable Story: Unit 1, Story 8

- This story reviews the sound/spellings /j/ spelled ge, gi_.
- Have students silently read *Decodable Stories and Comprehension Skills* page 8.
- Call on volunteers to read each paragraph aloud.
- For those students who need help, divide sentences according to natural phrases. Mark these phrases with diagonal slash marks on their worksheets.
- After students have read the story aloud, ask them questions and have them point to and read the answers in the story.
- Have students reread the story aloud with a partner.

HOMEWORK TIP

To help students build fluency, have them share with the class books, stories, and magazines that they have brought from home and read previously with their families.

19

SELECTION D • **Keeping Secrets**

OBJECTIVES

- Develop reading skills as the story is read to them.
- Gain knowledge of the comprehension skill Cause and Effect.
- Develop vocabulary by listening to and discussing a selection.
- Develop writing skills by writing a secret message.
- Identify subjects and predicates.

MATERIALS

Student Reader, pp. 12–13
Language Arts, p. T7
Decodable Stories and Comprehension Skills, p. 78
Transparencies 3, 9, 10
Listening Library Audiocassette/CD

Rereading the Selection

Comprehension Skills

Revisiting or rereading a selection allows students to learn and apply skills that give them a more complete understanding of a selection. For today's lesson, reread the selection to students. During the second reading, students will apply the following comprehension skill:

Cause and Effect: Good readers look for relationships between events in what they read. This helps them make accurate predictions about what will happen.

After Reading

Independent Reading

- Have students choose books from the **Classroom Library** or other available books to take home and read.
- Encourage students to read at least one book each week on their own.
- Set aside a few minutes each day for students to meet one-on-one with you to discuss their reading.
- Encourage students to record the titles of the books they are reading on the copy of **Transparency** 3.

TEACHER TIP

Have students listen to the selection recording on the **Listening Library Audiocassette/CD** for a proficient, fluent model of oral reading.

WRITING

Using the code on page 13 of the selection, write a secret message on the board. Tell students to figure out the message and write it on their paper. Call on a volunteer to read the secret message.

SELECTION D • **Keeping Secrets**

Assessment

Formal

At the conclusion of the lesson, have students complete the assessment Unit 1: Keeping Secrets. The Lesson Assessments are found in the **Assessment Guide.**

For all the items in this assessment, you should read both the question and answer choices out loud while students follow along silently. You may find it helpful to walk around the room while students are completing the assessment to provide them with any help they need to understand the questions.

By now, students should be familiar with the Unit Assessment selection "Story Time." Read Question 1 to students. Spend a few minutes discussing their favorite stories. Provide them with the help they need to write the names of their favorite stories. They will share their completed answers with other students during the Unit Assessment.

Informal

Be sure students understand what a homophone is. Write the words *see* and *sea* on the board. Have students explain the meanings of the two words. Ask students to name other homophone pairs. If they cannot easily do this, provide one word of a homophone pair, such as *here,* and have students define it. Ask students to name another word that sounds like *here* but is spelled differently and has a different meaning.

Ending the Lesson

Have students write messages using the code in the lesson selection. Be sure the messages are simple, and provide students with any help they need. Ask them when people might want to write messages in a code.

OBJECTIVES

- Complete lesson assessment.
- Review homophones.
- Visualize a character from a story.
- Demonstrate understanding of a code.

MATERIALS

Assessment Guide
Student Reader, pp. 12–13

SELECTION E • **Stories in the Sky**

Support Materials

LESSON 21

- Sound/Spelling Cards 10, 17, 21
- Decodable Stories and Comprehension Skills, p. 9
- Home Connection, p. 11
- High-Frequency Word Cards
- Sound/Spelling Card Stories Audiocassette/CD

LESSON 22

- Student Reader, pp. 14–17
- Language Arts, p. T10

LESSON 23

- Sound/Spelling Card 29
- Decodable Stories and Comprehension Skills, p. 10
- High-Frequency Word Cards
- Sound/Spelling Card Stories Audiocassette/CD

LESSON 24

- Student Reader, pp. 14–17
- Transparencies 3, 11
- Decodable Stories and Comprehension Skills, p. 79
- Listening Library Audiocassette/CD
- Language Arts, p. T9

LESSON 25

- Assessment Guide
- Student Reader, pp. 14–17

HOME CONNECTIONS

Distribute *Home Connection* page 11, which describes this week's classwork and suggests activities for families to do at home. This letter is available in English and Spanish.

Teacher Focus	Student Participation
• Conduct Listening Game. • Conduct Word Play. • Introduce Sight Words, blending procedure, and Set 1 blending words and sentences. • Conduct Oral Language Activity. • Dictate word lines. • Assist students with decodable text. • Assign writing activity.	• Take part in Listening Game. • Take part in Word Play. • Read Sight Words. • Blend words and sentences. • Suggest riddles and clues. • Write dictated words and sentences. • Read a decodable story. • Complete writing activity.
• Activate Prior Knowledge and provide background information. • Introduce and discuss selection vocabulary. • Preview selection. • Review Comprehension Strategies—Asking Questions and Monitoring and Clarifying. • Read the selection to students. • Introduce vocabulary skill. • Assign writing activity.	• Contribute to class discussion. • Read and discuss vocabulary words. Complete selection vocabulary activity. • Browse the selection. • Follow along as selection is read. • Complete vocabulary skill activity. • Complete writing activity.
• Conduct Repeating Word Parts game. • Conduct Listening for Vowel Sounds game. • Conduct Word Play. • Review blending procedure; introduce Set 2 blending words and sentences. • Provide riddle clues. • Dictate word lines. • Assist students with decodable text. • Assign writing activity.	• Participate in Repeating Word Parts game. • Participate in Listening for Vowel Sounds game. • Take part in Word Play. • Blend words and sentences. • Solve riddles. • Write dictated words and sentences. • Read a decodable story. • Complete writing activity.
• Introduce Comprehension Skill—Main Idea and Details. • Reread and discuss the selection with students. • Discuss Independent Reading. • Assign writing activity. • Introduce grammar skill.	• Follow along as selection is read again. • Discuss the selection. • Select a book to take home and read. • Complete writing activity. • Complete grammar skill activity.
• Administer weekly assessments. • Assess students' progress.	• Complete lesson assessment.

OBJECTIVES

- Identify and blend initial consonant sounds in words.
- Read sight words.
- Blend and break apart sounds in words.
- Participate in Word Play.
- Develop fluency by reading aloud.
- Apply decoding skills by reading *Unit 1, Decodable Story 9*.
- Develop writing skills by writing compound words.

MATERIALS

Sound/Spelling Cards:
10—Jump
17—Quacking Ducks
21—Tug
Decodable Stories and Comprehension Skills, p. 9
Home Connection, p. 11
High-Frequency Word Cards
Sound/Spelling Card Stories Audiocassette/CD

Phonemic Awareness

The goal of phonemic awareness activities is to help students understand that spoken words are made up of smaller sounds—word parts, syllables, and phonemes. Learning this concept is important to reading success because of the systematic relationship between speech sounds and written letters. If students cannot hear and manipulate the individual sounds in spoken words, they usually have difficulty deciphering that relationship. Phonemic awareness is also important to students' spelling success. Students who understand that sounds and letters are related usually are able to attach the sounds to letters and spell words.

Oral blending and segmentation are complementary processes in developing phonemic awareness and in learning to read and write. Just as learning to blend smaller units of sound into words is essential to decoding, learning to segment, or break apart, words into smaller units of sound is essential to spelling.

Oral Blending

Tell students that they are already good at listening; they obviously understand words they hear. Then explain that to be really good readers and writers, they need to learn to listen even more closely—they need to be able to hear the separate sounds that make up words. Tell them that when they can hear the separate sounds, they can read and spell most words.

Listening Game: Initial Consonant Sounds

The words in this activity begin with stop sounds. Stop sounds may be harder for you to hold and therefore harder for students to identify. However, do not distort the initial consonant by trying to stretch it out. Tell students that they are going to play the Initial Consonant Sounds Game again. Remind students that you will say some words, but you will say them in two parts. Then you will ask them to put the two parts together. Use the following example.

Teacher: */d/ . . . inner. What's the word?*

Students: *dinner*

Say the following word parts and have students say the complete word.

/p/ . . . eppermint	/d/ . . . aytime
/t/ . . . oothache	/b/ . . . owling
/t/ . . . estimony	/p/ . . . opcorn
/b/ . . . asement	/k/ . . . otton

TEACHER TIP

Listening Game To keep students' attention, switch unpredictably from group to individual responses.

SELECTION E • **Stories in the Sky**

Word Study

In this section of the lesson, students work on phonics, fluency, blending, and spelling. Increasing students' ability to work smoothly with printed words is one of the primary goals of the *Kaleidoscope* program.

Word Play

Provide pages from a newspaper to each student. Tell students to look for and circle words on the page that contain one of these sound/spellings: /j/ spelled *j, ge, gi_*; /s/ spelled *s, ce, ci_*; /k/ spelled *c, k, ■ck*. Call on individuals to read the words they have found and circled.

Sight Words

This week's sight words:

any	of	they

Use the following procedure for teaching sight words:

● Write this week's sight words on the board.
● Read the words to students, and then have them read the words.
● Pronounce any words with which students have difficulty.
● Have students use each sight word in a sentence.

Phonics—Blending: Set 1

/j/ spelled ■*dge*	/kw/ spelled *qu_*
/u/ spelled *u*	

● Display and discuss the **Sound/Spelling Cards.** Ask students what they know about these cards. For example, the letters on Card 21 are red, and the card has a green box—this means the card is for a vowel sound/spelling. For Card 10, point out the different spellings for /j/. Remind students that they have already worked with the /j/ spellings *j, ge,* and *gi_*. Explain that they will work with the ■*dge* spelling in this lesson. Ask them what the green box before the spelling means. If necessary, explain that the box means that a short-vowel spelling will always come before this spelling for /j/.

You will need the following *Sound/Spelling Cards* for blending the words in Set 1. 10—Jump, 17—Quacking Ducks, 21—Tug

Blending Exercise

● The words in the lines provide practice with the Set 1 sound/spellings. Write the following words and sentences on the board.

Line 1:	dodge edge budge ridge pledge
Line 2:	quiz quit quack quest quicksand
Line 3:	up jump bug trunk just
Line 4:	tax hilltop spell hotrod cutback
Sentence 1:	They left the truck on the edge of the cliff.
Sentence 2:	Did Quint cut any of the club's budget?

Teach the blending exercise using the procedure below, without varying from it. That way, students will become accustomed to the routine they will use to blend words.

● Blend the first two lines of words sound by sound. Write the first spelling, *d,* and ask students to give the sound. Then write the second spelling, *o,* and have students give the sound. Have students blend through the vowel, saying /d/ /o/ . . . /do/. Write the final spelling *dge,* and ask students to give the sound. Using a blending motion from left to right beneath the word, have students say all three sounds and blend the word *dodge.*

● Continue in this way for the remaining words on the first two lines.

● Begin Line 3 by doing whole-word blending. Write the word on the board. Have students say the sound as you point to each spelling. Then have students pronounce the word naturally—it is important for them to realize that blending sounds results in a word.

● Continue in this way for the remaining words and the sentences.

● If students have trouble reading a word, stop and do sound-by-sound blending.

● Then have a student use each word in a sentence. Extend the sentence by asking questions such as *where, when, why,* or *how.* Encourage students to extend sentences by adding information at the beginning and not just at the end of the sentence.

● Be sure to discuss the meanings of any unfamiliar words.

TEACHER TIP

Sound/Spelling Card Stories
Review today's sounds by using the *Sound/Spelling Card Stories.* Listening to the stories will help students understand how they can use the pictures on the *Sound/Spelling Cards* to remember the sounds associated with them. The stories are provided in the appendix and are also available on the *Sound/Spelling Card Stories Audiocassette/CD.*

SELECTION E • **Stories in the Sky**

About the Words and Sentences

- Have students identify each compound word on the lines (*quicksand, hilltop, hotrod, cutback*). Discuss with them the meaning of each word.

- The words on Line 4 review all short vowels. Have students identify the vowel sound/spelling in each word.

- Before reading a sentence, point to and read the underlined sight words. Have students reread the sentences to build fluency and comprehension.

- For the sentences, have students identify each subject and predicate.

WRITING

Ask students to choose two compound words from the word lines. Have them write the compound word and the two smaller words that make up each compound word.

Oral Language

Point to a word line, and invite a student to choose a word on the line and then give a riddle or clue for it, such as *It's the sound a duck makes (quack)* or *It's a promise (pledge)*. Have other students identify the word that solves the riddle.

Dictation

Dictation gives students an opportunity to spell words by using the sound/spellings that they have learned. For this dictation exercise, have students use writing paper. Dictate the words and sentence for them to write. Use the following whole-word procedure:

- Say the first word in the dictation word line. Use the word in a sentence, then say the word again. Have students say the word.

- Tell students to think about how to segment the word into sounds. Then have them write the spelling for each sound. Encourage them to check the **Sound/Spelling Cards.**

- After each word line, write (or have a student write) the words on the board. Have students proofread their words. Tell them to circle any incorrect words and to correct them.

- Next, dictate the sentence. Dictate one word at a time, following the sounds-in-sequence or whole-word dictation procedure, depending on your students. Remind students to start the sentence with a capital letter and to use correct end punctuation.

- Write (or have a student write) the sentence on the board. Have students proofread their work and correct any incorrect words.

Line 1:	bridge edge judge
Line 2:	quiz quick must
Sentence:	They will sell us the fudge.

Building Fluency

Decodable Story: Unit 1, Story 9

- This story reviews the sound/spellings /j/ spelled ▮dge; /kw/ spelled qu_; /u/ spelled u.

- Have students silently read **Decodable Stories and Comprehension Skills** page 9.

- Call on volunteers to read each paragraph aloud.

- For those students who need help, divide sentences according to natural phrases. Mark these phrases with diagonal slash marks on their worksheets.

- After students have read the story aloud, ask them questions and have them point to and read the answers in the story.

- Have students reread the story aloud with a partner. Rereading builds automaticity and fluency.

- Over the next few days, listen to each student reread the story.

TEACHER TIP

Phonics Skills As students read aloud, notice how they use the phonics skills they have learned. Remind them that the purpose of learning these skills is to help them decode unfamiliar words.

✓ QUICK CHECK

As a quick review of today's sound/spellings, say some sentences, and ask students to suggest words to fill the blanks. Sentences you might read aloud include:

My lazy dog won't _____ from the sofa. *(budge)*
I studied hard for my spelling _____ this week. *(quiz)*
His mom made him sign a _____ to keep his room clean. *(pledge)*

22

SELECTION E • **Stories in the Sky**

Before Reading

Build Background

Activate Prior Knowledge

● Ask students if they know what the word *astronomy* means. If no one does, have a student look up the word in a dictionary. Talk to students about the study of the stars.

Background Information

Use the following information to help students understand the selection you are about to read:

● Tell students that the selection you are going to read is fiction, but that it provides true information. Ask if they remember the name for this kind of fiction *(realistic)*.

● Ask them to tell any stories that they know about the stars or the night sky.

Selection Vocabulary

Write the following vocabulary words on the board. Before browsing the selection, introduce and discuss these words and their meanings:

ridge: the long and narrow raised part of something

fir: an evergreen tree that bears cones

chilly: cold

cinch: a fastening strap

Then have students read the words, stopping to blend any words that they have trouble reading. Demonstrate how to decode multisyllabic words by breaking the words into syllables and blending the syllables. Then have students try. If they still have trouble, refer them to the ***Sound/Spelling Cards.*** If the word is not decodable, give students the pronunciation.

As students study vocabulary, they will use a variety of skills to determine the meaning of a word. These skills include context clues, word structure, and apposition. In this unit, students will be learning about context clues. Write the following example on the board: *You should always wear your winter coat and gloves on chilly days.* Explain to students that they are going to use the context, or other words in the sentence, to help them decipher the meaning of the word *chilly.* Guide students until they can give a reasonable definition of the word.

OBJECTIVES

● Discuss vocabulary words and their meanings.
● Develop reading skills as the story is read to them.
● Gain knowledge of the comprehension strategies Asking Questions and Monitoring and Clarifying.
● Build vocabulary by identifying multiple-meaning words.
● Develop writing skills by writing a description of a story character.

MATERIALS

Student Reader, pp. 14–17
Language Arts, p. T10

Vocabulary Activity: Write the names of several articles of clothing on the board, such as *sweater, coat, bathing suit, shorts, t-shirt, hat, scarf, sandals*. Have students sort the clothing into two categories: *Clothes Worn on Chilly Days* and *Clothes Worn on Hot Days*.

Preview and Prepare

Before you read, use modeling and prompts such as:

Because it's fiction, we'll only browse the first page of this story. From the title and the first page, can you tell me what kind of stories Mom will tell when the family is outside? Let's read and find out.

During Reading

Read Aloud

For this lesson, read the entire selection aloud. As you read, stop at the points that are marked with numbers in magenta circles on the reduced student pages, and model for them how to use the indicated strategy. Encourage students to stop at any point in their reading if they don't understand something or want to talk about the meaning of a passage or word.

Comprehension Strategies

During the reading of "Stories in the Sky" on pages 14–17, you will model the following reading comprehension strategies:

Asking Questions: As they read, good readers ask themselves questions to see if they are making sense of what they are reading.

Monitoring and Clarifying: Good readers pay attention to how well they understand what they are reading. They stop to clarify the meanings of new words and to think about unfamiliar or difficult passages.

TEACHER TIP

Asking Questions Students should be encouraged to stop to ask questions. Have students take time to reflect on the text from time to time to see whether it makes sense.

First Read

Text Comprehension *strategies*

As you read the story, use modeling and prompts such as:

1 Asking Questions

Asking yourself questions is a good way to be sure you understand what you're reading. I have a question here: Why is Mom taking everybody outside to tell them a story? It's winter, and there's a fire inside. I'd rather stay there. I'll read on to see what the answer is.

2 Answering Questions

As we read, it is important to check whether our questions have been answered. Well, my question is answered: Mom is going to tell stories about the stars.

Stories in the Sky

by Elizabeth Sengel
illustrated by Pat Paris

It was a cold winter night. Rob and his parents sat by the fireplace.

"Please tell me a story," Rob said.

"Okay," Mom said. "Quick, put on your
1 coat. We are going outside."

14

WRITING

Have students look at the illustration on page 14 and choose one of the characters (Mom, Dad, Rob) to describe. Tell students to write a brief description of the character.

VOCABULARY

Tell students that some words are spelled the same but have different meanings. Tell them that the context of the story helps determine the meaning of these words. For a lesson on multiple-meaning words, use *Language Arts* page T10.

Dad had brought a blanket. He spread it out across the ground on the <u>ridge</u> by the <u>fir</u> tree. They all sat down. It was very <u>chilly</u>.

"Why are we out here?" Rob asked.

"Long ago," Mom began, "people thought that groups of stars made pictures. They made up stories about their sky pictures. I will show you."

 2

15

 Second Read

Text Comprehension

Main Idea and Details

Explain to students that good readers look for the main idea of a paragraph or passage. The main idea tells the most important idea. Finding the main idea helps the reader see how the author organized the ideas and lets the reader better understand what those ideas are.

● Reread the selection. Tell students to listen for the main idea of the story.

● After you have finished reading, ask them to identify the main idea of the story. *(Answers may vary. Possible answer: groups of stars make pictures.)*

● Use **Transparency** 11 to record their responses.

GRAMMAR

Ask students to recall what two components make up a complete sentence *(subject and predicate)*. For a lesson on complete and incomplete sentences, use *Language Arts* page T9.

First Read

Text Comprehension *Strategies*

❸ Monitoring and Clarifying

Good readers pay attention to how well they understand what they read. They stop to clarify, or to figure out, the meanings of words they don't know and of passages that confuse them. I don't know the word cinch. *Let's see if the context will help me—Mom's describing a group of stars called the Hunter. So I can picture a large hunter. A cinch is something he wears around his middle, so maybe it's a belt? I'd better check the dictionary to be sure. Yes, a cinch can be a belt.*

HOMEWORK TIP

Encourage students to find out information about the stars and the night sky. They might talk to family members or look in reference books and on approved Web sites. Allow time in class for them to share what they have learned.

Mom pointed to a group of stars. "Do you see how the stars form a picture of a man with a <u>cinch</u> around his middle?" she asked. "That star group is called the ❸ Hunter."

Dad pointed to another group of stars. "That one is the Hunter's dog," he said. "Do you see it?"

16

"Oh, yes!" Rob nodded. He pointed to a group of stars. It looked like a rabbit. "I see a sky picture!" he cried. "Now, I'll tell you its story."

17

Second Read

Main Idea and Details

Tell students that the details in the story give more information about the main idea.

● Ask students to identify some details that support the main idea. *(Answers may vary. Possible answers: a group of stars form a picture of a man called the Hunter; a group of stars form a picture of the Hunter's dog; a group of stars form a picture of a rabbit.)*

● Continue to record their responses on **Transparency** 11.

● For additional practice with Main Idea and Details, have students complete **Decodable Stories and Comprehension Skills** page 79.

Discussing the Selection

After you have read the story, discuss it with students. Use prompts such as:

● *What did you like about this selection?*

● *What did you learn from reading it?*

● *What kind of story do you think Rob will tell?*

● *How does this selection relate to the unit theme, Sharing Stories?*

QUICK CHECK

To review the comprehension skill Sequence, ask students to tell the sequence of events in "Stories in the Sky."

SELECTION E • **Stories in the Sky**

OBJECTIVES

- Repeat word parts.
- Identify /ī/ words.
- Blend and break apart sounds in words.
- Participate in Word Play activity.
- Develop fluency by reading aloud.
- Apply decoding skills by reading **Unit 1, Decodable Story 10.**
- Develop writing skills by writing rhyming words.

MATERIALS

Sound/Spelling Card:
29—Bird
Decodable Stories and Comprehension Skills, p. 10
High-Frequency Word Cards
Sound/Spelling Card Stories
  Audiocassette/CD

TEACHER TIP

Listening for Vowel Sounds The purpose of these listening activities is not to teach specific letter-sound correspondences, but to raise students' awareness of the presence of vowel sounds in words. For this reason, these activities are strictly oral.

Phonemic Awareness

Segmentation: Repeating Word Parts

Tell students that they are going to play the Repeating Word Parts Game again. Have students repeat only the rime (the last part of the syllable) of the one-syllable words that you say.

- Look at students and say very clearly the word *day*, exaggerating the /d/. Then have students respond by omitting the onset and saying /ā/.
- Continue with these words:

lie	we	new
mow	go	way
guy	jay	few
by	sow	no

Listening for Vowel Sounds

Listening for /ī/

Point to each long-vowel **Sound/Spelling Card** and remind students that these red letters, vowels, are special because they can say their names. As a review, have students say the sound of each long vowel as you point to the card.

- Write the letters *Ii* on the board and tell students that you will read a list of words aloud. Explain that you want them to listen carefully. If you say a word that has the sound of long *i*, such as *ice*, they are to clap their hands and say /ī/ if the word does not have that sound, they are to say and do nothing.

  - Say the following words:

meal	**tie**	**spike**	**pie**
fright	keep	came	**sight**
break	**like**	toe	he
chew	tool	**right**	**wide**
pail	**ripe**	slope	book

Word Study

Word Play

Say the following words sound by sound: *huddle* (/h/ /u/ /d/ /l/), *stump*
(/s/ /t/ /u/ /m/ /p/), *truck* (/t/ /r/ /u/ /k/), *bluff* (/b/ /l/ /u/ /f/), *luck* (/l/ /u/ /k/).
Call on volunteers to identify and say each word. After you say all the words,
ask students what sound was in every word that they heard. (*/u/*)

Phonics—Blending: Set 2

> /er/ spelled *er* | /or/ spelled *or*

Display and discuss the ***Sound/Spelling Card***. Point out the
various spellings for /er/. Tell them that in this lesson they will
work only with the *er* spelling. Tell them that they also will
work with another sound/spelling that does not have a card:
/or/ spelled *or*.

Blending Exercise

- Write the following words and sentences on the board.
- Have students blend the words and sentences using the whole-word
  procedure described on page 12F.

Line 1:	herd	fern	seller	manner
Line 2:	liver	quiver	silver	letter
Line 3:	orbit	cord	forget	corner
Line 4:	for	born	horn	corn
Sentence 1:	Did <u>any</u> <u>of</u> the joggers get blisters?			
Sentence 2:	<u>They</u> forgot to order dinner.			

- Before reading a sentence, point to and read the underlined sight words.
- Discuss with students that each sentence begins with a capital letter and
  ends with a punctuation mark.
- Have students reread the sentences to encourage fluency and
  comprehension.

TEACHER TIP

Sight Words Use the *High-Frequency Word Cards* to assess and review students' knowledge of sight words.

You will need the following *Sound/Spelling Card* for blending the words in Set 2. 29—Bird

SELECTION E • **Stories in the Sky**

About the Words and Sentences

- The words on the lines provide practice with the Set 2 sound/spellings.
- On Line 1, have students find the words that are *homophones*—words that sound like other words but are spelled differently and have different meanings *(herd, manner, seller).* Ask if they can spell the homophones for those words *(heard, manor, cellar).* Have them use each word in a sentence to show its meaning.
- For Line 3, have students find the word that has both target sound/spellings. *(corner)*
- Have students identify the subject and predicate of each sentence.

Oral Language

Give clues and have students find the words on the lines that the clues identify. Here are some possible clues.

> It's a type of plant. *(fern)*
>
> It means "to shake or tremble." *(quiver)*
>
> It's a vegetable that can be eaten on a cob. *(corn)*

Dictation

For the dictation exercise, have students use writing paper. Dictate the words and sentence for them to write.

Use the following whole-word procedure:

- Say the first word in the dictation word line. Use the word in a sentence, then say the word again. Have students say the word.
- Tell students to think about how to segment the word into sounds. Then have them write the spelling for each sound.
- After each word line, write (or have a student write) the words on the board. Have students proofread their words. Tell them to circle any incorrect words and to correct them.
- Next dictate the sentence. Dictate one word at a time, following the sounds-in-sequence or whole-word dictation procedure, depending on your students. Remind students to start the sentence with a capital letter and to use correct end punctuation.
- Write (or have a student write) the sentence on the board. Have students proofread their work and correct any incorrect words.

WRITING

Have students identify and write the three words that rhyme with *torn* on the word lines *(born, horn, corn).*

Line 1:	horn sort her
Line 2:	for order better
Sentence:	Bill sent a letter to his sister.

Building Fluency

Decodable Story: Unit 1, Story 10

● This story reviews the sound/spellings /er/ spelled *er;* /or/ spelled *or.*

● Have students silently read ***Decodable Stories and Comprehension Skills*** page 10.

● Call on volunteers to read each paragraph aloud.

● For those students who need help, divide sentences according to natural phrases. Mark these phrases with diagonal slash marks on their worksheets.

● After students have read the story aloud, ask them questions and have them point to and read the answers in the story.

● Have students reread the story aloud with a partner.

HOMEWORK TIP

To help students build fluency, have them take home the *Decodable Stories and Comprehension Skills* stories to read with their families.

24

SELECTION E • **Stories in the Sky**

OBJECTIVES

- Develop reading skills as the story is reread to them.
- Gain knowledge of the comprehension skill Main Idea and Details.
- Develop vocabulary by listening to and discussing a selection.
- Develop writing skills by writing a story title.
- Identify complete and incomplete sentences.

MATERIALS

Student Reader, pp. 14–17
Decodable Stories and Comprehension Skills, p. 79
Language Arts, p. T9
Transparencies 3, 11
Listening Library Audiocassette/CD

Rereading the Selection

Comprehension Skills

Revisiting or rereading a selection allows students to learn and apply skills that give them a more complete understanding of a selection. For today's lesson, reread the selection to students. During the second reading, students will apply the following comprehension skill:

Main Idea and Details: Good readers identify the most important points, or main ideas, in the selections that they read. This helps them organize information and better understand the selection.

After Reading

Independent Reading

- Have students choose books from the *Classroom Library* or other available books to take home and read.
- Encourage students to read at least one book on their own each week.
- Set aside a few minutes each day to meet one-on-one with students to discuss their reading.
- Encourage students to record the titles of the books they are reading on the copy of *Tranparency* 3.

TEACHER TIP

Have students listen to the selection recording on the *Listening Library Audiocassette/CD.*

WRITING

Remind students that Rob spots a rabbit in the stars and is going to tell its story. Tell students to make up and write a title for Rob's story. Have students share their titles with the class.

SELECTION E • **Stories in the Sky**

Assessment

Formal

At the conclusion of the lesson, have students complete the assessment Unit 1: Stories in the Sky. The Lesson Assessments are found in the *Assessment Guide.*

For all the items in this assessment, you should read both the question and answer choices out loud while students follow along silently. You may find it helpful to walk around the room while students are completing the assessment to provide them with any help they need to understand the questions.

Have students refer to the Unit Assessment selection "Story Time." Review the story briefly with students and then read Question 2 out loud. Help students decide which character they would like to draw and then let them complete their drawings. Encourage them to explain why they drew a specific character and why they drew the character as they did. This oral interaction will promote student engagement in both the selection and the assessment.

Informal

Discuss with students how some words have more than one meaning. A word from "Stories in the Sky," *long*, has several meanings. Talk about the various meanings of the word *long* with students using examples such as "a long time" and "a long road." Repeat the process with the words *like* and *coat*.

Ending the Lesson

Have students discuss the main idea of "Stories in the Sky" by asking them "What is this story mostly about?" You may find it helpful to prompt them by asking "Is it mostly about Rob?" Vary the question to help students differentiate between the main idea and details in the story.

OBJECTIVES

- Complete lesson assessment.
- Review multiple-meaning words.
- Visualize a character from a story.
- Differentiate the main idea and details.

MATERIALS

Assessment Guide
Student Reader, pp. 14–17

SELECTION F • **Kim Writes a Letter**

Support Materials

HOME CONNECTIONS

Distribute *Home Connection* page 13, which describes this week's classwork and suggests activities for families to do at home. This letter is available in English and Spanish.

LESSON 26

- Sound/Spelling Cards 27, 29
- Decodable Stories and Comprehension Skills, p. 11
- Home Connection, p. 13
- High-Frequency Word Cards
- Sound/Spelling Card Stories Audiocassette/CD

LESSON 27

- Student Reader, pp. 18–19
- Language Arts, p. T12

LESSON 28

- Sound/Spelling Cards
- Decodable Stories and Comprehension Skills, p. 12
- High-Frequency Word Cards
- Sound/Spelling Card Stories Audiocassette/CD

LESSON 29

- Student Reader, pp. 18–19, 20–21
- Transparencies 3, 12, 13
- Decodable Stories and Comprehension Skills, p. 80
- Listening Library Audiocassette/CD
- Language Arts, p. T11

LESSON 30

- Assessment Guide
- Student Reader, pp. 18–19

Teacher Focus	Student Participation
<ul><li>Conduct Listening Game.</li><li>Conduct Word Play.</li><li>Introduce Sight Words, blending procedure, and Set 1 blending words and sentences.</li><li>Conduct Oral Language activity.</li><li>Dictate word lines.</li><li>Assist students with decodable text.</li><li>Assign writing activity.</li></ul>	<ul><li>Take part in Listening Game.</li><li>Take part in Word Play.</li><li>Read Sight Words.</li><li>Blend words and sentences.</li><li>Create sentences.</li><li>Write dictated words and sentences.</li><li>Read a decodable story.</li><li>Complete writing activity.</li></ul>
<ul><li>Activate Prior Knowledge and provide background information.</li><li>Introduce and discuss selection vocabulary.</li><li>Preview selection.</li><li>Introduce Comprehension Strategies—Making Connections and Summarizing.</li><li>Read the selection to students.</li><li>Introduce vocabulary skill.</li><li>Assign writing activity.</li></ul>	<ul><li>Contribute to class discussion.</li><li>Read and discuss vocabulary words. Complete selection vocabulary activity.</li><li>Browse the selection.</li><li>Follow along as the selection is read.</li><li>Complete vocabulary skill activity.</li><li>Complete writing activity.</li></ul>
<ul><li>Conduct Restoring Initial Phonemes game.</li><li>Conduct Word Play.</li><li>Review blending procedure; introduce Set 2 blending words and sentences.</li><li>Conduct Oral Language activity.</li><li>Dictate word lines.</li><li>Assist students with decodable text.</li><li>Assign writing activity.</li></ul>	<ul><li>Participate in Restoring Initial Phonemes game.</li><li>Take part in Word Play.</li><li>Blend words and sentences.</li><li>Create sentences.</li><li>Write dictated words and sentences.</li><li>Read a decodable story.</li><li>Complete writing activity.</li></ul>
<ul><li>Introduce Comprehension Skill—Drawing Conclusions.</li><li>Reread and discuss the selection with students.</li><li>Discuss Independent Reading.</li><li>Assign writing activity.</li><li>Introduce grammar skill.</li><li>Discuss Reading Reflections.</li></ul>	<ul><li>Follow along as selection is read again.</li><li>Discuss the selection.</li><li>Select a book to take home and read.</li><li>Complete writing activity.</li><li>Complete grammar skill activity.</li><li>Discuss Reading Reflections.</li></ul>
<ul><li>Administer weekly assessments.</li><li>Assess students' progress.</li></ul>	<ul><li>Complete lesson and unit assessments.</li></ul>

SELECTION F • **Kim Writes a Letter**

OBJECTIVES

- Identify and blend initial consonant sounds in words.
- Read sight words.
- Blend and break apart sounds in words.
- Participate in Word Play activity.
- Develop fluency by reading aloud.
- Apply decoding skills by reading *Unit 1, Decodable Story 11.*
- Develop writing skills by writing words and identifying sound/spellings.

MATERIALS

Sound/Spelling Cards:
27—Armadillo
29—Bird
Decodable Stories and Comprehension Skills, p. 11
Home Connection, p. 13
High-Frequency Word Cards
Sound/Spelling Card Stories Audiocassette/CD

Phonemic Awareness

The goal of phonemic awareness activities is to help students understand that spoken words are made up of smaller sounds—word parts, syllables, and phonemes. Learning this concept is important to reading success because of the systematic relationship between speech sounds and written letters. If students cannot hear and manipulate the individual sounds in spoken words, they usually have difficulty deciphering that relationship. Phonemic awareness is also important to students' spelling success. Students who understand that sounds and letters are related usually are able to attach the sounds to letters and spell words.

Oral blending and segmentation are complementary processes in developing phonemic awareness and in learning to read and write. Just as learning to blend smaller units of sound into words is essential to decoding, learning to segment, or break apart, words into smaller units of sound is essential to spelling.

Oral Blending

Tell students that they are already good at listening; they obviously understand words they hear. Then explain that to be really good readers and writers, they need to learn to listen even more closely—they need to be able to hear the separate sounds that make up words. Tell them that when they can hear the separate sounds, they can read and spell most words.

Listening Game: Initial Consonant Sounds

The words in this activity may be difficult. Many of them are only one syllable, so their endings do not give strong clues.

Tell students to listen very carefully as you say each of the following word parts distinctly. Have students say the complete word.

/p/. . . aper	/d/. . . octor
/t/. . . ape	/g/. . . ift
/k/. . . ard	/p/. . . ill
/t/. . . est	/k/. . . ite
/b/. . . ean	/p/. . . et
/g/. . . oal	/d/. . . ine

TEACHER TIP

Responses To keep students' attention, switch unpredictably from group to individual responses.

SELECTION F • **Kim Writes a Letter**

Word Study

In this section of the lesson, students work on phonics, fluency, blending, and spelling. Increasing students' ability to work smoothly with printed words is one of the primary goals of the *Kaleidoscope* program.

Word Play

Play the I'm Thinking of Something game again. Choose a previously taught sound/spelling. Look around the room until you see something that contains—but does not begin with—the sound. Say, for example, "I'm thinking of something in the room that ends with /er/." Give a clue, such as the object's size or color, or direct students' attention to the correct part of the room. Objects you might name include *sweater, marker, locker.* Turn the game over to students to find and give clues for other objects that contain a previously taught sound/spelling.

Sight Words

This week's sight words:

| been | often | never |

Use the following procedure for teaching sight words:
- Write this week's sight words on the board.
- Read the words to students, and then have them read the words.
- Pronounce any words with which students have difficulty.
- Have students use each word in a sentence.

Phonics—Blending: Set 1

| /ar/ spelled *ar* | /er/ spelled *er, ir, ur* |

This section of the phonics lesson provides practice in building sounds and spellings into words.

- Display and discuss each new **Sound/Spelling Card** to be used. Ask students what they know about these cards.
- Touch each card, and tell students the name of the card, the sound, and the spelling. (For detailed information on how to introduce **Sound/Spelling Cards,** see Getting Started.)

You will need the following **Sound/Spelling Cards** for blending the words in Set 1. 27—Armadillo, 29—Bird

Blending Exercise

The words in the lines provide practice with the Set 1 sound/spellings. Write the following words and sentences on the board.

Line 1:	bark	art	barn	yarn
Line 2:	collar	dollar	cellar	lizard
Line 3:	girl	twirl	fir	first
Line 4:	fur	burn	curb	blur
Sentence 1:	The car had <u>been</u> left to rust in the yard.			
Sentence 2:	The ginger cat <u>often</u> bats the yarn.			
Sentence 3:	Art <u>never</u> stops for beggars.			

Teach the blending exercise using the procedure below, without varying from it. That way, students will become accustomed to the routine they will use to blend words.

- Blend the first two lines of words sound by sound. Write the first spelling, *b,* and ask students to give the sound. Then write the second sound/spelling, *ar,* and have students give the sound. Have students blend these sounds together, saying /b/ /ar/ . . . /bar/. Write the final spelling, *k,* and ask students to give the sound. Using a blending motion from left to right beneath the word, have students say the sounds and blend the word *bark.*

- Continue in this way for the remaining words on the first two lines.

- Begin Line 3 by doing whole-word blending. Write the word on the board. Have students say the sound as you point to each spelling. Then have students pronounce the word naturally—it is important for them to realize that blending sounds results in a word.

- Continue in this way for the remaining words and the sentences.

- If students have trouble reading a word, stop and do sound-by-sound blending.

- Then have students use each word in a sentence. Extend the sentence by asking questions such as *where, when, why,* or *how.* Encourage students to extend sentences by adding information at the beginning and not just at the end of the sentence.

- Be sure to discuss the meanings of any unfamiliar words.

WRITING

Have students identify the words on the lines with /er/ spelled *ir.* Tell them to write those words and circle the sound/spelling for /er/ in each word.

SELECTION F • **Kim Writes a Letter**

About the Words and Sentences

● On Line 1, have students identify the words that have multiple meanings (bark, art). Ask them to give two meanings for each word. Have them use each word in a sentence.

● Have students find two words on the lines that are homophones (fir, fur). Ask them to tell the meaning of each word.

● Before reading a sentence, point to and read the underlined sight word. Have students reread the sentences to build fluency and comprehension.

Oral Language

Have students take turns choosing a word from the lines, reading it, using it in a sentence, and calling on a classmate to extend the sentence.

Dictation

Dictation gives students an opportunity to spell words by using the sound/spellings that they have learned. For this dictation exercise, have students use writing paper. Dictate the words and sentence for them to write. Use the following whole-word procedure:

● Say the first word in the dictation word line. Use the word in a sentence, and then say the word again. Have students say the word.

● Tell students to think about how to segment the word into sounds. Then have them write the spelling for each sound. Encourage them to check the **Sound/Spelling Cards.**

● After each word line, write (or have a student write) the words on the board. Have students proofread their words. Tell them to circle any incorrect words and to correct them.

● Next, dictate the sentence. Dictate one word at a time, following the sounds-in-sequence or whole-word dictation procedure, depending on your students. Remind students to start the sentence with a capital letter and to use correct end punctuation.

● Write (or have a student write) the sentence on the board. Have students proofread their work and correct any incorrect words.

Line 1:	dirt	turn	farm
Line 2:	star	dollar	hurt
Sentence:	Did the girl twirl her skirt?		

Building Fluency

Decodable Story: Unit 1, Story 11

- This story reviews the sound/spellings /ar/ spelled *ar;* /er/spelled *ar, ir, ur.*
- Have students silently read **Decodable Stories and Comprehension Skills** page 11.
- Call on volunteers to read each paragraph aloud.
- For those students who need help, divide sentences according to natural phrases. Mark these phrases with diagonal slash marks on their worksheets.
- After students have read the story aloud, ask them questions and have them point to and read the answers in the story.
- Have students reread the story aloud with a partner. Rereading builds automaticity and fluency.
- Over the next few days, listen to each student reread the story.

Sound/Spelling Card Stories Review today's sounds by using the *Sound/Spelling Card Stories.* Listening to the stories will help students understand how they can use the pictures on the *Sound/Spelling Cards* to remember the sounds associated with them. The stories are provided in the appendix and are also available on the *Sound/Spelling Card Stories Audiocassette/CD.*

 QUICK CHECK

As a quick review of today's sound/spellings, say some sentences, and ask students to suggest words to fill the blanks. Sentences you might read aloud include:

The horses are kept in the _____. *(barn)*
A is the _____ letter in the alphabet. *(first)*
Sally's dress has a lace _____. *(collar)*

SELECTION F • **Kim Writes a Letter**

Before Reading

Build Background

Activate Prior Knowledge

Ask students to recall the selections they have read so far. Ask them how each selection relates to the unit theme, Sharing Stories.

Background Information

Use the following information to help students understand the selection you are about to read.

● Tell students that the selection you are going to read is unusual because it is a friendly letter.

● Ask them if they ever write letters. If so, to whom do they write? Why do they write? Do they send the letters through the regular mail or do they send them electronically?

Selection Vocabulary

Write the following vocabulary words on the board. Before browsing the selection, introduce and discuss these words and their meanings.

hint: a clue or suggestion

car lot: a place where cars are sold

sniffing: taking short, quick breaths through the nose

Then have students read the words, stopping to blend any words that they have trouble reading. Demonstrate how to decode multisyllabic words by breaking the words into syllables and blending the syllables. Then have students try. If they still have trouble, refer them to the *Sound/Spelling Cards.* If the word is not decodable, give students the pronunciation.

As students study vocabulary, they will use a variety of skills to determine the meaning of a word. These skills include context clues, word structure, and apposition. In this unit, students will be learning about context clues. Write the following example on the board: *If you can't solve the riddle, I'll give you a hint.* Explain to students that they are going to use the context, or other words in the sentence, to help them decipher the meaning of the word *hint.* Guide students until they can give a reasonable definition of the word.

Vocabulary Activity: Bring in several objects that have distinct smells, such as an orange, an onion, or a scented candle. Have students close their eyes and sniff each object. Ask students if they can guess what each object is.

Preview and Prepare

Before you read, use modeling and prompts such as:

Because this is a letter, we'll only browse it to find to whom it was written. From the title, we know that it was written by Kim. Let's read it to see why she wrote her grandparents.

WRITING

Have students write a short prediction about why they think Kim wrote her grandparents. Tell students to refer back to their prediction as the selection is read to see if their prediction is true.

During Reading

Read Aloud

For this lesson, read the entire selection aloud. As you read, stop at the points that are marked with numbers in magenta circles on the reduced student pages, and model for them how to use the indicated strategy. Encourage students to stop at any point in their reading if they don't understand something or want to talk about the meaning of a passage or word.

Comprehension Strategies

During the reading of "Kim Writes a Letter" on pages 18–19, you will model the following reading comprehension strategies:

Making Connections: Good readers improve their understanding of a selection by making connections between what they already know and what they are reading.

Summarizing: Good readers often pause during reading to summarize. After reading, they may make a mental summary of the entire selection. Summarizing helps them make sense of what they read.

First
Read

Text Comprehension *Strategies*

As you read the story, use modeling and prompts such as:

❶ Making Connections

I can certainly make connections to Kim's eagerness to tell her grandparents about something new in her life. Don't you enjoy sharing good news with people you care about?

❷ Making Connections

This reminds me of what happens when I give my dog a bath. She splashes water everywhere, and I get as wet as she does.

❸ Summarizing

Good readers stop now and then as they read so that they can summarize what they have read and make sure they understand it. I'm going to summarize what we've read so far: Kim has a new dog, his name is Nick, he can do tricks, and he has his own pet—a kitten. Kim takes good care of Nick.

❹ Summarizing

I'm going to summarize again: Kim has a new dog that she loves. She and her friends are going to have a dog show soon. So now I see that Kim is writing to her grandparents not just to tell them about the new dog but to invite them to come for a visit.

HOMEWORK
TIP

Encourage students to bring pictures of their pets to class. Set aside a few minutes for them to share and talk about the pictures.

Kim Writes a Letter

by Grace Long

illustrated by Doug Knutson

18

VOCABULARY

For a review lesson on rhyming words and compound words, use *Language Arts* page T12.

Dear Grandma and Grandpa,

I want to tell you about my new dog, Nick. He is great. His fur is the same color as my hair. **1**

Nick can do lots of tricks. He can walk forward AND backward. I have been working on a new trick with Nick. I won't tell you what it is until he's got it just right. I'll give you a <u>hint</u>. Nick uses a giant ball in the trick.

I try to take good care of Nick. I feed him and take him for walks. When he needs it, I give him a bath. He loves to splash! **2**

Nick has his own pet, a kitten named Angel. He found Angel at the <u>car lot</u>. Now Angel likes Nick best of all. Angel sleeps right next to Nick's head. **3**

Nick is <u>sniffing</u> this letter. I think he knows it is about him.

Soon my friends and I will have a dog show in the park. Please try to come. **4**

Love,
Kim

19

GRAMMAR

For a review lesson on kinds of sentences and end marks, use *Language Arts* page T11.

Second Read

Text Comprehension

skills

Drawing Conclusions

Explain to students that authors do not always provide complete and clear information about a topic, character, thing, or event. They do, however, provide clues or suggestions that readers can use to "read between the lines" by drawing conclusions that are based on the information in the selection.

● Ask students to use clues from the text to draw conclusions about:

> how Kim knows that Angel likes Nick.

> what Kim and her friends have in common.

● Use **Transparency** 12 to record their responses.

● For additional practice with Drawing Conclusions, have students complete *Decodable Stories and Comprehension Skills* page 80.

Discussing the Selection

After you have read the story, discuss it with students. Use prompts such as:

● *What did you like about this selection?*

● *How did the reading strategies and skills that you've learned help you to understand it?*

● *How does this selection relate to the unit theme, Sharing Stories?*

✓ QUICK CHECK

Quickly review with students the comprehension strategies and skills that they've learned so far.

Unit 1 • LESSON

28

SELECTION F • **Kim Writes a Letter**

OBJECTIVES

- Restore initial phonemes.
- Blend and break apart sounds in words.
- Participate in Word Play activity.
- Review the sound/spellings introduced in this unit.
- Develop fluency by reading aloud.
- Apply decoding skills by reading **Unit 1, Decodable Story 12.**
- Develop writing skills by writing a caption.

MATERIALS

Sound/Spelling Cards
Decodable Stories and
  Comprehension Skills, p. 12
High-Frequency Word Cards
Sound/Spelling Card Stories
  Audiocassette/CD

Segmentation Remember to move quickly through these activities. Do not hold the class back waiting on all students to catch on. Return to the same activity often. Frequent repetition is very beneficial and allows students additional opportunities to catch on.

Phonemic Awareness

Segmentation: Restoring Initial Phonemes

In this activity you are introducing students to the more difficult task of segmenting, or isolating the initial phonemes in words. Tell students that you are going to challenge them by asking them to say the initial sound of a word.

● Use the following to demonstrate.

Teacher:	*zip . . . ip*
Teacher:	*zzzzzzip. I forgot the /z/.*

● After demonstrating, ask students to repeat the word and to say what sound was left off.

Teacher:	*zap . . . ap*
Teacher:	*Help me. What's the word? What sound did I leave off?*
Students:	*zzzzzap, /z/.*
Teacher:	*That's right, the word is* zap. *I left off the /z/.*

● Continue with the following words:

sea	clip
lips	ring
fit	pit
sip	tea
bath	disk
sound	zipper

TEACHER TIP

Word Study

Word Play

Play the I'm Thinking of Something game again. Choose a previously taught sound/spelling. Look around the room until you see something that contains—but does not begin with—the sound. Say, for example, "I'm thinking of something in the room that has /ar/." Give a clue, such as the object's size or color, or direct students' attention to the correct part of the room. Objects you might name include *art, yarn, star.* Turn the game over to students to find and give clues for other objects that contain a previously taught sound/spelling.

Phonics—Blending: Set 2

Display and discuss any **Sound/Spelling Cards** that you particularly want students to review. Tell them that in this lesson, they will review the sound/spellings that they have learned so far.

Blending Exercise

● Write the following words and sentences on the board.
● Have students blend the words and sentences using the whole-word procedure described on page 12F.

Line 1:	lizard	zipper	turn	girl	her
Line 2:	west	snack	drill	dump	stop
Line 3:	quick	neck	kick	click	car
Line 4:	judge	lodge	jump	gem	ginger
Line 5:	backyard	popcorn	blackbird		
Sentence 1:	Rick has <u>never been</u> to the large bridge.				
Sentence 2:	Dad and Mom <u>often</u> visit the farm.				

TEACHER TIP

Sight Words Use the *High-Frequency Word Cards* to assess and review students' knowledge of sight words.

● Before reading a sentence, point to and read the underlined sight words.
● Discuss with students that each sentence begins with a capital letter and ends with a punctuation mark.
● Have students reread the sentences to encourage fluency and comprehension.

SELECTION F • **Kim Writes a Letter**

About the Words and Sentences

- For Line 1, have students identify the various spellings for /er/.
- For Line 2, have students identify the short-vowel spelling in each word.
- For Line 3, have students identify the various spellings for /k/.
- For Line 4, have students identify the various spellings for /j/.
- For Line 5, have students identify each smaller word that makes up the compound word. Have them tell the meanings of the compound words.

Oral Language

Have students take turns choosing a word, reading it, using it in a sentence, and calling on a classmate to extend the sentence.

Dictation

For the dictation exercise, have students use writing paper. Dictate the words and sentence for them to write.

Use the following whole-word procedure:

- Say the first word in the dictation word line. Use the word in a sentence, then say the word again. Have students say the word.

  - Tell students to think about how to segment the word into sounds. Then have them write the spelling for each sound.
  - After each word line, write (or have a student write) the words on the board. Have students proofread their words. Tell them to circle any incorrect words and to correct them.
  - Next dictate the sentence. Dictate one word at a time, following the sounds-in-sequence or whole-word dictation procedure, depending on your students. Remind students to start the sentence with a capital letter and to use correct end punctuation.
  - Write (or have a student write) the sentence on the board. Have students proofread their work and correct any incorrect words.

WRITING

Have students select a word from the word lines and create an illustration and a short caption using the word. Ask students to share their drawings and captions with the class.

Line 1:	for job dollar steps
Line 2:	fix zest drip quiz
Line 3:	ridge grin since loft
Sentence:	Will Liz win part of the big jackpot?

Building Fluency

Decodable Story: Unit 1, Story 12

- This story reviews the sound/spellings introduced in the unit.
- Have students silently read *Decodable Stories and Comprehension Skills* page 12.
- Call on volunteers to read each paragraph aloud.
- For those students who need help, divide sentences according to natural phrases. Mark these phrases with diagonal slash marks on their worksheets.
- After students have read the story aloud, ask them questions and have them point to and read the answers in the story.
- Have students reread the story aloud with a partner.

HOMEWORK TIP

To help students build fluency, have them take home the *Decodable Stories and Comprehension Skills* stories to read with their families.

SELECTION F • **Kim Writes a Letter**

OBJECTIVES

- Develop reading skills as the story is read to them.
- Gain knowledge of the comprehension skill Drawing Conclusions.
- Develop vocabulary by listening to and discussing a selection.
- Develop writing skills by writing a letter.
- Review kinds of sentences and end marks.

MATERIALS

Student Reader, pp. 18–19, 20–21
Decodable Stories and Comprehension Skills, p. 80
Language Arts, p. T11
Transparencies 3, 12, 13
Listening Library Audiocassette/CD

Rereading the Selection

Comprehension Skills

Revisiting or rereading a selection allows students to learn and apply skills that give them a more complete understanding of a selection. For today's lesson, reread the selection to students. During the second reading, students will apply the following comprehension skill:

Drawing Conclusions: Good readers often "read between the lines," using clues provided by the author to draw conclusions about a selection's meaning.

After Reading

Reading Reflections

Have students discuss with a partner the Reading Reflections questions on pages 20–21. After partner discussions, have students discuss the answers to the questions as a class.

Independent Reading

- Have students choose books from the *Classroom Library* or other available books to take home and read. Encourage students to read at least one book on their own each week.
- Spend some time discussing students' independent reading with them.
- Encourage students to use the comprehension skill of Drawing Conclusions as they read independently.
- Encourage students to record the titles of the books they are reading on the copy of *Transparency* 3.

TEACHER TIP

Have students listen to the selection recording on the *Listening Library Audiocassette/CD*.

WRITING

To practice writing a letter, ask students to write a brief reply that Kim might expect to receive from her grandparents. Have students share their letters with the class.

Assessment

Formal

At the conclusion of the lesson, have students complete the assessment Unit 1: Kim Writes a Letter. The Lesson Assessments are found in the *Assessment Guide.*

For all the items in this assessment, you should read both the question and answer choices out loud while students follow along silently. You may find it helpful to walk around the room while students are completing the assessment to provide them with any help they need to understand the questions.

Ask students to refer to Question 3 of the Unit Assessment. Have them think of several different fairy tales and then choose the one they like best. Brainstorm plot, characters, and setting with students. Provide them with the help they need to describe their fairy tale. Have students complete the rest of the unit assessment questions. Review the answers as a group activity and give students an opportunity to share the performance items with the rest of the group.

Informal

Identify several sentences in "Kim Writes a Letter" that are either statements or questions. Point out the structure of the sentences and the end punctuation. Spend a moment discussing exclamations. When you are confident students know the different types of sentences, have them work together to create at least one of each type of sentence. Write the sentences on the board and emphasize the correct end punctuation.

Ending the Lesson

Ask students to talk about letters they have written or received. If they have not written a letter, ask them to think about a person they would like to write a letter to and what they would say in the letter.

OBJECTIVES

- Complete lesson and unit assessments.
- Plan to write a fairy tale.
- Review kinds of sentences and end punctuation.
- Plan to write a letter.

MATERIALS

Assessment Guide
Student Reader, pp. 18–19

Reading Reflections

Focus on the Characters

- Possible answers: Her father begins the story and Pam does insist that he tells a much better story; however, Pam's constant interruptions during the story show that she has her own plan for storytelling.

- By going outside, the family can gaze at the stars. Then they can make up stories using the "pictures" made by a group of stars.

- The statement "so did the elephant" adds humor to the story and makes Rosa's tale a silly story.

Focus on the Stories

- Possible answers: making marks on rocks, writing on plant leaves, using codes, sending smoke signals, telling stories from star pictures, using oral storytelling, writing books to share with others.

- "A Story for Pam" and "An Elephant Story" are used to entertain the reader. "From Rocks to Books," "Keeping Secrets," and "Stories in the Sky" inform the reader of various aspects of the history of storytelling.

- "Stories in the Sky," "A Story for Pam," and "Kim Writes a Letter"

Reading Reflections

These questions can help you think about the stories you just read. After you write your responses, discuss them with a partner.

Focus on the Characters

- In "A Story for Pam," which character is the real storyteller? Is it Pam or her father? Explain your choice.
- In "Stories in the Sky," Rob's mother suggests that they go outside to tell a story. Why is it necessary for the family to tell the story outside?
- Why does Rosa ask Ned to say "so did the elephant" after each addition to her story in "An Elephant Story"?

Focus on the Stories

- People share stories in different ways. After reading this unit, list at least three ways that people have communicated with each other.

20

Sharing Stories

- Which selections from the unit show people sharing stories to entertain others and make them laugh? Which selections are used to share more information about the history of storytelling?
- Which stories in this unit include family members sharing stories with one another?

Focus on the Theme

- What advantages does reading a book have over other forms of storytelling that are discussed in this unit?
- Of the various types of storytelling discussed in this unit, which way did you find most interesting and unique? Explain your choice.
- Another way to tell a story is by using body language instead of words. Retell the story "An Elephant Story" by using gestures to act out the silly story.

21

Focus on the Theme

- Possible answers: Stories on rocks would be very heavy to carry around. Mud and leaves are not permanent ways to record a story. Star pictures are only available at night. Codes can take a long time to decode and read. Reading a book is an easy way to share the same story with many people over time.
- Answers will vary.
- Answers will vary.

UNIT ②

Overview

HOME CONNECTIONS

Distribute *Home Connection* page 15, which describes the unit theme and suggests activities for families to do at home. This letter is available in English and Spanish.

Unit Goals

Throughout the *Kaleidoscope* program, students will be introduced to a variety of reading and writing skills. In this unit students will

- develop phonemic awareness through oral blending and segmentation activities.
- learn to decode by introducing and reviewing the phonic elements /ā/, /ē/, /ī/, /ō/, /ū/, /hw/ spelled *wh,* /f/ spelled *ph,* /sh/, /th/, /n/ spelled *kn_,* /r/ spelled *wr_.*
- increase their proficiency in decoding and word attack skills through practice with decodable text highlighting introduced phonic elements.
- build reading fluency through repeated reading of decodable text.
- expand their vocabulary through instruction and practice in using antonyms, synonyms, homophones, and multiple-meaning words.
- acquire an understanding of basic English grammar through work with common and proper nouns, regular and irregular plural nouns, and possessive nouns.
- improve reading comprehension by working with the comprehension strategies Making Connections, Visualizing, Predicting, Monitoring and Clarifying, Asking Questions, Monitoring and Adjusting Reading Speed, and Summarizing; and the comprehension skills Sequence, Reality and Fantasy, Compare and Contrast, Making Inferences, Cause and Effect, and Drawing Conclusions.
- engage in daily writing activities related to the phonics and reading lessons.

Theme

At a very early age, most children are taught that being kind to others is important. Yet few children ever think for themselves about what kindness really means or when, how, and why it is appropriate and necessary to be kind.

Learning about kindness is crucial to children's social and personal growth and to their long-term development. They need to acquire both an understanding of what it is to be kind and to be unkind. They also need to learn that kindness is more than an act. It involves intentions—we are kind only if we behave intentionally, not if our kindness was unintentional.

In this unit students will read and talk about kindness. They will examine ways of showing kindness to others, consider some possible motivations and rewards for kindness, and look at ways in which kindness can sometimes be misused.

Introducing the Unit

- Tell students they will be talking and reading about kindness in this unit.
- Ask students what it means to be kind.
- Encourage them to talk about different ways in which people show kindness.
- Have students think about whether people who look kind always are.
- Encourage them to share examples of kindness that they have experienced.

Selection	Overview of Selection	Link to Theme
A A Nature Adventure	Tanya and her dad show kindness when they encounter a hurt rabbit at the nature park.	Kindness should be shown toward Earth's creatures.
B The Lion and the Mouse	This fable tells of a tiny mouse who helps a lion when he gets tangled in a net.	Kindness returns to people (and animals) in ways they do not expect.
C Helping Others	This realistic fiction piece describes how a young girl helps out her neighbor.	Helping others is an important act of kindness.
D Tyler's Bad Day	Mr. Chang helps Tyler's bad day get better when he repairs a bicycle chain.	When we see others in need, it is right to show kindness.
E Marta Helps at Home	A young girl helps out at home by washing the dinner dishes.	Everyone can perform simple acts of kindness.
F Special Ears for Susan	Susan, who can't hear, and her dog take good care of each other.	People and animals can show kindness toward each other.

CLASSROOM LIBRARY

Fat Cat Tompkin
by Diana Noonan. Nelson Thomson Learning, 1994.
A kind neighbor helps Miss Pots take her cat to the vet.

Mr. Clutterbus
by Cecily Matthews. Nelson Thomson Learning, 1994.
On his way into town, Mr. Clutterbus encounters several people who need supplies, which he kindly agrees to pick up while he is in town.

The Giving Tree
by Shel Silverstein. Harper/Collins Publishers, 1964.
A tree shows unconditional love and kindness toward a little boy. As the boy grows, the tree gives and gives until there is nothing left to give.

SELECTION A • **A Nature Adventure**

Support Materials

LESSON 1
- Sound/Spelling Cards 28, 33, 34, 37
- Decodable Stories and Comprehension Skills, p. 13
- Home Connection, p. 17
- High-Frequency Word Cards
- Sound/Spelling Card Stories Audiocassette/CD

LESSON 2
- Student Reader, pp. 22–25
- Language Arts, p. T14

LESSON 3
- Sound/Spelling Cards 35, 36, 38
- Decodable Stories and Comprehension Skills, p. 14
- High-Frequency Word Cards
- Sound/Spelling Card Stories Audiocassette/CD

LESSON 4
- Student Reader, pp. 22–25
- Transparencies 3, 14, 15
- Decodable Stories and Comprehension Skills, p. 81
- Listening Library Audiocassette/CD
- Language Arts, p. T13

LESSON 5
- Assessment Guide
- Student Reader, pp. 22–25

HOME CONNECTIONS

Distribute *Home Connection* page 17, which describes this week's classwork and suggests activities for families to do at home. This letter is available in English and Spanish.

Teacher Focus	Student Participation
• Conduct Listening Game. • Conduct Word Play. • Introduce Sight Words and Set 1 blending words and sentences. • Provide riddle clues. • Dictate word lines. • Assist students with decodable text. • Assign writing activity.	• Take part in Listening Game. • Take part in Word Play. • Read Sight Words. • Blend words and sentences. • Solve riddles. • Write dictated words and sentences. • Read a decodable story. • Complete writing activity.
• Activate Prior Knowledge and provide background information. • Introduce and discuss selection vocabulary. • Preview selection. • Review Comprehension Strategies—Making Connections and Visualizing. • Read the selection to students. • Introduce vocabulary skill. • Assign writing activity.	• Contribute to class discussion. • Read and discuss vocabulary words. Complete selection vocabulary activity. • Browse the selection. • Follow along as selection is read. • Complete vocabulary skill activity. • Complete writing activity.
• Conduct Restoring Initial Phonemes game. • Conduct Listening for Vowel Sounds game. • Conduct Word Play. • Introduce Set 2 blending words and sentences. • Provide riddle clues. • Dictate word lines. • Assist students with decodable text. • Assign writing activity.	• Participate in Restoring Initial Phonemes game. • Participate in Listening for Vowel Sounds game. • Take part in Word Play. • Blend words and sentences. • Solve riddles. • Write dictated words and sentences. • Read a decodable story. • Complete writing activity.
• Review Comprehension Skill—Sequence. • Reread and discuss the selection with students. • Discuss Independent Reading. • Assign writing activity. • Introduce grammar skill.	• Follow along as selection is read again. • Discuss the selection. • Select a book to take home and read. • Complete writing activity. • Complete grammar skill activity.
• Administer weekly assessments. • Assess students' progress.	• Complete lesson assessment.

Unit 2 • LESSON

1

OBJECTIVES

- Identify and blend final consonant sounds in words.
- Read sight words.
- Participate in Word Play activity.
- Blend and break apart sounds in words.
- Develop fluency by reading aloud.
- Apply decoding skills by reading *Unit 2, Decodable Story 1*.
- Develop writing skills by writing color words.

MATERIALS

Sound/Spelling Cards:
28—Whales
33—Long A
34—Long I
37—Long E
Decodable Stories and Comprehension Skills, p. 13
Home Connection, p. 17
High-Frequency Word Cards
Sound/Spelling Card Stories Audiocassette/CD

Phonemic Awareness

The basic purpose of providing structured practice in phonemic awareness is to help students hear and understand the sounds from which words are made. Before students can be expected to understand the sound/symbol correspondence that forms the base of written English, they need to have a strong working knowledge of the sound relationships that make up the spoken language. This understanding of spoken language lays the foundation for the transition to written language. Phonemic awareness activities provide students with easy practice in discriminating the sounds that make up words. Once students begin reading and writing, this experience with manipulating sounds will help them use what they know about sounds and letters to sound out and spell unfamiliar words.

The two main formats for teaching phonemic awareness are oral blending and segmentation. These are supported by occasional discrimination activities and general word play. From these playful activities, students derive serious knowledge about language.

Oral Blending

In oral blending, students are led through a progression of activities designed to help them hear how sounds are put together to make words. The tone of the activities should be playful and informal and should move quickly. Although these activities will provide information about student progress, they are not diagnostic tools. Do not expect mastery.

Listening Game: Final Consonant Sounds

In this activity, the focus is on separating the final consonant sound from the first part of the word. The example words in this lesson are easily recognizable, so they should be easy for students to blend.

Tell students that you are going to ask them to put together some sounds to make words. Explain that you will say the beginning part of a word, pause, then say the ending sound. Then you will ask them to put the parts together and say the word. Demonstrate with the following example.

Teacher: *treehou . . . /s/. What's the word?*

Students: *treehouse*

Tell students to listen very carefully as you say each of the following words distinctly. Then ask students to tell you what the word is.

superma . . . /n/	acroba . . . /t/
sailboa . . . /t/	intersectio . . . /n/
windowpa . . . /n/	elephan . . . /t/
astronau . . . /t/	lighthou . . . /s/
tremendou . . . /s/	environmen . . . /t/

TEACHER TIP

Pacing Phonemic Awareness
Phonemic awareness activities should be quick and snappy. Do not let these activities drag, and do not expect mastery before moving on to the day's next activity. Students' ability to master phonemic awareness varies greatly and is normal. Many students who do not catch on at first will learn how to respond by observing their classmates.

SELECTION A • **A Nature Adventure**

Word Study

In this section of the lesson, students work on phonics, fluency, blending, and spelling. Increasing students' ability to work smoothly with printed words is one of the primary goals of the *Kaleidoscope* program.

Word Play

Teach students the Go Fish game. Ahead of time, cut large fish shapes from construction paper. On the back of each fish, print a word that contains a sound/spelling that students have learned. Underline the target sound/spelling. Attach a metal paper clip to the tail of each "fish." Place the fish front side up on a low table. Tie a short length of string to the end of a dowel rod. On the other end of the string, attach a small magnet. Call on students one by one to go fishing. When a student "catches" a fish, have him or her read the word and say the target sound/spelling.

Sight Words

This week's sight words:

give   many   some

Use the following procedure for teaching sight words:

- Write this week's sight words on the board.
- Read the words to students, and then have them read the words.
- Pronounce any words with which students have difficulty.
- Have students use each sight word in a sentence.

Phonics—Blending: Set 1

/ā/ spelled *a_e*	/ē/ spelled *e_e*
/ī/ spelled *i_e*	/hw/ spelled *wh_*

This section of the phonics lesson provides practice in building sounds and spellings into words.

- Point out and discuss each **Sound/Spelling Card** to be used.
- For **Card 28—Whales,** tell students that the two letters in this spelling, *wh,* represent one sound, /hw/. Have them say the sound several times. To help them distinguish /hw/ from /w/, have them hold their hands in front of their mouths and say pairs of words such as *wind* and *when, watt* and *what.* Explain that they should feel the difference in the amount of air on their hands, with little air for /w/ words and more air for /hw/ words.

You will need the following *Sound/Spelling Cards* for blending the words in Set 1.
28—Whales, 33—Long A, 34—Long I, 37—Long E

Blending Exercise

- The words in the lines provide practice with the Set 1 sound/spellings. Write the following words and sentences on the board.

- Have students blend the words and sentences using the sound-by-sound or whole-word procedure described in Unit 1 on page 12F.

Line 1:	age	flame	save	state
Line 2:	nice	mine	like	wide
Line 3:	eve	Pete	extreme	trapeze
Line 4:	whip	wave	white	will
Sentence 1:	Many of us crave fame.			
Sentence 2:	Give Steve some cake and put ice in his cup.			

About the Words and Sentences

- Have students find multiple-meaning words on the lines (for example, *flame, mine, eve, whip, wave, will*).

- Ask students to say the words on Line 4 and to distinguish the words that begin with /hw/ and those that begin with /w/.

- Have students find the words on the lines that have more than one syllable. *(extreme, trapeze)*

- Before reading a sentence, point to and read the underlined sight words. Have students reread the sentences to encourage fluency and comprehension.

Oral Language

Give clues for words on the lines for students to find and read. Here are some possible clues:

> It's a boy's name. *(Pete)*
> It might be seen at a circus. *(trapeze)*
> It's made by a fire. *(flame)*

TEACHER TIP

Blending Because this unit introduces long-vowel spellings for the first time, have students blend the words sound by sound, spelling by spelling. Continue using sound-by-sound blending, and gradually begin whole-word blending, depending on your students.

WRITING

Have students find the word on the word lines that is a color *(white)*. Tell students to write three other color words.

TEACHER TIP

Sound/Spelling Cards Remind students of any special features on the cards. For Card 33, point out the *a_e* spelling and explain that a consonant goes in the blank. Illustrate by writing *a_e* on the board. Have students say the sound for the spelling. Then write *t* in the blank. Have students blend the sounds to make the word *ate*. Explain that the letter *e* is silent in spellings such as this and it makes the *a* "say its name," or have a long sound. Point out similar vowel-blank-*e* spellings on *Card 34—Long I* and *Card 37—Long E.*

SELECTION A • **A Nature Adventure**

Dictation

Dictation gives students an opportunity to spell words by using the sound/spellings that they have learned. For this dictation exercise, have students use writing paper. Dictate the words and sentence for them to write. Use the following procedure:

- Say the first word in the Dictation word lines. Use the word in a sentence, then say the word again. Have students say the word.

- Tell students to think about how to segment the word into sounds. Then have them write the spelling for each sound. Encourage them to check the **Sound/Spelling Cards.**

- After each word line, write (or have a student write) the words on the board. Have students proofread their words. Tell them to circle any incorrect words and to correct them.

- Next, dictate the sentence. Dictate one word at a time, following the sounds-in-sequence or whole-word dictation procedure, depending on your students. Remind students to start the sentence with a capital letter and to use correct end punctuation.

- Write (or have a student write) the sentence on the board. Have students proofread their work and correct any incorrect words.

Line 1:	ate	life	whiz
Line 2:	place	five	when
Sentence:	Did Pete give Eve a ride on his white bike?		

TEACHER TIP

Sound/Spelling Card Stories Review today's sounds by using the *Sound/Spelling Card Stories.* Listening to the stories will help students understand how they can use the pictures on the *Sound/Spelling Cards* to remember the sounds associated with them. The stories are provided in the appendix and are also available on the *Sound/Spelling Card Stories Audiocassette/CD.*

Building Fluency

Decodable Story: Unit 2, Story 1

- This story reviews the sound/spellings /ā/ spelled *a_e;* /ē/ spelled *e_e;* /ī/ spelled *i_e;* /hw/ spelled *wh_.*
- Have students silently read **Decodable Stories and Comprehension Skills** page 13.
- Call on volunteers to read each paragraph aloud.
- For those students who need help, divide sentences according to natural phrases. Mark these phrases with diagonal slash marks on their worksheets.
- After students have read the story aloud, ask them questions and have them point to and read the answers in the story.
- Have students reread the story aloud with a partner. Rereading builds automaticity and fluency.
- Over the next few days, listen to each student reread the story.

Develop Fluency Some students may find it difficult to read with fluency because they do not recognize the importance of grouping words into natural meaning units, such as phrases, as they read. Model fluent reading frequently for students, showing them how pausing in the right places and adding expression can make a passage easier to understand.

 QUICK CHECK

As a quick review of today's sound/spellings, say some sentences, and ask students to suggest words to fill the blanks. Sentences you might read aloud include:

I had to _____ the leaves. *(rake)*
It took a long _____ for us to solve the problem. *(time)*
Jason is a _____ at math. *(whiz)*

OBJECTIVES

- Discuss vocabulary words and their meanings.
- Develop reading skills as the story is read to them.
- Gain knowledge of the comprehension strategies Making Connections and Visualizing.
- Build vocabulary by determining word meanings from context.
- Develop writing skills by writing a description.

MATERIALS

Student Reader, pp. 22–25
Language Arts, p. T14

SELECTION A • **A Nature Adventure**

Before Reading

Build Background

Activate Prior Knowledge

- Remind students that this unit is about kindness. Explain that kindness can be shown in many ways, to animals as well as to people.
- Ask students to share any stories that involve kindness—or a lack of kindness—to animals.

Background Information

Use the following information to help students understand the selection you are about to read:

- Ask students to tell what they know about nature parks. Ask them what animals they might see in a nature park.
- Tell students that many large nature parks rely on park rangers to take care of the park and to keep them safe. Explain that park rangers protect trees and other plants in the park, and that they look after the animals who may live there as well. In addition, they help people who visit the parks by giving directions and warning them of possible dangers.

Selection Vocabulary

Write the following vocabulary words on the board. Before browsing the selection, introduce and discuss these words and their meanings.

retraced: went back over

recall: to remember

disabled: unable to move or act as usual

Then have students read the words, stopping to blend any words that they have trouble reading. Demonstrate how to decode multisyllabic words by breaking the words into syllables and blending the syllables. Then have students try. If they still have trouble, refer them to the *Sound/Spelling Cards.* If the word is not decodable, give students the pronunciation.

As students study vocabulary, they will use a variety of skills to determine the meaning of a word. These skills include context clues, word structure, and apposition. In this unit, students will be learning about apposition. Write the following example on the board: *Tanya was able to recall, or remember, exactly where the bunny was.* Explain to students that they are going to use apposition to help them decipher the meaning of the word *recall.* Tell students that when they use apposition, they are looking for a word or group of words in the sentence that help define the word in question. Guide students until they can give a reasonable definition of the word.

Vocabulary Activity: Explain to students that a prefix is a word part that is added to the beginning of a base word. Tell students that the three selection vocabulary words have prefixes. Show students the prefix and the base word for each vocabulary word. Tell students they will learn more about prefixes throughout the year.

Preview and Prepare

Before you read, use modeling and prompts such as:

This is a story, so we'll only browse the first page. We can see that the story is about a girl named Tanya and her father, and they are spending a day in a nature park. Let's read to find out what happens.

WRITING

Tell students to think about a time when they have been in the woods or a nature park. Have students write a short description of their experience.

During Reading

Read Aloud

For this lesson, read the entire selection aloud. If you feel your students are ready to read the selection orally, have them do so. As you read, stop at the points that are marked with numbers in magenta circles on the reduced student pages, and model for them how to use the indicated strategy. Encourage students to stop at any point in their reading if they don't understand something or want to talk about the meaning of a passage or word.

Comprehension Strategies

During the reading of "A Nature Adventure" on pages 22–25, you will model the following reading comprehension strategies:

Making Connections: Good readers improve their understanding of a selection by making connections between what they already know and what they are reading about.

Visualizing: As they read, good readers often make pictures in their minds of the characters, events, and places of a story to help them better understand what they're reading.

TEACHER TIP

Enlarge the Comprehension Strategy Cards found in the appendix, and display them in a prominent place in the classroom. As they are reading, remind students that using the posted strategies will help them better understand what they read.

2

Text Comprehension *Strategies*

As you read the selection, use modeling and prompts such as:

❶ Making Connections

Good readers relate past experiences to what they read to make the selection more interesting and easier to understand. I love hiking, so I can connect with Tanya's excitement about spending the day in a nature park. Share with the class any connections you are making.

❷ Visualizing

Good readers make mental pictures, or visualize, as they read. By picturing in their minds the characters and what they're doing in the story, readers are better able to understand a story. I've made a picture here. I can see Tanya carefully walking back down the trail, trying to find whatever made the noises in the bushes.

A Nature Adventure

by Pamela Bliss
illustrated by Linda Pierce

It was eight o'clock in the morning. Tanya and her dad were going to spend the whole day in the nature park.

Tanya ran down the trail. She knew the way.

❶ "Wait for me!" called her dad.

22

VOCABULARY

Explain to students that when they see an unfamiliar word in something they are reading, they can sometimes figure out its meaning by looking at the words around it. For a lesson on word meanings from context, use *Language Arts* page T14.

"Hurry, Dad! Let's race." Tanya yelled. Suddenly, she heard a noise in the bushes. She retraced her steps to where she heard the noise and waited for her dad. ❷

"Look, Dad! There's a rabbit. It looks hurt."

Tanya's dad saw the rabbit. "I think you are right," he said. "Let's return to the ranger's station and get some help."

23

GRAMMAR

Tell students that a *common noun* names any person, place, thing, or idea. Explain to them that common nouns do not begin with a capital letter. For a lesson on common nouns, use **Language Arts** page T13.

Text Comprehension *skills*

Sequence

Remind students that events in a reading selection usually happen in a certain order, or a *sequence*. Sequence can mean that the author tells what happens from the first to the last event, from one day to the next day, or in some other kind of order. The author may use words such as *first, then, next,* and *last* or *first, second, third,* and *finally* to help readers follow the order of events. If authors do not use these words, readers need to pay close attention to what they are reading to figure out the sequence of events.

- Reread these pages of the selection. Tell students to listen for the order in which the events take place.
- When you have finished reading, call on volunteers to tell what happened to Tanya and her dad first, second, third, and fourth.
- Use **Transparency** 14 to record their responses.
- Review the events with students. Have them respond using the words *first, second, third,* and *fourth.*

First
Read

Text Comprehension *strategies*

❸ Visualizing

Can you picture the baby rabbit? I can. It's tiny and soft, and it's afraid, so it's trembling. Poor little rabbit. I hope the ranger can help it.

❹ Making Connections

When I was about eight, my dad and I found a baby raccoon on a busy road. We were afraid that it would get hurt, so we called the Animal Control Department. They took the raccoon back to its home in the woods.

As you are reading, be aware of how events in the story remind you of things that have happened to you. What connections are you making?

HOMEWORK
TIP

Ask students to look through magazine articles, newspaper stories, and books as they read at home for examples of ways that authors sequence the information in their writing. Have them bring to class and share their examples.

They returned to the ranger's station. They told the ranger, Joyce, about the rabbit. She went with Tanya and her dad to find it. Tanya was able to <u>recall</u> exactly where it was. The rabbit was still hiding in the bushes.

"It's just a baby," said Ranger Joyce. ❸ "It hardly weighs anything."

24

"Can you help it?" Tanya's dad asked.

"Yes," the ranger replied. "It is disabled. Its leg is hurt. But we can fix it at the animal hospital."

"Where will you take the rabbit when it is better?" Tanya asked.

"Why, the best place of all," the ranger said. "I will bring the rabbit back here—to its home in the park." ❹

25

 Second Read

Text Comprehension *skills*

Sequence

- Reread these pages of the selection. Tell students to listen for the order in which the events take place.
- When you have finished reading, call on volunteers to tell what happened to Tanya and her dad.
- Use **Transparency** 14 to record their responses.
- Review the events with students. Have them respond using the words *first, then, next,* and *finally*.
- For additional practice with Sequence, have students complete **Decodable Stories and Comprehension Skills** page 81.

Discussing the Selection

After you have read the story, discuss it with students. Use prompts such as:

- *What did you like about this selection?*
- *What act of kindness did Tanya and her father perform?*
- *Did anyone else show kindness? Who?*
- *What two kind things did the ranger do for the baby rabbit?*
- *How does this selection relate to the unit theme, Kindness?*

 ## ✓ QUICK CHECK

As a quick review, ask students to retell the events in the selection in the correct order.

3

OBJECTIVES

- Restore initial sounds.
- Identify long-vowel sounds in words.
- Blend and break apart sounds.
- Participate in Word Play activity.
- Develop fluency by reading aloud.
- Apply decoding skills by reading *Unit 2, Decodable Story 2.*
- Develop writing skills by writing words and identifying sound/spellings.

MATERIALS

Sound/Spelling Cards:
35—Long O
36—Long U
38—Gong
Decodable Stories and Comprehension Skills, p. 14
High-Frequency Word Cards
Sound/Spelling Card Stories Audiocassette/CD

Phonemic Awareness

Segmentation: Restoring Initial Phonemes

- Tell students they are going to play the Restoring Initial Phonemes game again.
- Demonstrate for students to remind them how the game is played.

  Teacher: moose . . . oose

  Teacher: mmmmoose. I forgot the /m/.

- Ask students to repeat the word and to say what sound was left off.
- Continue with the following words:

bee	we
lake	say
shoe	sea
boat	low
meet	take

Listening for Vowel Sounds

Listening for /ē/ and /ō/

Point to each long-vowel **Sound/Spelling Card** and remind students that these red letters, vowels, are special because they can say their names.

- Tell students that for this lesson they will respond to all the words by repeating the vowel sound in each word. Explain that the words contain either /ē/ or /ō/.
- Use the following words:

see	feel	loan
mow	peach	gross
reed	bow	toast
bean	no	mole
peace	toe	eat
feet	load	me
peal	groan	road
boats	boast	lean
so	meal	grease
tea	each	feast
lead	row	pole
green	knee	oats

Word Study

Word Play

Play the Go Fish game once again. On the backs of several "fish," write *a_e, e_e, i_e,* and *wh_* spellings. (Use each spelling more than once.) One by one, give students the fishing pole and tell them to "go fish." When a student catches a fish, have him or her read the spelling, say the sound, and say a word that contains the sound/spelling.

Phonics—Blending: Set 2

/ō/ spelled o_e	/ū/ spelled u_e
/ng/ spelled ■ng	

- Point out and discuss the new **Sound/Spelling Cards.**

- For the long-vowel cards, point out the vowel-blank-*e* spelling and ask students to explain what the blank means. Ask them what the letter *e* does in spellings such as this. *(It makes the vowel "say its name," or have a long sound.)*

Blending Exercise

- Write the following words and sentences on the board.

- Have students blend the words and sentences using the sound-by-sound or whole-word procedure described in Unit 1 on page 12F.

Line 1:	slope spoke joke rope
Line 2:	cute amuse mute huge
Line 3:	wing ring fling spring
Sentence 1:	Make <u>some</u> ice cubes and <u>give</u> them to Steve.
Sentence 2:	Sam sang <u>many</u> songs as he drove.
Sentence 3:	Bring <u>some</u> logs to put in the stove.

- Before reading a sentence, point to and read the underlined sight words.

- Discuss with students that each sentence begins with a capital letter and ends with a punctuation mark.

- Have students reread the sentences to encourage fluency and comprehension.

You will need the following **Sound/Spelling Cards** for blending the words in Set 2. 35—Long O, 36—Long U, 38—Gong

3

SELECTION A • **A Nature Adventure**

About the Words and Sentences

- The words on the lines provide practice with the Set 2 sound/spellings.
- On Line 1, have students find the pairs of words that rhyme. *(slope, rope; spoke, joke)*
- Have students find words on the lines that have multiple meanings *(spoke, ring, spring)*. Have them use the words in sentences to show their different meanings.
- For Sentence 1, have students identify the different long-vowel sound/spellings.

Oral Language

Give clues and have students find the words on the lines that the clues identify. Here are some possible clues:

> It can make you laugh. *(joke)*
> It means "not speaking." *(mute)*
> It helps a bird to fly. *(wing)*

Dictation

For the dictation exercise, have students use writing paper. Dictate the words and sentence for them to write.

Use the following procedure:

- Say the first word in each word line. Use the word in a sentence, then say the word again. Have students say the word.
- Tell students to think about how to segment the word into sounds. Then have them write the spelling for each sound.
- After each word line, write (or have a student write) the words on the board. Have students proofread their words. Tell them to circle any incorrect words and to correct them.
- Next dictate the sentence. Dictate one word at a time, following the sounds-in-sequence or whole-word dictation procedure, depending on your students. Remind students to start the sentence with a capital letter and to use correct end punctuation.
- Write (or have a student write) the sentence on the board. Have students proofread their work and correct any incorrect words.

WRITING

Have students write the words from Line 3. Tell them to circle the spelling for /ng/ in each word.

Line 1:	use hope bring
Line 2:	spring hang home
Sentence:	Put the hose next to the roses.

Building Fluency

Decodable Story: Unit 2, Story 2

- This story reviews the sound/spellings /ō/ spelled *o_e;* /ū/ spelled *u_e;* /ng/ spelled ■*ng.*
- Have students silently read ***Decodable Stories and Comprehension Skills*** page 14.
- Call on volunteers to read each paragraph aloud.
- For those students who need help, divide sentences according to natural phrases. Mark these phrases with diagonal slash marks on their worksheets.
- After students have read the story aloud, ask them questions and have them point to and read the answers in the story.
- Have students reread the story aloud with a partner.

HOMEWORK TIP

Encourage students to use what they are learning about sound/spellings as they read at home.

SELECTION A • **A Nature Adventure**

OBJECTIVES

- Develop reading skills as the story is reread to them.
- Gain knowledge of the comprehension skill Sequence.
- Develop vocabulary by listening to and discussing the selection.
- Identify common nouns.
- Develop writing skills by writing the first event in a sequence.

MATERIALS

Transparencies 3, 14, 15
Decodable Stories and Comprehension Skills, p. 81
Student Reader, pp. 22–25
Listening Library Audiocassette/CD
Language Arts, p. T13

Rereading the Selection

Comprehension Skills

Revisiting or rereading a selection allows students to learn and apply skills that give them a more complete understanding of a selection. For today's lesson, reread the selection to students. During the second reading, students will apply the following comprehension skill:

Sequence: Good readers identify the order in which the events of the story take place.

After Reading

Independent Reading

- Have students choose books from the *Classroom Library* or other available books to take home and read.
- Encourage students to read at least one book each week on their own.
- Encourage students to use the comprehension strategies they are learning as they read independently.
- On the bulletin board, post the copy of *Transparency* 3 and encourage students to record on it the titles of the books they are reading.

TEACHER TIP

Have students listen to the selection recording on the *Listening Library Audiocassette/CD* for a proficient, fluent model of oral reading.

WRITING

Tell students to think about the sequence of events in the selection. Have them write what happens *first* to Tanya at the nature park.

SELECTION A • **A Nature Adventure**

Assessment

Formal

At the conclusion of the lesson, have students complete the assessment Unit 2: A Nature Adventure. The Lesson Assessments are found in the *Assessment Guide.*

For all the items in this assessment, you should read both the question and answer choices out loud while students follow along silently. You may find it helpful to walk around the room while students are completing the assessment to provide them with any help they need to understand the questions.

Students should have the lesson selection in front of them when they answer the questions. When a question refers to information in the selection, you may find it useful to show students the portion of the selection that will help them find the answer.

Informal

Choose words from the selection that have regular long- and short-vowel sounds. Say these words clearly, write them on the board, and have students repeat the vowel sound in each word and identify the letter that makes the sound. Repeat the process by having students choose words from the selection.

Ending the Lesson

Have students attempt to recall the events in "A Nature Adventure" from memory. Then have them repeat the process with the story in front of them. Discussions like this help students recognize the importance of understanding the sequence of a story without implying that it is necessary to memorize all the events as you read.

OBJECTIVES

- Complete lesson assessment.
- Identify regular vowel sounds.
- Review sequence of events.

MATERIALS

Assessment Guide
Student Reader, pp. 22–25

SELECTION B • **The Lion and the Mouse**

Support Materials

HOME CONNECTIONS

Distribute *Home Connection* page 19, which describes this week's classwork and suggests activities for families to do at home. This letter is available in English and Spanish.

LESSON 6
- Sound/Spelling Cards 6, 30, 31
- Decodable Stories and Comprehension Skills, p. 15
- Home Connection, p. 19
- High-Frequency Word Cards
- Sound/Spelling Card Stories Audiocassette/CD

LESSON 7
- Student Reader, pp. 26–29
- Language Arts, p. T16

LESSON 8
- Sound/Spelling Card 32
- Decodable Stories and Comprehension Skills, p. 16
- High-Frequency Word Cards
- Sound/Spelling Card Stories Audiocassette/CD

LESSON 9
- Student Reader, pp. 26–29
- Transparencies 3, 6, 16
- Decodable Stories and Comprehension Skills, p. 82
- Listening Library Audiocassette/CD
- Language Arts, p. T15

LESSON 10
- Assessment Guide
- Student Reader, pp. 26–29

Teacher Focus	Student Participation
• Conduct Listening Game. • Conduct Word Play. • Introduce Sight Words and Set 1 blending words and sentences. • Conduct Oral Language activity. • Dictate word lines. • Assist students with decodable text. • Assign writing activity.	• Take part in Listening Game. • Take part in Word Play. • Read Sight Words. • Blend words and sentences. • Create sentences. • Write dictated words and sentences. • Read a decodable story. • Complete writing activity.
• Activate Prior Knowledge and provide background information. • Introduce and discuss selection vocabulary. • Preview selection. • Review Comprehension Strategies—Predicting and Monitoring and Clarifying. • Read the selection to students. • Introduce vocabulary skill. • Assign writing activity.	• Contribute to class discussion. • Read and discuss vocabulary words. Complete selection vocabulary activity. • Browse the selection. • Follow along as selection is read. • Complete vocabulary skill activity. • Complete writing activity.
• Conduct Listening for Vowel Sounds game. • Conduct Alliterative Word game. • Conduct Word Play. • Introduce Set 2 blending words and sentences. • Provide riddle clues. • Dictate word lines. • Assist students with decodable text. • Assign writing activity.	• Participate in Listening for Vowel Sounds game. • Participate in Alliterative Word game. • Take part in Word Play. • Blend words and sentences. • Solve riddles. • Write dictated words and sentences. • Read a decodable story. • Complete writing activity.
• Review Comprehension Skill—Reality and Fantasy. • Reread and discuss the selection with students. • Discuss Independent Reading. • Assign writing activity. • Introduce grammar skill.	• Follow along as selection is read again. • Discuss the selection. • Select a book to take home and read. • Complete writing activity. • Complete grammar skill activity.
• Administer weekly assessments. • Assess students' progress.	• Complete lesson assessment.

6

SELECTION B • **The Lion and the Mouse**

OBJECTIVES

- Identify and blend final consonant sounds in words.
- Read sight words.
- Participate in Word Play activity.
- Blend and break apart sounds in words.
- Develop fluency by reading aloud.
- Apply decoding skills by reading *Unit 2, Decodable Story 3.*
- Develop writing skills by identifying and writing words.

MATERIALS

Sound/Spelling Cards:
6—Fan
30—Shell
31—Thimble
Decodable Stories and Comprehension Skills, p. 15
Home Connection, p. 19
High-Frequency Word Cards
Sound/Spelling Card Stories Audiocassette/CD

Phonemic Awareness

The basic purpose of providing structured practice in phonemic awareness is to help students hear and understand the sounds from which words are made. Before students can be expected to understand the sound/symbol correspondence that forms the base of written English, they need to have a strong working knowledge of the sound relationships that make up the spoken language. This understanding of spoken language lays the foundation for the transition to written language. Phonemic awareness activities provide students with easy practice in discriminating the sounds that make up words. Once students begin reading and writing, this experience with manipulating sounds will help them use what they know about sounds and letters to sound out and spell unfamiliar words.

The two main formats for teaching phonemic awareness are oral blending and segmentation. These are supported by occasional discrimination activities and general word play. From these playful activities, students derive serious knowledge about language.

Oral Blending

In oral blending, students are led through a progression of activities designed to help them hear how sounds are put together to make words. The tone of the activities should be playful and informal and should move quickly. Although these activities will provide information about student progress, they are not diagnostic tools. Do not expect mastery.

Listening Game: Final Consonant Sounds

In this activity, the focus is on separating the final consonant sound from the first part of the word. The example words in this lesson may be harder for students to blend because the first part of each word does not give strong clues to the final consonant sounds.

Tell students that you are going to ask them to put together some sounds to make words. Explain that you will say the beginning part of a word, pause, then say the ending sound. Then you will ask them to put the parts together and say the word.

> Tell students to listen very carefully as you say each of the following words distinctly, pausing before the final sound. Then ask students to tell you what the word is.
>
> | | |
> |---|---|
> | cabba . . . /j/ | panca . . . /k/ |
> | liqui . . . /d/ | bathro . . . /b/ |
> | mushroo . . . /m/ | carpe . . . /t/ |

TEACHER TIP

Oral Blending Find time to review the oral blending activities with small groups of students who need extra practice.

SELECTION B • **The Lion and the Mouse**

Word Study

In this section of the lesson, students work on phonics, fluency, blending, and spelling. Increasing students' ability to work smoothly with printed words is one of the primary goals of the *Kaleidoscope* program.

Word Play

Play Go Fish once again. To the "fish" used in Lesson 3, add fish that contain vowel-blank-*e* spellings for /ō/ and /ū/, as well as the ■*ng* spelling.

Sight Words

This week's sight words:

from	once	want

Use the following procedure for teaching sight words:

● Write this week's sight words on the board.
● Read the words to students, and then have them read the words.
● Pronounce any words with which students have difficulty.
● Have students use each sight word in a sentence.

Phonics—Blending: Set 1

/f/ spelled *ph*	/sh/ spelled *sh*	/th/ spelled *th*

This section of the phonics lesson provides practice in building sounds and spellings into words.

● Point out and discuss the *Sound/Spelling Cards.* Ask students what they know about these cards. (For detailed information on how to introduce *Sound/Spelling Cards*, see Getting Started.)

You will need the following *Sound/Spelling Cards* for blending the words in Set 1. 6—Fan, 30—Shell, 31—Thimble

Blending Exercise

● The words in the lines provide practice with the Set 1 sound/spellings. Write the following words and sentences on the board.

● Have students blend the words and sentences using the sound-by-sound or whole-word procedure described in Unit 1 on page 12F.

Line 1:	ship fresh shop squash
Line 2:	phone graph orphan alphabet
Line 3:	thing thump with thick
Sentence 1:	Phil <u>once</u> had <u>many</u> shellfish <u>from</u> the shore.
Sentence 2:	When will Thad <u>want</u> to go shopping?

About the Words and Sentences

● For Line 1, have students identify each short-vowel sound/spelling.

● For Line 2, have students clap out and count the syllables in each word.

● Ask students to find words on the lines that have multiple meanings (for example: *ship, shop, squash*). Have them use the words in sentences to show their different meanings.

● Before reading a sentence, point to and read the underlined sight words. Have students reread the sentences to encourage fluency and comprehension.

● Have students identify the subject and predicate of each sentence.

Oral Language

To review the words, have students take turns coming to the board, touching a word, and using it in a sentence. Encourage them to extend their sentences by asking *when, where, how,* and *why* questions.

WRITING

Give clues to words on the word lines and have students write the words that the clues identify. Clues you might use include:
It's a large boat. *(ship)*
It's a yellow or green vegetable. *(squash)*
It can be used to talk to other people. *(phone)*

6

SELECTION B • **The Lion and the Mouse**

Dictation

Dictation gives students an opportunity to spell words by using the sound/spellings that they have learned. For this dictation exercise, have students use writing paper. Dictate the words and sentence for them to write. Use the following procedure:

● Say the first word in the Dictation word lines. Use the word in a sentence, then say the word again. Have students say the word.

● Tell students to think about how to segment the word into sounds. Then have them write the spelling for each sound. Encourage them to check the **Sound/Spelling Cards.**

● After each word line, write (or have a student write) the words on the board. Have students proofread their words. Tell them to circle any incorrect words and to correct them.

● Next, dictate the sentence. Dictate one word at a time, following the sounds-in-sequence or whole-word dictation procedure, depending on your students. Remind students to start the sentence with a capital letter and to use correct end punctuation.

● Write (or have a student write) the sentence on the board. Have students proofread their work and correct any incorrect words.

Line 1:	bath shape thunder
Line 2:	wish phrase crash
Sentence:	Did Ralph finish fifth in the race?

TEACHER TIP

Sound/Spelling Card Stories Review today's sounds by using the **Sound/Spelling Card Stories.** Listening to the stories will help students understand how they can use the pictures on the **Sound/Spelling Cards** to remember the sounds associated with them. The stories are provided in the appendix and are also available on the **Sound/Spelling Card Stories Audiocassette/CD.**

Building Fluency

Decodable Story: Unit 2, Story 3

- This story reviews the sound/spellings /f/ spelled *ph;* /sh/ spelled *sh;* /th/ spelled *th.*
- Have students silently read *Decodable Stories and Comprehension Skills* page 15.
- Call on volunteers to read each paragraph aloud.
- For those students who need help, divide sentences according to natural phrases. Mark these phrases with diagonal slash marks on their worksheets.
- After students have read the story aloud, ask them questions and have them point to and read the answers in the story.
- Have students reread the story aloud with a partner. Rereading builds automaticity and fluency.
- Over the next few days, listen to each student reread the story.

Building Fluency To help students build fluency, have them share with the class books, stories, and magazines that they have brought from home and read previously with their families.

QUICK CHECK

As a quick review of today's sound/spellings, say some sentences, and ask students to suggest words to fill the blanks. Sentences you might read aloud include:

Will you help me draw this _____ for math? *(graph)*
Seth ripped a button from the front of his _____. *(shirt)*
Listen, can you hear the _____? *(thunder)*

7

OBJECTIVES

- Discuss vocabulary words and their meanings.
- Develop reading skills as the story is read to them.
- Gain knowledge of the comprehension strategies Predicting and Monitoring and Clarifying.
- Build vocabulary by learning about antonyms.
- Develop writing skills by writing a prediction.

MATERIALS

Student Reader, pp. 26–29
Language Arts, p. T16

SELECTION B • **The Lion and the Mouse**

Before Reading

Build Background

Activate Prior Knowledge

- Remind students that this unit is about kindness. Review what they have learned so far about kindness.
- Ask students if they know any stories that have animal characters who can talk and act the way that people do. If necessary, talk to them about stories such as "Little Red Riding Hood," "The Three Pigs," and the Frog and Toad stories. Call on volunteers to retell their favorite stories.

Background Information

Use the following information to help students understand the selection you are about to read:

- Ask students to recall what they know about fiction. Tell them that the story you are going to read is a kind of fiction called a *fable*. Explain that a fable is a story that usually has animal characters who talk and act just like people. Explain that the purpose of a fable is to teach a lesson about life, called a *moral*.

Selection Vocabulary

Write the following vocabulary words on the board. Before reading the selection, introduce and discuss these words and their meanings.

unwise: foolish

predawn: before daybreak

tangled: caught in something

gnaw: to bite again and again

Then have students read the words, stopping to blend any words that they have trouble reading. Demonstrate how to decode multisyllabic words by breaking the words into syllables and blending the syllables. Then have students try. If they still have trouble, refer them to the *Sound/Spelling Cards.* If the word is not decodable, give students the pronunciation.

As students study vocabulary, they will use a variety of skills to determine the meaning of a word. These skills include context clues, word structure, and apposition. In this unit, students will be learning about apposition. Write the following example on the board: *In the predawn hours, before daybreak, the mouse heard a cry.* Explain to students that they are going to use apposition to help them decipher the meaning of the word *predawn*. Tell students that when they use apposition, they are looking for a word or group of words in the sentence that help define the word in question. Guide students until they can give a reasonable definition of the word.

Vocabulary Activity: Write the word *gnaw* on the board. Have students suggest items that animals might gnaw, such as grass, trees, leaves, or bones. Discuss which animals might gnaw on the items they suggest.

Preview and Prepare

Before you read, use modeling and prompts such as:

This is a story, so we'll only browse the title and the first page. From the title, we can see that the characters in the story are a lion and a mouse. What do you think the story will be about? Can you tell from browsing the first page? Let's read the whole story to find out what happens.

During Reading

Read Aloud

For this lesson, read the entire selection aloud. As you read, stop at the points that are marked with numbers in magenta circles on the reduced student pages, and model for them how to use the indicated strategy. Encourage students to stop at any point in their reading if they don't understand something or want to talk about the meaning of a passage or word.

Comprehension Strategies

During the reading of "The Lion and the Mouse" on pages 26–29, you will model the following reading comprehension strategies:

Predicting: Good readers know when to pause during reading to think about what is going on and to use their own knowledge and information from what they read to decide what will happen next. Good readers also return to their predictions to see whether the reading confirms them.

Monitoring and Clarifying: Good readers pay attention to how well they understand what they are reading. They stop to clarify the meanings of new words and to think about unfamiliar or difficult passages.

TEACHER TIP

Asking Questions Students should be encouraged to stop to ask questions. Have students take time to reflect on the text from time to time to see if it makes sense.

First Read

Text Comprehension *Strategies*

As you read the selection, use modeling and prompts such as:

❶ Making Predictions

Readers make predictions constantly about what's going to happen next in a story, and then they confirm or change their predictions as they read. This keeps them interested in what is happening in the story and helps them to understand it better. I predict that the lion won't let the mouse go. He will argue with her, then end up eating her. After all, that's what lions do. Share any predictions you are making.

❷ Confirming Predictions

Well, my prediction was not confirmed! I forgot that this is a fable, and that animals in fables don't always do what they might do if they were real. Remember to confirm the predictions you have made.

HOMEWORK TIP

Ask students to talk with family members about their favorite fables or stories that involve talking animals. Set aside time in class for students to share some of these stories with classmates.

The Lion and the Mouse

a fable by Aesop retold by Jane Cummings
illustrated by Dave Blanchette

Once a lion was sleeping. A mouse ran on his paw. The lion woke up. He grabbed the mouse.

"Now I'll eat you!" the lion cried.

The tiny mouse was frightened.

"Don't eat me," the mouse sighed.

❶ "That would be <u>unwise</u>."

26

VOCABULARY

Tell students that *antonyms* are words that have opposite meanings. Discuss some common antonyms, such as *light/dark, big/little,* and *easy/hard.* For a lesson on antonyms, use ***Language Arts*** page T16.

"Why?" the lion asked.

"One day I might be able to help you," said the mouse.

The lion smiled his widest smile.

"You are too tiny to help me," he said. "But I believe I will be kind anyhow."

And so the lion let the mouse go. **2**

27

Text Comprehension

Reality and Fantasy

Remind students that *fantasy* refers to something that is made up and that could not possibly happen in the real world.

● For these pages, ask students to identify what the lion and the mouse do that could not possibly happen in the real world. *(Answers may vary. Possible answer: The lion and the mouse talk.)* Ask students to identify what is realistic about the lion and the mouse. *(Answers may vary. Possible answer: The lion grabs and wants to eat the mouse.)*

● Use **Transparency** 6 to record their responses.

GRAMMAR

Review common nouns with students. Tell them that a *proper noun* names a particular person, place, thing, or idea. Point out that proper nouns always start with a capital letter. For a lesson on proper nouns, use *Language Arts* page T15.

First Read

Text Comprehension *strategies*

❸ Monitoring and Clarifying

Good readers pay attention to how well they understand what they read. They stop to clarify, or to figure out the meanings of words they don't know and of passages that confuse them. The lion is calling for help, so he must be in trouble. But I'm not sure exactly what kind of trouble. I'm going to reread this section to see if I can find out. Oh, I missed the line about the net. Now I understand that the lion is caught in a net and can't get out.

❹ Making Predictions

The lion is helpless. I predict that the mouse will find a way to help him as a way to return his act of kindness to her.

❺ Monitoring and Clarifying

The mouse is doing something to the net, but I don't know the word gnaw. Let's see, I know that mice have strong, sharp teeth, and that they can chew up just about anything. I think that gnaw means "chew," and that the mouse is chewing through the net to free the lion. Just to be sure, though, I'm going to check the word in a dictionary.

❻ Confirming Predictions

My prediction that the mouse would help the lion was confirmed. He was kind to her, and now she is kind to him.

The next day, in the <u>predawn</u> hours, the mouse heard a cry. "Who could that be?" the mouse asked.

❸ She saw the lion in a net. He tried to get out but could not.

❹ "Help me! Help me! These nets are very strong. My feet are <u>tangled</u>. I can't get them untangled," the lion cried.

28

W R I T I N G

After you have read page 28, have students write a short prediction about what they think will happen next in the story. Remind students to check their predictions to see if the reading confirms them.

The mouse was prepared to help. She began to <u>gnaw</u> at the net. Soon there was **5** a wide hole. The lion leaped out. The escape was complete! He smiled at the mouse.

"You are a very kind friend," the lion sighed in relief.

"It pays to be nice," said the mouse. **6**

29

Second Read

Text Comprehension

Reality and Fantasy

● For these pages, have students identify what the lion and the mouse do that could not possibly happen in the real world. *(Answers may vary. Possible answer: The mouse gnaws through a large net to free the lion.)* Have students identify the ways that the two animal characters are like people. *(Answers may vary. Possible answer: The lion and the mouse are kind to one another; they help each other.)*

● For additional practice with Reality and Fantasy, have students complete ***Decodable Stories and Comprehension Skills*** page 82.

Discussing the Selection

After you have read the story, discuss it with students. Use prompts such as:

● *What did you like about this selection?*
● *What act of kindness did the lion perform? What act of kindness did the mouse perform?*
● *What do you think is the lesson, or moral, of the story? (It pays to be nice.)*
● *How does this selection relate to the unit theme, Kindness?*
● *How does this selection add to what you already know about kindness?*

✓QUICK CHECK

Reread small sections of the story and ask students to identify what each character does in that section.

Unit 2 • LESSON 8

SELECTION B • **The Lion and the Mouse**

OBJECTIVES

- Change long-vowel sounds in words.
- Identify words with initial consonant sounds.
- Blend and break apart sounds in words.
- Participate in Word Play activity.
- Develop fluency by reading aloud.
- Apply decoding skills by reading *Unit 2, Decodable Story 4.*
- Develop writing skills by writing words and identifying sound/spellings.

MATERIALS

Sound Spelling Card:
32—Chipmunk
*Decodable Stories and
  Comprehension Skills,* p. 16
*High-Frequency Word Cards
Sound/Spelling Card Stories
  Audiocassette/CD*

Phonemic Awareness

Listening for Vowel Sounds

"Apples and Bananas"

This activity is intended to show students the important role that vowels play in syllables. "Apples and Bananas" is ideal for this purpose. The song requires students to control consciously the vowel sounds in the words while leaving the consonant sounds unchanged.

- Begin by pointing to each long-vowel *Sound/Spelling Card* and reviewing the sounds.

- Tell students to listen as you sing or say the song slowly, announcing each vowel change. After going through the entire song, have students join in as you repeat it. Have them sing or say the song several times.

    I like to eat, eat, eat,
    apples and bananas.
    I like to eat, eat, eat,
    apples and bananas.

    (/ā/)
    I like to ate, ate, ate,
    aypples and baynaynays.

    (/ē/)
    I like to eat, eat, eat,
    eepples and beeneenees.

    (/ī/)
    I like to ite, ite, ite,
    eyepples and beyeneyeneyes.

    (/ō/)
    I like to oat, oat, oat,
    oapples and boanoanoas.

Alliterative Word Game

This game focuses on the first sound in a word. It is a simple activity in which students say any words they can think of that begin with a target consonant sound. It complements the Listening for Vowel Sounds activities in which you produce the words and ask students to identify sounds.

- Explain that you are going to say some words that begin with the same sound, and that when you stop, you want them to add words that begin with that same sound. Begin with these words:

    dog   doodle

    door   delicious

    doctor   dangerous

- When students run out of words, begin again with another initial sound.

29A   Lesson 8 • UNIT 2

Word Study

Word Play

Play the I Spy game. Choose a previously taught sound/spelling. Look around the room until you see something that contains—but does not begin with—the sound/spelling. Say, for example, *I spy something that ends with o_e.* Give a clue, such as the object's size or color, or direct students' attention to the correct part of the room. Objects you might name include *globe, rope, phone.* Turn the game over to students to find and give clues for other objects that contain a previously taught sound/spelling.

Phonics—Blending: Set 2

```
/ch/ spelled ch, ■tch
```

Point out and discuss the **Sound/Spelling Card.** Ask students what they know about this card.

You will need the following *Sound/Spelling Card* for blending the words in Set 2.
32—Chipmunk

Blending Exercise

● Write the following words and sentences on the board.

● Have students blend the words and sentences using the sound-by-sound or whole-word procedure described in Unit 1 on page 12F.

Line 1:	chop chin chime chimp
Line 2:	hatch patch latch itch
Line 3:	chum chest crutch clutch
Sentence 1:	Did Chuck <u>want</u> any of the squash <u>from</u> the chest?
Sentence 2:	Get the batch of papers <u>from</u> the hutch.

● Before reading a sentence, point to and read the underlined sight words.

● Discuss with students that each sentence begins with a capital letter and ends with a punctuation mark.

● Have students reread the sentences to encourage fluency and comprehension.

WRITING

Have students write the words on Line 3. Tell them to circle the sound/spelling for /ch/ in each word.

Unit 2 • LESSON 8

SELECTION B • **The Lion and the Mouse**

About the Words and Sentences

- For Line 2, have students find the words that rhyme. *(hatch, patch, latch)*
- Have students find words on the lines that are names for body parts. *(chin, chest)*
- Ask students to find and give two meanings for multiple-meaning words. *(for example, chop, hatch, patch, chest)*
- Have students identify each kind of sentence. *(question, statement)*

Oral Language

To review the words, give clues and have students find the words on the lines that the clues identify. Here are some possible clues:

>It can be used to repair holes. *(patch)*
>
>It's another word for *friend* or *pal*. *(chum)*
>
>It rhymes with *shrimp*. *(chimp)*

Dictation

For the dictation exercise, have students use writing paper. Dictate the words and sentences for them to write.

Line 1:	such	pitch	chip
Line 2:	much	stitch	catch
Sentence:	Which pitcher lives on a ranch?		

Multiple Spellings For sounds that have multiple spellings, remind students to ask *Which spelling?* when they are unsure which one to use in a given word. Remind them to use the *Sound/Spelling Cards* and to ask for help when they need it.

Use the following procedure:

- Say the first word in each word line. Use the word in a sentence, then say the word again. Have students say the word.
- Tell students to think about how to segment the word into sounds. Then have them write the spelling for each sound.
- After each word line, write (or have a student write) the words on the board. Have students proofread their words. Tell them to circle any incorrect words and to correct them.
- Next dictate the sentence. Dictate one word at a time, following the sounds-in-sequence or whole-word dictation procedure, depending on your students. Remind students to start the sentence with a capital letter and to use correct end punctuation.
- Write (or have a student write) the sentence on the board. Have students proofread their work and correct any incorrect words.

Building Fluency

Decodable Story: Unit 2, Story 4

● This story reviews the sound/spellings /ch/ spelled *ch*, ■*tch*.

● Have students silently read ***Decodable Stories and Comprehension Skills*** page 16.

● Call on volunteers to read each paragraph aloud.

● For those students who need help, divide sentences according to natural phrases. Mark these phrases with diagonal slash marks on their worksheets.

● After students have read the story aloud, ask them questions and have them point to and read the answers in the story.

● Have students reread the story aloud with a partner.

HOMEWORK TIP

To help students build fluency, have them take home the ***Decodable Stories and Comprehension Skills*** stories to read with their families.

Unit 2 • LESSON

9

SELECTION B • **The Lion and the Mouse**

OBJECTIVES

- Develop reading skills as the story is reread to them.
- Gain knowledge of the comprehension skill Reality and Fantasy.
- Develop vocabulary by listening to and discussing a selection.
- Develop writing skills by writing about Reality and Fantasy.
- Identify proper nouns.

MATERIALS

Transparencies 3, 6, 16
Decodable Stories and Comprehension Skills, p. 82
Student Reader, pp. 26–29
Listening Library Audiocassette/CD
Language Arts, p. T15

Rereading the Selection

Comprehension Skills

Revisiting or rereading a selection allows students to learn and apply skills that give them a more complete understanding of a selection. For today's lesson, reread the selection to students. During the second reading, students will apply the following comprehension skill:

Reality and Fantasy: Good readers are able to find clues in their reading to let them know if the characters, events, and places are real or if they are just the product of the author's imagination and could not possibly exist.

After Reading

Independent Reading

- Have students choose books from the *Classroom Library* or other available books to take home and read. Encourage students to read at least one book each week on their own.
- Sit with each student and talk about the independent reading that she or he is doing.
- Encourage students to use the comprehension strategies they are learning as they read independently.
- Encourage students to record the titles of the books they are reading on the copy of *Transparency* 3.

TEACHER TIP

Have students listen to the selection recording on the *Listening Library Audiocassette/CD* for a proficient, fluent model of oral reading.

WRITING

Have students write about one event in the selection that shows that "The Lion and the Mouse" is a fantasy. Have students share their examples with the class.

SELECTION B • **The Lion and the Mouse**

Assessment

Formal

At the conclusion of the lesson, have students complete the assessment Unit 2: The Lion and the Mouse. The Lesson Assessments are found in the *Assessment Guide.*

For all the items in this assessment, you should read both the question and answer choices out loud while students follow along silently. You may find it helpful to walk around the room while students are completing the assessment to provide them with any help they need to understand the questions.

After completing the lesson assessment, discuss the answers with students. Reinforce students' correct answers and discuss their mistakes. Help them correct their mistakes and reinforce the belief that making mistakes is an important part of learning and that no one is always right.

Informal

Have an "antonym bee." Say a common word and have students name an antonym. Allow students to challenge one another to find an antonym for a word they know. You can enhance the activity by helping students find unusual antonyms in a dictionary. Be sure to write all the words on the board and have students read them out loud.

Ending the Lesson

If you are confident students are familiar with the story, have them read it out loud as a readers' theater. Allow them to practice the voices of the animals and have them read as they think the animals would speak. Provide them with any help they need to pronounce words with which they are struggling.

OBJECTIVES

- Complete lesson assessment.
- Review antonyms.
- Read selection aloud as a readers' theater.

MATERIALS

Assessment Guide
Student Reader, pp. 26–29

SELECTION C • **Helping Others**

Support Materials

LESSON 11
- Sound/Spelling Cards 14, 18
- Decodable Stories and Comprehension Skills, p. 17
- Home Connection, p. 21
- High-Frequency Word Cards
- Sound/Spelling Card Stories Audiocassette/CD

LESSON 12
- Student Reader, pp. 30–31
- Language Arts, p. T18
- Transparency 17

LESSON 13
- Sound/Spelling Cards
- Decodable Stories and Comprehension Skills, p. 18
- High-Frequency Word Cards
- Sound/Spelling Card Stories Audiocassette/CD

LESSON 14
- Student Reader, pp. 30–31
- Transparencies 3, 18
- Decodable Stories and Comprehension Skills, p. 83
- Listening Library Audiocassette/CD
- Language Arts, p. T17

LESSON 15
- Assessment Guide
- Student Reader, pp. 30–31

HOME CONNECTIONS

Distribute *Home Connection* page 21, which describes this week's classwork and suggests activities for families to do at home. This letter is available in English and Spanish.

Teacher Focus

- Conduct Listening Game.
- Conduct Word Play.
- Introduce Sight Words and Set 1 blending words and sentences.
- Conduct Oral Language activity.
- Dictate word lines.
- Assist students with decodable text.
- Assign writing activity.

- Activate Prior Knowledge and provide background information.
- Introduce and discuss selection vocabulary.
- Preview selection.
- Review Comprehension Strategies—Predicting and Asking Questions.
- Read the selection to students.
- Introduce vocabulary skill.
- Assign writing activity.

- Conduct Initial Consonant Sounds game.
- Conduct Listening for Vowel Sounds game.
- Conduct Word Play.
- Introduce Set 2 blending words and sentences.
- Provide riddle clues.
- Dictate word lines.
- Assist students with decodable text.
- Assign writing activity.

- Introduce Comprehension Skill—Compare and Contrast.
- Reread and discuss the selection with students.
- Discuss Independent Reading.
- Assign writing activity.
- Introduce grammar skill.

- Administer weekly assessments.
- Assess students' progress.

Student Participation

- Take part in Listening Game.
- Take part in Word Play.
- Read Sight Words.
- Blend words and sentences.
- Identify vowel sounds.
- Write dictated words and sentences.
- Read a decodable story.
- Complete writing activity.

- Contribute to class discussion.
- Read and discuss vocabulary words. Complete selection vocabulary activity.
- Browse the selection.
- Follow along as selection is read.
- Complete vocabulary skill activity.
- Complete writing activity.

- Participate in Initial Consonant Sounds game.
- Participate in Listening for Vowel Sounds game.
- Take part in Word Play.
- Blend words and sentences.
- Solve riddles.
- Write dictated words and sentences.
- Read a decodable story.
- Complete writing activity.

- Follow along as selection is read again.
- Discuss the selection.
- Select a book to take home and read.
- Complete writing activity.
- Complete grammar skill activity.

- Complete lesson assessment.

OBJECTIVES

- Identify and blend final consonant sounds in words.
- Blend and break apart sounds in words.
- Read sight words.
- Participate in Word Play activity.
- Develop fluency by reading aloud.
- Apply decoding skills by reading *Unit 2, Decodable Story 5*.
- Develop writing skills by writing compound words.

MATERIALS

Sound/Spelling Cards:
14—Nose
18—Robot
Decodable Stories and Comprehension Skills, p. 17
Home Connection, p. 21
High-Frequency Word Cards
Sound/Spelling Card Stories Audiocassette/CD

Phonemic Awareness

The basic purpose of providing structured practice in phonemic awareness is to help students hear and understand the sounds from which words are made. Before students can be expected to understand the sound/symbol correspondence that forms the base of written English, they need to have a strong working knowledge of the sound relationships that make up the spoken language. This understanding of spoken language lays the foundation for the transition to written language. Phonemic awareness activities provide students with easy practice in discriminating the sounds that make up words. Once students begin reading and writing, this experience with manipulating sounds will help them use what they know about sounds and letters to sound out and spell unfamiliar words.

The two main formats for teaching phonemic awareness are oral blending and segmentation. These are supported by occasional discrimination activities and general word play. From these playful activities, students derive serious knowledge about language.

Oral Blending

In oral blending, students are led through a progression of activities designed to help them hear how sounds are put together to make words. The tone of the activities should be playful and informal and should move quickly. Although these activities will provide information about student progress, they are not diagnostic tools. Do not expect mastery.

Listening Game: Final Consonant Sounds

In this activity, the focus is on separating the final consonant sound from the first part of the word. This lesson uses one-syllable words, which may be difficult for students to identify without paying close attention to each word part. Repeat the words if necessary, but do not distort the final sound by stretching it out.

Tell students that you are going to play the Final Consonant Sounds listening game again. Remind them that you will say the beginning part of a word, pause, then say the ending sound. Then you will ask them to put the parts together and say the word.

Tell students to listen very carefully as you say each of the following words distinctly, pausing before the final sound. Then ask students to tell you what the word is.

mea . . . /t/	tra . . . /p/
be . . . /d/	ta . . . /b/
tu . . . /g/	fee . . . /t/
ca . . . /b/	ma . . . /d/

TEACHER TIP

Student Responses To keep students' attention, switch unpredictably between individual and group response.

Unit 2 • LESSON 11

Word Study

In this section of the lesson, students work on phonics, fluency, blending, and spelling. Increasing students' ability to work smoothly with printed words is one of the primary goals of the *Kaleidoscope* program.

Word Play

Have students work in teams of three or four. On the board, write the spellings *ch* and ■*tch*. Give the teams five or so minutes to write as many words as they can that contain one of these spellings. Have each team read its list as you write the words on the board. Award a point for each correct word.

Sight Words

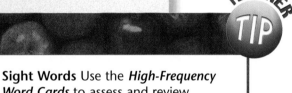

Sight Words Use the *High-Frequency Word Cards* to assess and review students' knowledge of sight words.

This week's sight words:

again	answer	who

Use the following procedure for teaching sight words:
- Write this week's sight words on the board.
- Read the words to students, and then have them read the words.
- Pronounce any words with which students have difficulty.
- Have students use each sight word in a sentence.

Phonics—Blending: Set 1

> /n/ spelled *kn_* | /r/ spelled *wr_*

This section of the phonics lesson provides practice in building sounds and spellings into words.

- Point out and discuss the *Sound/Spelling Cards.* Ask students what they know about these cards.

You will need the following *Sound/Spelling Cards* for blending the words in Set 1. 14—Nose, 18—Robot

Blending Exercise

- The words in the lines provide practice with the Set 1 sound/spellings. Write the following words and sentences on the board.

- Have students blend the words and sentences using the whole-word procedure described in Unit 1 on page 12F.

Line 1:	knot not wring ring
Line 2:	wrap rap wrung rung
Line 3:	knapsack wristband knothole
Sentence 1:	Do not knock <u>again</u>!
Sentence 2:	Ron did not <u>answer</u> the letter I wrote to him.
Sentence 3:	<u>Who</u> has the hammer and the wrench?

About the Words and Sentences

- On Lines 1 and 2, have students notice the pairs of words in which a sound is represented by two different spellings. Ask them what words that sound the same but are spelled differently and have different meanings are called *(homophones)*.

- For Line 3, ask students what they know about compound words, and then have them tell the meanings of the compound words.

- Before reading a sentence, point to and read the underlined sight words. Have students reread the sentences to encourage fluency and comprehension.

- For the sentences, have students identify the end punctuation marks. Ask them what the marks tell them about how the sentences should be read.

Oral Language

- Remind students that every word must have a vowel sound. Say words from the lines and have students identify the vowel sound in each word.

- Have students take turns choosing a word and asking each other to identify the vowel sound it contains.

WRITING

Have students write the compound words on Line 3. Then have them write the two smaller words that make up each compound word. Discuss the meanings of each smaller word and each compound word.

SELECTION C • **Helping Others**

Dictation

Dictation gives students an opportunity to spell words by using the sound/spellings that they have learned. For this dictation exercise, have students use writing paper. Dictate the words and sentence for them to write. Use the following procedure:

● Say the first word in the word lines. Use the word in a sentence, then say the word again. Have students say the word.

● Tell students to think about how to segment the word into sounds. Then have them write the spelling for each sound. Encourage them to check the **Sound/Spelling Cards.**

● After each word line, write (or have a student write) the words on the board. Have students proofread their words. Tell them to circle any incorrect words and to correct them.

● Next, dictate the sentence. Dictate one word at a time, following the sounds-in-sequence or whole-word dictation procedure, depending on your students. Remind students to start the sentence with a capital letter and to use correct end punctuation.

● Write (or have a student write) the sentence on the board. Have students proofread their work and correct any incorrect words.

Line 1:	wreck	knob	wrote
Line 2:	knit	write	knock
Sentence:	He broke the knickknack with a wrench.		

Sound/Spelling Card Stories Review today's sounds by using the **Sound/Spelling Card Stories.** Listening to the stories will help students understand how they can use the pictures on the **Sound/Spelling Cards** to remember the sounds associated with them. The stories are provided in the appendix and are also available on the **Sound/Spelling Card Stories Audiocassette/CD.**

Building Fluency

Decodable Story: Unit 2, Story 5

- This story reviews the sound/spellings /n/ spelled *kn_*; /r/ spelled *wr_*.
- Have students silently read ***Decodable Stories and Comprehension Skills*** page 17.
- Call on volunteers to read each paragraph aloud.
- For those students who need help, divide sentences according to natural phrases. Mark these phrases with diagonal slash marks on their worksheets.
- After students have read the story aloud, ask them questions and have them point to and read the answers in the story.
- Have students reread the story aloud with a partner. Rereading builds automaticity and fluency.
- Over the next few days, listen to each student reread the story.

Develop Fluency Model fluent reading frequently for students, showing them how pausing in the right places and adding expression can make a passage easier to understand.

QUICK CHECK

As a quick review of today's sound/spellings, say some sentences, and ask students to suggest words to fill the blanks. Sentences you might read aloud include:

Always _____ before you enter the office. *(knock)*
I like to _____ packages with pretty paper. *(wrap)*
Did he break his _____ when he fell on his arm? *(wrist)*

12

SELECTION C • **Helping Others**

Before Reading

Build Background

Activate Prior Knowledge

Remind students that this unit is about kindness. Review what they have learned so far about kindness from each selection they have read.

Background Information

Use the following information to help students understand the selection you are about to read:

● Ask students to talk about things that they have done to help family members, neighbors, and friends.

● Ask students how they felt after helping someone.

Selection Vocabulary

Write the following vocabulary words on the board. Before browsing the selection, introduce and discuss these words and their meanings.

spend: to pay out money

spied: noticed

Then have students read the words, stopping to blend any words that they have trouble reading. Demonstrate how to decode multisyllabic words by breaking the words into syllables and blending the syllables. Then have students try. If they still have trouble, refer them to the ***Sound/Spelling Cards.*** If the word is not decodable, give students the pronunciation.

As students study vocabulary, they will use a variety of skills to determine the meaning of a word. These skills include context clues, word structure, and apposition. In this unit, students will be learning about apposition. Write the following example on the board: *David spied, or noticed, the ball that had rolled into the bushes.* Explain to students that they are going to use apposition to help them decipher the meaning of the word *spied.* Tell students that when they use apposition, they are looking for a word or group of words in the sentence that help define the word in question. Guide students until they can give a reasonable definition of the word.

Vocabulary Activity: Write the word *spend* on the board and make two columns under the word *spend*—one column labeled *Needs* and the other column labeled *Wants.* Have students give examples of items that people spend money on and write their examples under the appropriate column. Discuss the list as a class.

OBJECTIVES

• Discuss vocabulary words and their meanings.
• Develop reading skills as the story is read to them.
• Gain knowledge of the comprehension strategies Asking Questions and Predicting.
• Build vocabulary by learning about synonyms.
• Develop writing skills by writing a prediction.

MATERIALS

Student Reader, pp. 30–31
Language Arts, p. T18
Transparency 17

Preview and Prepare

Before you read, use modeling and prompts such as:

● *This is a very short story, so we'll only browse the title and the first paragraph.*

● *What can you tell from the title? What do you think the story will be about? Let's read the whole story to find out what happens.*

During Reading

Read Aloud

For this lesson, read the entire selection aloud. As you read, stop at the points that are marked with numbers in magenta circles on the reduced student pages, and model for them how to use the indicated strategy. Encourage students to stop at any point in their reading if they don't understand something or want to talk about the meaning of a passage or word.

Comprehension Strategies

During the reading of "Helping Others" on pages 30–31, you will model the following reading comprehension strategies:

Asking Questions: As they read, good readers ask themselves questions to see if they are making sense of what they are reading.

Predicting: Good readers know when to pause during reading to think about what is going on and to use their own knowledge and information from what they read to decide what will happen next. Good readers also return to their predictions to see whether the reading confirms them.

WRITING

Dictate the following sentence to students: *This selection looks like it might be about* _____. Have students write their ideas about the selection's content based on their browsing.

Text Comprehension *strategies*

As you read the selection, use modeling and prompts such as:

❶ Asking Questions

I have questions about this title: Who is doing the helping? Who are the "others"? I'll keep these questions in mind as we read the story.

❷ Making Predictions

I predict that Pat will spend the money that's left on candy. Share with the class any predictions you are making.

❸ Asking Questions

I wonder who Spot is. I must have missed something, so I'll go back and reread to see if I can answer this question. Oh, there it is in the third paragraph. Spot is Pat's dog.

❹ Confirming Predictions

Well, my prediction didn't come true. Pat didn't buy candy with the leftover money. I should have paid more attention to the characters. Pat was kind to run an errand for Mike's mom, so I could have predicted that she would spend the money on something for someone else.

Remind students that they should spend at least 20 minutes each day reading outside of school.

❶ Helping Others

by Beth Adkins
illustrated by Sally Schaedler

One day Mike's mom called Pat. She said, "Pat, I need some things from the store. Mike can't go now. Could you come by and get the things for me?"

"I will ask my mom," Pat replied.

Her mom said yes, so Pat rode to Mike's on her bike. Her dog, Spot, walked with her. Mike's mom gave Pat some money. "Pat," she said. "My things won't cost this much. You may <u>spend</u>

❷ what is left."

30

VOCABULARY

Tell students that *synonyms* are words that have the same or nearly the same meaning. Discuss some common synonyms, such as *happy/glad, large/huge, easy/simple.* For a lesson on synonyms, use **Language Arts** page T18.

At the store, Pat found the things for Mikc's mom right away. She also got a good bone for Spot. Then she <u>spied</u> a red  ball. Spot had one, but Mike's dog, Flash, didn't. He might like a ball. She got the ball for Flash.

Pat was glad to be helping.

31

Text Comprehension

Compare and Contrast

Tell students that to *compare* is to tell how things are alike and to *contrast* is to say how they are different. Explain that as they read, good readers both compare and contrast characters, things, and events to get a better understanding of the story.

● Ask students to compare and contrast the following:

   Pat and Mike's mom

   Spot and Flash

● Use **Transparency** 18 to record their responses.

● For additional practice with Compare and Contrast, have students complete **Decodable Stories and Comprehension Skills** page 83.

Discussing the Selection

After you have read the story, discuss it with students. Use prompts such as:

● *What does the title of the story mean?*

● *What did Pat do to help Mike's mom?*

● *Why did Pat buy the red ball for Flash and not for Spot?*

● *How does this selection relate to the unit theme, Kindness?*

● *How does this selection add to what you already know about kindness?*

GRAMMAR

Remind students that nouns name persons, places, things, and ideas. Explain to them that a *singular* noun names one person, place, thing, or idea and a *plural* noun names more than one. For a lesson on plural nouns, use **Language Arts** page T17.

QUICK CHECK

Ask students to retell the story event by event.

SELECTION C • **Helping Others**

Phonemic Awareness

Segmentation: Initial Consonant Sounds

● Tell students they are going to play another game. Explain that you will say a word and repeat the beginning consonant. Then you will ask them to repeat the word and to say what sounds were left off. Use this example:

Teacher:	top . . . /t/
Teacher:	What's the word? What sounds were left off?
Students:	top . . . /o/ /p/

● Continue with the following words:

goat	she	fight
pie	light	go
neat	boom	kite
boat	show	my
right	day	feet

Listening for Vowel Sounds

Listening for /ā/ and /ī/

● Tell students that once again they will respond to each word that you say by repeating its vowel sound after you read the word. Tell them that the vowel sounds they are listening for are /ā/ and /ī/.

● Use the following words:

pie	race	way
stay	say	bite
gray	nine	ice
my	lace	hay
try	bait	pay
rice	light	tray
name	high	bike

TEACHER TIP

Segmentation Find time to review segmenting initial sounds with small groups of students who need extra practice.

Word Study

Word Play

Have students work in teams of three or four. On the board, write the word *cut*. Ask them to say the word, then ask them to say its short-vowel sound, /u/. Then add *e* to the word and ask them to say the new word *(cute)* and vowel sound, /ū/ . Call on volunteers to tell the different meanings of the two words. Give the teams five or so minutes to write as many real short-vowel/long-vowel word pairs as they can make by adding an *e* to the word. Then have each team read its list as you write the words on the board. Award a point for each correct pair. Some pairs they might create include *Sam/same, kit/kite, bit/bite, dim/dime, pin/pine, rod/rode, rob/robe, cub/cube.*

Phonics—Blending: Set 2

Point out and discuss any **Sound/Spelling Cards** that you particularly want students to review. Tell them that in this lesson, they will review the sound/spellings that they have learned so far in this unit.

Blending Exercise

● Write the following words and sentences on the board.

● Have students blend the words and sentences using the whole-word procedure described in Unit 1 on page 12F.

Line 1:	size	rate	chose	eve	pride
Line 2:	shine	phone	whiz	bath	shell
Line 3:	switch	match	catch	ranch	branch
Line 4:	knit	knot	swing	wrong	write
Sentence 1:	Who wrote notes to Kate and Pete?				
Sentence 2:	Answer the phone when it rings again.				

● Before reading a sentence, point to and read the underlined sight words.

● Discuss with students that each sentence begins with a capital letter and ends with a punctuation mark.

● Have students reread the sentences to encourage fluency and comprehension.

TEACHER TIP

Sight Words Use the *High-Frequency Word Cards* to assess and review students' knowledge of sight words.

WRITING

Have students select a word from the word lines and create an illustration and a short caption using the word. Ask students to share their drawings and captions with the class.

SELECTION C • **Helping Others**

About the Words and Sentences

- For Line 1, have students identify the long-vowel sound/spellings in each word.
- For Line 3, have students identify the sound/spellings for /ch/ in each word.
- Ask students to find words on the lines that have multiple meanings and to give at least two meanings of each word. *(for example, eve, pride, switch, match)*
- For Sentence 1, have students identify the proper nouns. *(Kate, Pete)*
- For Sentence 2, have students identify the common noun. *(phone)*

Oral Language

Give clues and have students find words on the lines that the clues identify. Here are some possible clues:

> It can be found at the seashore. *(shell)*
>
> It can be tied in a rope. *(knot)*
>
> It's a place with cattle. *(ranch)*

Line 1:	trash	when	home	like
Line 2:	gave	spring	with	chum
Sentence:	Phil hung his spaceship from the knob.			

Multiple Spellings For sounds that have multiple spellings, remind students to ask *Which spelling?* when they are unsure which one to use in a given word. Remind them to use the *Sound/Spelling Cards* and to ask for help when they need it.

Dictation

For the dictation exercise, have students use writing paper. Dictate the words and sentences for them to write.

Use the following procedure:

- Say the first word in each word line. Use the word in a sentence, then say the word again. Have students say the word.
- Tell students to think about how to segment the word into sounds. Then have them write the spelling for each sound.
- After each word line, write (or have a student write) the words on the board. Have students proofread their words. Tell them to circle any incorrect words and to correct them.
- Next dictate the sentence. Dictate one word at a time, following the sounds-in-sequence or whole-word dictation procedure, depending on your students. Remind students to start the sentence with a capital letter and to use correct end punctuation.
- Write (or have a student write) the sentence on the board. Have students proofread their work and correct any incorrect words.

Building Fluency

Decodable Story: Unit 2, Story 6

● This story reviews the sound/spellings introduced in this unit.

● Have students silently read ***Decodable Stories and Comprehension Skills*** page 18.

● Call on volunteers to read each paragraph aloud.

● For those students who need help, divide sentences according to natural phrases. Mark these phrases with diagonal slash marks on their worksheets.

● After students have read the story aloud, ask them questions and have them point to and read the answers in the story.

● Have students reread the story aloud with a partner.

Tell students to look through the books, magazines, and newspapers they read at home for words that contain the vowel-blank-*e* spelling for the long vowels. Have them make lists of the words and share the lists with the class.

SELECTION C • **Helping Others**

OBJECTIVES

- Develop reading skills as the story is reread to them.
- Gain knowledge of the comprehension skill Compare and Contrast.
- Develop vocabulary by listening to and discussing a selection.
- Develop writing skills by writing a grocery list.
- Identify and correctly use plural nouns.

MATERIALS

Transparencies 3, 18
Decodable Stories and Comprehension Skills, p. 83
Student Reader, pp. 30–31
Listening Library Audiocassette/CD
Language Arts, p. T17

Rereading the Selection

Comprehension Skills

Revisiting or rereading a selection allows students to learn and apply skills that give them a more complete understanding of a selection. For today's lesson, reread the selection to students. During the second reading, students will apply the following comprehension skill:

Compare and Contrast: Good readers deepen their understanding of what they read by looking for ways in which characters, things, and events in a selection are alike and ways they are different.

After Reading

Independent Reading

- Have students choose books from the *Classroom Library* or other available books to take home and read. Encourage students to read at least one book each week on their own.
- Invite students to sit with partners and talk about the independent reading that they are doing.
- Encourage students to use the comprehension strategies they are learning as they read independently.
- Encourage students to record the titles of the books they are reading on the copy of *Transparency* 3.

TEACHER TIP

Have students listen to the selection recording on the *Listening Library Audiocassette/CD* for a proficient, fluent model of oral reading.

WRITING

Remind students that Pat is helping Mike's mom by going to the store for her. Have students write a short grocery list that Mike's mom might have given to Pat. Have students share their lists with the class.

SELECTION C • **Helping Others**

Assessment

Formal

At the conclusion of the lesson, have students complete the assessment Unit 2: Helping Others. The Lesson Assessments are found in the *Assessment Guide.*

For all the items in this assessment, you should read both the question and answer choices out loud while students follow along silently. If you notice any students having trouble with a question, ask them to repeat the question to be sure they understand it. If they do not understand the question, clarify it for them.

In the Unit Assessment, students will answer reading and language arts questions about a new selection, "A Place for Cats." Even though this assessment won't take place for several weeks, we recommend reading the story out loud several times in advance while students follow along silently. If you start this process now, students should be familiar with the story by the end of the unit.

Informal

Choose words from the selection that you believe students know. Read the words out loud and have students repeat the initial or final consonant sounds. Have volunteers write the words on the board as you spell them and then point out the letters that make the sounds.

Ending the Lesson

Have students compare the stories "The Lion and the Mouse" and "Helping Others." Ask them to consider the characters, the setting, the kind of story, and so on.

OBJECTIVES

- Complete lesson assessment.
- Preview the unit assessment selection.
- Review initial and final consonant sounds.
- Compare two selections.

MATERIALS

Assessment Guide
Student Reader, pp. 30–31

SELECTION D • **Tyler's Bad Day**

Support Materials

LESSON 16

- Sound/Spelling Card 33
- Decodable Stories and Comprehension Skills, p. 19
- Home Connection, p. 23
- High-Frequency Word Cards

HOME CONNECTIONS

Distribute *Home Connection* page 23, which describes this week's classwork and suggests activities for families to do at home. This letter is available in English and Spanish.

LESSON 17

- Student Reader, pp. 32–35
- Language Arts, p. T20

LESSON 18

- Sound/Spelling Card 37
- Decodable Stories and Comprehension Skills, p. 20
- High-Frequency Word Cards

LESSON 19

- Student Reader, pp. 32–35
- Transparencies 3, 19, 20
- Decodable Stories and Comprehension Skills, p. 84
- Listening Library Audiocassette/CD
- Language Arts, p. T19

LESSON 20

- Assessment Guide
- Student Reader, pp. 32–35

Teacher Focus	Student Participation
• Conduct Listening Game. • Conduct Word Play. • Introduce Sight Words and Set 1 blending words and sentences. • Conduct Oral Language activity. • Dictate word lines. • Assist students with decodable text. • Assign writing activity.	• Take part in Listening Game. • Take part in Word Play. • Read Sight Words. • Blend words and sentences. • Create sentences. • Write dictated words and sentences. • Read a decodable story. • Complete writing activity.
• Activate Prior Knowledge and provide background information. • Introduce and discuss selection vocabulary. • Preview selection. • Review Comprehension Strategies—Monitoring and Clarifying and Monitoring and Adjusting Reading Speed. • Read the selection to students. • Introduce vocabulary skill. • Assign writing activity.	• Contribute to class discussion. • Read and discuss vocabulary words. Complete selection vocabulary activity. • Browse the selection. • Follow along as selection is read. • Complete vocabulary skill activity. • Complete writing activity.
• Conduct Listening for Vowel Sounds game. • Conduct Word Play. • Introduce Set 2 blending words and sentences. • Conduct Oral Language activity. • Dictate word lines. • Assist students with decodable text. • Assign writing activity.	• Participate in Listening for Vowel Sounds game. • Take part in Word Play. • Blend words and sentences. • Identify antonyms. • Write dictated words and sentences. • Read a decodable story. • Complete writing activity.
• Introduce Comprehension Skill—Making Inferences. • Reread and discuss the selection with students. • Discuss Independent Reading. • Assign writing activity. • Introduce grammar skill.	• Follow along as selection is read again. • Discuss the selection. • Select a book to take home and read. • Complete writing activity. • Complete grammar skill activity.
• Administer weekly assessments. • Assess students' progress.	• Complete lesson assessment.

SELECTION D • **Tyler's Bad Day**

OBJECTIVES

- Identify and blend initial consonant sounds in words.
- Blend and break apart sounds in words.
- Read sight words.
- Participate in Word Play activity.
- Develop fluency by reading aloud.
- Apply decoding skills by reading **Unit 2, Decodable Story 7**.
- Develop writing skills by identifying and writing words.

MATERIALS

Sound/Spelling Card:
33—Long A
Decodable Stories and Comprehension Skills, p. 19
Home Connection, p. 23
High-Frequency Word Cards

Phonemic Awareness

The basic purpose of providing structured practice in phonemic awareness is to help students hear and understand the sounds from which words are made. Before students can be expected to understand the sound/symbol correspondence that forms the base of written English, they need to have a strong working knowledge of the sound relationships that make up the spoken language. This understanding of spoken language lays the foundation for the transition to written language. Phonemic awareness activities provide students with easy practice in discriminating the sounds that make up words. Once students begin reading and writing, this experience with manipulating sounds will help them use what they know about sounds and letters to sound out and spell unfamiliar words.

The two main formats for teaching phonemic awareness are oral blending and segmentation. These are supported by occasional discrimination activities and general word play. From these playful activities, students derive serious knowledge about language.

Oral Blending

In oral blending, students are led through a progression of activities designed to help them hear how sounds are put together to make words. The tone of the activities should be playful and informal and should move quickly. Although these activities will provide information about student progress, they are not diagnostic tools. Do not expect mastery.

Listening Game: Initial Consonant Sounds

In this lesson, students will replace initial consonant sounds in words to make nonsense words. The point of the activity is to increase students' awareness of initial consonant sounds. It builds on the initial consonant segmentation and blending activities and on the Alliterative Word Game.

To start this activity, you will say a common word, then have students rapidly change its initial consonant sound to make nonsense words. Write the word changes on the board to show students the words they are making. Tell students that you will show them how changing just one sound can make a new word. Use the following example:

Teacher:	[Write *dinosaur* on the board.] *This word is* dinosaur. *What's the word?*
Students:	*dinosaur*
Teacher:	*I'm going to change the word.* [Erase *d*.] *It now starts with /m/. What's the new word?*
Students:	*minosaur*
Teacher:	[Write *m*.] *That's right,* minosaur. *Now I'm going to change the word again.*

Continue erasing the initial letter and telling students what new sound you will put at the beginning of the word. Ask them to tell what the word will be before you write the letter in place. Use these words, replacing the initial consonant with a series of sounds such as /p/, /f/, /k/, /g/, /n/, /m/, and /sh/:

butterfly	television	ladybug
doorbell	rainbow	saddlebag

TEACHER TIP

Listening Game Note the suggestion that you write the new letter after you have said the sound and students have pronounced the new word. The focus of this lesson is on sounds.

SELECTION D • **Tyler's Bad Day**

Word Study

In this section of the lesson, students work on phonics, fluency, blending, and spelling. Increasing students' ability to work smoothly with printed words is one of the primary goals of the **Kaleidoscope** program.

Word Play

Provide each student with a newspaper page. Tell students to look for and circle words on their pages that contain any of the long-vowel sound/spellings they have learned. Call on individuals to read and spell the words they find.

Sight Words

This week's sight words:

| enough | what | where |

Use the following procedure for teaching sight words:
- Write this week's sight words on the board.
- Read the words to students, and then have them read the words.
- Pronounce any words with which students have difficulty.
- Have students use each sight word in a sentence.

Phonics—Blending: Set 1

:::
/ā/ spelled *a, ai_ , _ay, eigh*
:::

This section of the phonics lesson provides practice in building sounds and spellings into words.

Point out and discuss the **Sound/Spelling Card.** Ask students what they know about this card. Remind students that they have learned the *a_e* spelling. Tell them that today they will focus on the remaining spellings for /ā/. Explain that the *_ay* spelling only comes at the end of words or syllables. Write the *eigh* spelling on the board. Explain that although this spelling is not on the card, it sometimes represents /ā/.

TEACHER TIP

Sight Words Use the *High-Frequency Word Cards* to assess and review students' knowledge of sight words.

You will need the following *Sound/Spelling Card* for blending the words in Set 1. 33—Long A

Blending Exercise

● The words in the lines provide practice with the Set 1 sound/spellings. Write the following words and sentences on the board.

● Have students blend the words and sentences using the whole-word procedure described in Unit 1 on page 12F.

Line 1:	paper	able	agent	stranger
Line 2:	aid	rain	chain	wait
Line 3:	way	day	stay	tray
Line 4:	weigh	weight	eight	sleigh
Sentence 1:	What train will the players take?			
Sentence 2:	Where did Kay make the paper planes?			
Sentence 3:	Did Jane pay enough for the layer cakes?			

About the Words and Sentences

● Have students identify the spelling for /ā/ in each line.

● Have students find words on the lines that are homophones *(way, weigh; wait, weight)*. Have them use the words in sentences to show their different meanings.

● Before reading a sentence, point to and read the underlined sight words. Have students reread the sentences to encourage fluency and comprehension.

● Have students identify the plural nouns in each sentence. *(players, planes, cakes)*

Oral Language

Have students take turns coming to the board, touching a word, and using it in a sentence. Encourage them to extend their sentences by asking *When? Where? How?* and *Why?* questions.

WRITING

Give clues for the words on the lines and have students write the word that the clue identifies. Some possible clues are:
You can write on this. *(paper)*
It's a number. *(eight)*
It's someone you don't know. *(stranger)*

SELECTION D • Tyler's Bad Day

Dictation

Dictation gives students an opportunity to spell words by using the sound/spellings that they have learned. For this dictation exercise, have students use writing paper. Dictate the words and sentence for them to write. Use the following procedure:

● Say the first word in the Dictation word lines. Use the word in a sentence, then say the word again. Have students say the word.

● Tell students to think about how to segment the word into sounds. Then have them write the spelling for each sound. Encourage them to check the **Sound/Spelling Cards.**

● After each word line, write (or have a student write) the words on the board. Have students proofread their words. Tell them to circle any incorrect words and to correct them.

● Next, dictate the sentence. Dictate one word at a time, following the sounds-in-sequence or whole-word dictation procedure, depending on your students. Remind students to start the sentence with a capital letter and to use correct end punctuation.

● Write (or have a student write) the sentence on the board. Have students proofread their work and correct any incorrect words.

Line 1:	layer	maid	freight
Line 2:	paid	player	trail
Sentence:	What made the mail late yesterday?		

Building Fluency

Decodable Story: Unit 2, Story 7

- This story reviews the sound/spellings /ā/ spelled *a*, *ai_*, *_ay*, *eigh*.
- Have students silently read ***Decodable Stories and Comprehension Skills*** page 19.
- Call on volunteers to read each paragraph aloud.
- For those students who need help, divide sentences according to natural phrases. Mark these phrases with diagonal slash marks on their worksheets.
- After students have read the story aloud, ask them questions and have them point to and read the answers in the story.
- Have students reread the story aloud with a partner. Rereading builds automaticity and fluency.
- Over the next few days, listen to each student reread the story.

Building Fluency Model fluent reading frequently for students, showing them how pausing in the right places and adding expressions can make a passage easier to understand.

QUICK CHECK

As a quick review of today's sound/spellings, say some sentences and ask students to suggest words to fill the blanks. Sentences you might read aloud include:

I hope it doesn't _____ today! *(rain)*
May I have a sheet of _____? *(paper)*
My bicycle _____ is broken. *(chain)*

SELECTION D • **Tyler's Bad Day**

Before Reading

Build Background

Activate Prior Knowledge

● Remind students that this unit is about kindness. Review what they have learned so far about kindness from each selection they have read.

● Ask students what people mean when they say, "I've had a bad day."

Background Information

Use the following information to help students understand the selection you are about to read:

● Have students talk about bicycles. What are some things that can go wrong with a bicycle? *(flat tires, broken chain)*

● Ask students if they have ever broken or lost something that they borrowed from a family member or friend. What did they do?

● Have them talk about unexpected kind things that people have done for them.

Selection Vocabulary

Write the following vocabulary words on the board. Before browsing the selection, introduce and discuss these words and their meanings.

roaming: wandering

disbelief: refusal to believe

echoed: repeated

reattached: connected again

Then have students read the words, stopping to blend any words that they have trouble reading. Demonstrate how to decode multisyllabic words by breaking the words into syllables and blending the syllables. Then have students try. If they still have trouble, refer them to the **Sound/Spelling Cards.** If the word is not decodable, give students the pronunciation.

As students study vocabulary, they will use a variety of skills to determine the meaning of a word. These skills include context clues, word structure, and apposition. In this unit, students will be learning about apposition. Write the following example on the board: *The students echoed, or repeated, the words of their teachers.* Explain to students that they are going to use apposition to help them decipher the meaning of the word *echoed.* Tell students that when they use apposition, they are looking for a word or group of words in the sentence that help define the word in question. Guide students until they can give a reasonable definition of the word.

Vocabulary Activity: Have students choose one of the vocabulary words and write a sentence using the word. Remind students to begin their sentence with a capital letter and to use correct end punctuation. Ask students to share their sentences with the class.

Preview and Prepare

Before you read, use modeling and prompts such as:

● *This is a story, so we'll only browse the title and the first page.*

● *What does the title tell you? Who are the characters in the story? Let's read the whole story to find out what happens to them.*

During Reading

Read Aloud

For this lesson, read the entire selection aloud. As you read, stop at the points that are marked with numbers in magenta circles on the reduced student pages, and model for them how to use the indicated strategy. Encourage students to stop at any point in their reading if they don't understand something or want to talk about the meaning of a passage or word.

Comprehension Strategies

During the reading of "Tyler's Bad Day" on pages 32–35, you will model the following reading comprehension strategies:

Monitoring and Clarifying: Good readers pay attention to how well they understand what they are reading. They stop to clarify the meanings of new words and to think about unfamiliar or difficult passages.

Monitoring and Adjusting Reading Speed: If they notice that they are having trouble understanding what they read, good readers slow down. They also may reread passages.

TEACHER
TIP

Comprehension Strategies It is important for you to let students know that, as you read, you also use the comprehension strategies that you are teaching them. Let them see you using these strategies often.

First Read

Text Comprehension *Strategies*

As you read the selection, use modeling and prompts such as:

❶ Monitoring and Clarifying

Something's confusing me. There are three characters in the story so far: Tyler, his brother, and Mr. Chang. This last sentence I read says that Tyler waved to him. I can't figure out who Tyler is waving to. Is he waving to his brother or Mr. Chang? I'll go back and reread to see if I can figure it out. Yes, I see now that Tyler is waving to Mr. Chang, who is in the window.

❷ Monitoring and Adjusting Reading Speed

When they don't understand what they're reading, good readers go back and reread part of a selection. Then they read slower until they do understand what's happening. A lot is happening in the story, and I don't understand all of it. I'll reread, but slower this time. OK, Tyler has borrowed his big brother's bike to ride to school. His big brother is worried that Tyler will break it. Mr. Chang is a neighbor. I can read on now.

❸ Monitoring and Clarifying

There is a lot of information in this paragraph. I need to reread it to make sure I understand everything that's happened. I'll put things in order: first, Tyler locked the bike to a tree when he got to school—he was being very careful with it, wasn't he? Then he starts home, but something makes him stop. What? Oh, I see, the bike's chain is broken. Next, he banged his elbow. So that's why the story is called "Tyler's Bad Day"—so many bad things are happening to him.

Tyler's Bad Day

by Sheri Cooper Sinykin
illustrated by Susan Spellman

"Thank you," Tyler said to his big brother. "I will take good care of your bike."

He saw Mr. Chang in the window. Tyler waved to him as he got on his
❶ brother's bike.

"Stay on the road and don't go <u>roaming</u> off after school," said his brother. "And whatever you do, don't
❷ break my bike!"

32

VOCABULARY

Remind students that a *homophone* is a word that sounds the same as another word but has a different spelling and meaning. For a review lesson on homophones, use **Language Arts** page T20.

Tyler was careful on the way to school. He locked the bike to a tree. When Tyler was returning home, a noise made him look down by his toe. A look of <u>disbelief</u> crossed his face. The bike's chain was broken! This was not good. His brother's words <u>echoed</u> in his head—"Don't break my bike!" Tyler banged his elbow jumping off the bike. This was not a good day. He would be in a world of trouble when his brother saw the bike. ❸

33

Text Comprehension

Making Inferences

Tell students that authors do not always tell readers everything that they need to know to understand a story. Explain that good readers learn to use what they already know along with information from what they're reading to figure things out—or make inferences—on their own.

● For these pages ask students the following questions:

What happened just before the story begins? (Tyler's brother let him borrow his bike to ride to school.)

What information in the story lets you figure out what happened? (Tyler says "Thank you" and promises to take good care of the bike.)

Who is Mr. Chang? (a neighbor)

How do you know? (He is looking out of the window.)

What happened to the bike? Was Tyler responsible for what happened? (The chain came off. Tyler didn't do anything to cause it to happen.)

GRAMMAR

Remind students that plural nouns name more than one person, place, thing, or idea. Tell students that some plural nouns are *irregular* and do not follow the rules about adding *-s* or *-es*. These plural words have to be learned and remembered. For a lesson on irregular plural nouns, use **Language Arts** page T19.

First Read

Text Comprehension Strategies

④ Monitoring and Adjusting Reading Speed

I got so caught up reading about Tyler's problems, I think I missed some important information on this page. I'll reread it more slowly to make sure I understand what else is happening to make Tyler's day so bad.

⑤ Monitoring and Clarifying

When you don't understand what a word, a group of words, or a sentence means, you should stop to clarify it or figure it out. What words do you need to clarify?

Student Sample

I don't really know what the word reattached *means. Maybe if I look at the different parts of the word, I can figure out the meaning. I know the prefix* re- *means "again" and the word* attach *means "to connect." So,* reattached *must mean "connected again." Now I understand. Mr. Chang put the chain back on the bike.*

Tyler walked the bike home. Mr. Chang was at the window when Tyler walked by. Tyler raced into the house. He got some of his father's tools to fix the bike. How could he replace the chain?

The bike was gone! Where could it be? Maybe Mr. Chang saw what happened to the bike. He rang Mr. Chang's bell. Mr. ④ Chang did not come. Where was he?

34

HOMEWORK TIP

Remind students that they should spend at least 20 minutes each day reading outside of school.

TEACHER TIP

Student Sample The student sample is only one example of many possible student responses. Accept other responses that are reasonable and appropriate.

A noise came from the garage. Tyler opened the door. There was Mr. Chang. There was the bike! Mr. Chang had <u>reattached</u> the chain.

"There you go," said Mr. Chang. "It's as good as new." He smiled and gave Tyler the bike. "Have you had a bad day?"

"Yes," Tyler said. "But it just got better. Thank you, Mr. Chang!"

⑤

35

WRITING

Ask students to think about Mr. Chang. Have them write a short answer to the following question: *How was Mr. Chang kind to Tyler?*

Text Comprehension

Making Inferences

- For these pages, ask students to use their own knowledge to explain the following:

  What happens on these pages that the author does not tell us about directly? (Mr. Chang is fixing the bike.)

- Use **Transparency** 19 to record their responses.
- For additional practice with Making Inferences, have students complete **Decodable Stories and Comprehension Skills** page 84.

Discussing the Selection

After you have read the story, discuss it with students. Use prompts such as:

- *What does the title of the story mean? In what ways was Tyler's day bad?*
- *What made the day better for Tyler?*
- *How does this selection relate to the unit theme, Kindness?*
- *How does this selection add to what you already know about kindness?*

 QUICK CHECK

Ask students to compare and contrast Mr. Chang with other characters they've read about so far.

SELECTION D • **Tyler's Bad Day**

Phonemic Awareness

Listening for Vowel Sounds

Listening for /ī/ and /o͞o/

● Tell students that once again they will respond to each word that you say by repeating its vowel sound after you read the word. Tell them that the vowel sounds they are listening for are /ī/ and /o͞o/. Start by repeating the vowel sounds yourself: /ī/, /o͞o/.

● Use the following words:

truth	June	hide
item	truce	rule
rude	plume	diet
tile	prune	juice
crime	wipe	stripe
like	clue	trial
true	tune	chime

OBJECTIVES

- Identify long-vowel sounds in words.
- Blend and break apart sounds in words.
- Participate in Word Play activity.
- Develop fluency by reading aloud.
- Apply decoding skills by reading **Unit 2, Decodable Story 8.**
- Develop writing skills by writing number words.

MATERIALS

Sound/Spelling Card:
37—Long E
Decodable Stories and
  Comprehension Skills, p. 20
High-Frequency Word Cards

Listening for Vowel Sounds The purpose of this activity is not to teach specific letter-sound correspondences. Rather, the goal is to increase students' sensitivity to the sounds of vowels in words. Developing vowel awareness is important preparation for reading and writing.

Word Study

Word Play

Play the Go Fish game once again. On the backs of several "fish" write the spellings for /ā/. (Use each spelling more than once.) One by one, give students the fishing pole and tell them to "go fish." When a student catches a fish, have her or him read the spelling, say the sound, and then say a word that contains the sound/spelling.

Phonics—Blending: Set 2

> /ē/ spelled *e, ea, ee, _ie_, _y*

Point out and discuss the **Sound/Spelling Card.** Ask students what they know about it. Remind students that they have learned one spelling for this sound, *e_e*.

Blending Exercise

You will need the following **Sound/Spelling Card** for blending the words in Set 2. 37—Long E

- Write the following words and sentences on the board.

- Have students blend the words and sentences using the whole-word procedure described in Unit 1 on page 12F.

Line 1:	three	tree	see	fifteen	she
Line 2:	be	me	scream	easy	creamy
Line 3:	thief	chief	bunnies	puppies	happy
Line 4:	read	reed	seem	seam	
Sentence 1:	Did Pete clean <u>enough</u> of the leaves from the street?				
Sentence 2:	<u>What</u> do Gene and Mandy believe Jean did?				
Sentence 3:	<u>Where</u> did she leave her peanut butter sandwich?				

- Before reading a sentence, point to and read the underlined sight words.

- Discuss with students that each sentence begins with a capital letter and ends with a punctuation mark.

- Have students reread the sentences to encourage fluency and comprehension.

Unit 2 • LESSON

18

SELECTION D • **Tyler's Bad Day**

About the Words and Sentences

- Have students identify the spelling for /ē/ in each word.
- For Line 4, have students notice that the words on the line are pairs of homophones. Have them use the words in sentences to show their different meanings.
- Have students find words on the lines that are number names. *(three, fifteen)*
- For the sentences, have students identify the proper nouns. *(Pete, Gene, Mandy, Jean)*

Oral Language

Have students find, read, and erase words that are antonyms for these words: *hard (easy), lumpy (creamy), whisper (scream).*

Dictation

For the dictation exercise, have students use writing paper. Dictate the words and sentence for them to write.

Use the following procedure:

- Say the first word in each word line. Use the word in a sentence, and then say the word again. Have students say the word.
- Tell students to think about how to segment the word into sounds. Then have them write the spelling for each sound.
- After each word line, write (or have a student write) the words on the board. Have students proofread their words. Tell them to circle any incorrect words and to correct them.
- Next dictate the sentence. Dictate one word at a time, following the sounds-in-sequence or whole-word dictation procedure, depending on your students. Remind students to start the sentence with a capital letter and to use correct end punctuation.
- Write (or have a student write) the sentence on the board. Have students proofread their work and correct any incorrect words.

WRITING

Remind students of the number words on the word lines *(three, fifteen)*. Have students write three more number words.

Line 1:	we	knee	clean
Line 2:	street	bead	baby
Sentence:	The breeze made the tree sway.		

35C   Lesson 18 • UNIT 2

Building Fluency

Decodable Story: Unit 2, Story 8

● This story reviews the sound/spellings /ē/ spelled *e, ea, ee, _ie_, _y*.

● Have students silently read ***Decodable Stories and Comprehension Skills*** page 20.

● Call on volunteers to read each paragraph aloud.

● For those students who need help, divide sentences according to natural phrases. Mark these phrases with diagonal slash marks on their worksheets.

● After students have read the story aloud, ask them questions and have them point to and read the answers in the story.

● Have students reread the story aloud with a partner.

HOMEWORK TIP

Tell students to look through the books, magazines, and newspapers they read at home for words that contain spellings for /ē/. Have them make lists of the words and share the lists with the class.

SELECTION D • **Tyler's Bad Day**

OBJECTIVES

- Develop reading skills as the story is reread to them.
- Gain knowledge of the comprehension skill Making Inferences.
- Develop vocabulary by listening to and discussing a selection.
- Develop writing skills by identifying and writing characters' names.
- Identify irregular plural nouns.

MATERIALS

Transparencies 3, 19, 20
Decodable Stories and Comprehension Skills, p. 84
Student Reader, pp. 32–35
Listening Library Audiocassette/CD
Language Arts, p. T19

Rereading the Selection

Comprehension Skills

Revisiting or rereading a selection allows students to learn and apply skills that give them a more complete understanding of a selection. For today's lesson, reread the selection to students. During the second reading, students will apply the following comprehension skill:

Making Inferences: Authors do not always tell readers everything. Good readers use what they already know along with what they read to figure out things that aren't made clear in a selection.

After Reading

Independent Reading

- Have students choose books from the **Classroom Library** or other available books to take home and read. Encourage students to read at least one book each week on their own.
- Find time to sit with students and talk with them about the independent reading they are doing.
- Encourage students to use the comprehension strategies and skills they are learning as they read independently.
- Encourage students to record the titles of the books they are reading on the copy of **Transparency** 3.

TEACHER TIP

Have students listen to the selection recording on the *Listening Library Audiocassette/CD* for a proficient, fluent model of oral reading.

WRITING

Discuss with students the characters in the selection (*Tyler, Tyler's brother, Mr. Chang*). Give descriptions of the characters and have students write the name of the character you are describing.

SELECTION D • **Tyler's Bad Day**

Assessment

Formal

At the conclusion of the lesson, have students complete the assessment Unit 2: Tyler's Bad Day. The Lesson Assessments are found in the *Assessment Guide.*

For all the items in this assessment, you should read both the question and answer choices out loud while students follow along silently. For the extended response items, have students explain their answers before they write them. Keep in mind that their oral answers will probably be more extensive than their written answers.

By now, students should be familiar with the Unit Assessment selection "A Place for Cats." Read Question 1 to students. Have volunteers explain their answer to the question. If they don't get it right, guide them to the correct answer. After the discussion, have students write their answers. They will share their completed answers with other students during the Unit Assessment.

Informal

Have a volunteer explain what a homophone is. If the volunteer or others can't recall what a homophone is, explain the meaning to them. Write the following homophone pairs on the board: *meet/meat, new/knew, rode/road.* Help students explain the meaning of each word and then have them create sentences for the words. Be sure they understand that the words are spelled differently, are pronounced the same, and have different meanings.

Ending the Lesson

Have a volunteer summarize "Tyler's Bad Day." Allow other students to add details they recall. Ask students if they have ever had bad days that turned out good, as Tyler's did.

OBJECTIVES

- Complete lesson assessments.
- Plan an extended response.
- Review homophones.
- Share a personal experience.

MATERIALS

Assessment Guide
Student Reader pp. 32–35

SELECTION E • **Marta Helps at Home**

Support Materials

LESSON 21
- Sound/Spelling Card 34
- Decodable Stories and Comprehension Skills, p. 21
- Home Connection, p. 25
- High-Frequency Word Cards

LESSON 22
- Student Reader, pp. 36–37
- Language Arts, p. T22

LESSON 23
- Sound/Spelling Card 35
- Decodable Stories and Comprehension Skills, p. 22
- High-Frequency Word Cards

LESSON 24
- Student Reader, pp. 36–37
- Transparencies 3, 21, 22
- Decodable Stories and Comprehension Skills, p. 85
- Listening Library Audiocassette/CD
- Language Arts, p. T21

LESSON 25
- Assessment Guide
- Student Reader, pp. 36–37

HOME CONNECTIONS

Distribute *Home Connection* page 25, which describes this week's classwork and suggests activities for families to do at home. This letter is available in English and Spanish.

Teacher Focus	Student Participation
• Conduct Listening Game. • Conduct Word Play. • Introduce Sight Words and Set 1 blending words and sentences. • Conduct Oral Language Activity. • Dictate word lines. • Assist students with decodable text. • Assign writing activity.	• Take part in Listening Game. • Take part in Word Play. • Read Sight Words. • Blend words and sentences. • Identify synonyms. • Write dictated words and sentences. • Read a decodable story. • Complete writing activity.
• Activate Prior Knowledge and provide background information. • Introduce and discuss selection vocabulary. • Preview selection. • Review Comprehension Strategies—Predicting and Monitoring and Clarifying. • Read the selection to students. • Introduce vocabulary skill. • Assign writing activity.	• Contribute to class discussion. • Read and discuss vocabulary words. Complete selection vocabulary activity. • Browse the selection. • Follow along as selection is read. • Complete vocabulary skill activity. • Complete writing activity.
• Conduct Initial Consonant Sounds game. • Conduct Word Play. • Introduce Set 2 blending words and sentences. • Conduct Oral Language activity. • Dictate word lines. • Assist students with decodable text. • Assign writing activity.	• Participate in Initial Consonant Sounds game. • Take part in Word Play. • Blend words and sentences. • Create sentences. • Write dictated words and sentences. • Read a decodable story. • Complete writing activity.
• Review Comprehension Skill—Cause and Effect. • Reread and discuss the selection with students. • Discuss Independent Reading. • Assign writing activity. • Introduce grammar skill.	• Follow along as selection is read again. • Discuss the selection. • Select a book to take home and read. • Complete writing activity. • Complete grammar skill activity.
• Administer weekly assessments. • Assess students' progress.	• Complete lesson assessment.

SELECTION E • **Marta Helps at Home**

Phonemic Awareness

The basic purpose of providing structured practice in phonemic awareness is to help students hear and understand the sounds from which words are made. Before students can be expected to understand the sound/symbol correspondence that forms the base of written English, they need to have a strong working knowledge of the sound relationships that make up the spoken language. This understanding of spoken language lays the foundation for the transition to written language. Phonemic awareness activities provide students with easy practice in discriminating the sounds that make up words. Once students begin reading and writing, this experience with manipulating sounds will help them use what they know about sounds and letters to sound out and spell unfamiliar words.

The two main formats for teaching phonemic awareness are oral blending and segmentation. These are supported by occasional discrimination activities and general word play. From these playful activities, students derive serious knowledge about language.

Oral Blending

In oral blending, students are led through a progression of activities designed to help them hear how sounds are put together to make words. The tone of the activities should be playful and informal and should move quickly. Although these activities will provide information about student progress, they are not diagnostic tools. Do not expect mastery.

OBJECTIVES

- Identify and blend initial consonant sounds in words.
- Blend and break apart sounds in words.
- Read sight words.
- Participate in Word Play activity.
- Develop fluency by reading aloud.
- Apply decoding skills by reading **Unit 2, Decodable Story 9.**
- Develop writing skills by writing rhyming words.

MATERIALS

Sound/Spelling Card:
34—Long I
Decodable Stories and Comprehension Skills, p. 21
Home Connection, p. 25
High-Frequency Word Cards

Listening Game: Initial Consonant Sounds

Have students continue to replace the initial consonant sounds in words to make nonsense words. The point of the activity is to make students conscious of the **sounds** of words and to give them some skill in manipulating the sounds—not in identifying word meanings.

Say a common word, then have students rapidly change its initial consonant sound to make nonsense words. Write the word changes on the board to show students the words they are making. Use the following example.

Teacher:	*[Write hamburger on the board.] This word is hamburger. What's the word?*
Students:	*hamburger*
Teacher:	*I'm going to change the word. [Erase h.] It now starts with /s/. What's the new word?*
Students:	*samburger*

Continue erasing the first letter and substituting other consonants, pronouncing each sound and then writing the letters. Ask students to say each new word. Words that can be used for this activity include:

rabbit	**visitor**	**cinnamon**
railroad	**building**	**sailboat**

TEACHER TIP

Responses To keep students' attention, switch unpredictably from group to individual responses.

SELECTION E • **Marta Helps at Home**

Word Study

In this section of the lesson, students work on phonics, fluency, blending, and spelling. Increasing students' ability to work smoothly with printed words is one of the primary goals of the **Kaleidoscope** program.

Word Play

Provide each student with a newspaper page. Tell students to look for and circle words on the page that contain any of the spellings for /ē/ that they have learned. Call on individuals to read and spell the words they find.

Sight Words

This week's sight words:

> **buy**   **have**   **great**

Use the following procedure for teaching sight words:

- Write this week's sight words on the board.
- Read the words to students, and then have them read the words.
- Pronounce any words with which students have difficulty.
- Have students use each sight word in a sentence.

Phonics—Blending: Set 1

> /ī/ spelled *i, _ie, _igh, _y*

This section of the phonics lesson provides practice in building sounds and spellings into words.

- Point out the new **Sound/Spelling Card.** Ask students what they know about it. Focus attention on the three spellings that follow blanks. Explain that a letter must come before these sound/spellings.

HOMEWORK TIP

Sight Words Use the **High-Frequency Word Cards** to assess and review students' knowledge of sight words.

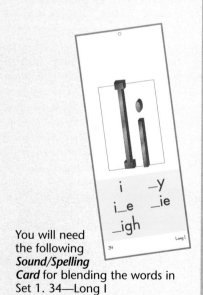

You will need the following **Sound/Spelling Card** for blending the words in Set 1. 34—Long I

Blending Exercise

- The words in the lines provide practice with the Set 1 sound/spellings. Write the following words and sentences on the board.

- Have students blend the words and sentences using the whole-word procedure described in Unit 1 on page 12F.

Line 1:	fried	tie	lie	blind	kind
Line 2:	I	timer	try	my	skyline
Line 3:	sigh	sight	light	tight	bright
Line 4:	night	knight	write	right	
Sentence 1:	The night sky was great!				
Sentence 2:	Jamie wants to buy a white tie.				
Sentence 3:	Iris and I will have a slice of lime pie.				

About the Words and Sentences

- Have students identify the spelling for /ī/ in each word.
- For Line 1, have students find words that have multiple meanings. *(tie, lie, blind, kind)*
- For Line 4, ask students to notice that the words are sets of homophones. Ask them to tell the meaning of each word.
- Before reading a sentence, point to and read the underlined sight words. Have students reread the sentences to build fluency and comprehension.
- For Sentence 3, have students identify the various spellings for /ī/.

Oral Language

Have students find, read, and erase words that are synonyms for these words: *nice (kind), weightless (light), evening (night), attempt (try).*

WRITING

Have students identify and write the two pairs of rhyming words on Line 1 *(tie, lie; blind, kind)*. As a class, discuss other words that rhyme with these words.

SELECTION E • **Marta Helps at Home**

Dictation

Dictation gives students an opportunity to spell words by using the sound/spellings that they have learned. For this dictation exercise, have students use writing paper. Dictate the words and sentence for them to write. Use the following procedure:

- Say the first word in each word line. Use the word in a sentence, then say the word again. Have students say the word.
- Tell students to think about how to segment the word into sounds. Then have them write the spelling for each sound. Encourage them to check the **Sound/Spelling Cards.**
- After each word line, write (or have a student write) the words on the board. Have students proofread their words. Tell them to circle any incorrect words and to correct them.
- Next, dictate the sentence. Dictate one word at a time, following the sounds-in-sequence or whole-word dictation procedure, depending on your students. Remind students to start the sentence with a capital letter and to use correct end punctuation.
- Write (or have a student write) the sentence on the board. Have students proofread their work and correct any incorrect words.

Line 1:	tiger by sight
Line 2:	myself tie might
Sentence:	Did the spider frighten Ida?

Building Fluency

Decodable Story: Unit 2, Story 9

- This story reviews the sound/spellings /ī/ spelled *i, _ie, _igh, _y.*
- Have students silently read **Decodable Stories and Comprehension Skills** page 21.
- Call on volunteers to read each paragraph aloud.
- For those students who need help, divide sentences according to natural phrases. Mark these phrases with diagonal slash marks on their worksheets.
- After students have read the story aloud, ask them questions and have them point to and read the answers in the story.
- Have students reread the story aloud with a partner. Rereading builds automaticity and fluency.
- Over the next few days, listen to each student reread the story.

TEACHER TIP

Phonics Skills As students read aloud, notice how they use the phonics skills they have learned. Remind them that the purpose of learning these skills is to help them decode unfamiliar words.

✓ QUICK CHECK

As a quick review of today's sound/spellings, say some sentences, and ask students to suggest words to fill the blanks. Sentences you might read aloud include:

I bought my Dad a colorful _____ for his birthday. *(tie)*
Please turn off the _____ when you leave the room. *(light)*
What type of stories do you like to _____? *(write)*

22

SELECTION E • **Marta Helps at Home**

Before Reading

Build Background

Activate Prior Knowledge

Remind students that this unit is about kindness. Review what they have learned so far about kindness from each selection they have read.

Background Information

Use the following information to help students understand the selection you are about to read:

- Ask students to talk about the things that they do to help their families around the house.
- Ask them if they volunteer to do things or if they have to be asked to do them.

Selection Vocabulary

Write the following vocabulary words on the board. Before browsing the selection, introduce and discuss these words and their meanings.

unusual: not common

future: the time that is to come

argue: to have a discussion and disagree

Then have students read the words, stopping to blend any words that they have trouble reading. Demonstrate how to decode multisyllabic words by breaking the words into syllables and blending the syllables. Then have students try. If they still have trouble, refer them to the *Sound/Spelling Cards.* If the word is not decodable, give students the pronunciation.

As students study vocabulary, they will use a variety of skills to determine the meaning of a word. These skills include context clues, word structure, and apposition. In this unit, students will be learning about apposition. Write the following example on the board: *It is unusual, or uncommon, for Susan to be late.* Explain to students that they are going to use apposition to help them decipher the meaning of the word *unusual.* Tell students that when they use apposition, they are looking for a word or group of words in the sentence that help define the word in question. Guide students until they can give a reasonable definition of the word.

OBJECTIVES

- Discuss vocabulary words and their meanings.
- Develop reading skills as the story is read to them.
- Gain knowledge of the comprehension strategies Monitoring and Clarifying and Predicting.
- Build vocabulary by expanding their knowledge of multiple-meaning words.
- Develop writing skills by writing a question.

MATERIALS

Student Reader, pp. 36–37
Language Arts, p. T22

Vocabulary Activity: Write the three vocabulary words on the board. Have students suggest words that are antonyms for each of the vocabulary words (*for example, usual, common; past; agree*). Write their suggestions under the appropriate word on the board and discuss the words as a class.

Preview and Prepare

Before you read, use modeling and prompts such as:

● *This is a very short story, so we'll only browse the title and the first paragraph.*
● *What does the title tell you? Who do you think Marta is? How do you think she helps at home? Let's read the whole story to find out.*

During Reading

Read Aloud

For this lesson, read the entire selection aloud. As you read, stop at the points that are marked with numbers in magenta circles on the reduced student pages, and model for them how to use the indicated strategy. Encourage students to stop at any point in their reading if they don't understand something or want to talk about the meaning of a passage or word.

Comprehension Strategies

During the reading of "Marta Helps at Home" on pages 36–37, you will model the following reading comprehension strategies:

Predicting: Good readers know when to pause during reading to think about what is going on and to use their own knowledge and information from what they read to decide what will happen next. Good readers also return to their predictions to see whether the reading confirms them.

Monitoring and Clarifying: Good readers pay attention to how well they understand what they are reading. They stop to clarify the meanings of new words and to think about unfamiliar or difficult passages.

First Read

Text Comprehension *strategies*

As you read the selection, use modeling and prompts such as:

❶ Making Predictions

Making predictions about what's going to happen next in a story keeps readers interested in reading more and helps them to understand the story better. Do you have any predictions to make?

Student Sample

Marta wants to help out, so I predict that she will do a good job of washing the dishes.

❷ Monitoring and Clarifying

When I read this paragraph for the first time, I thought that Marta's dad was unhappy with her for taking so long to do the dishes. But I don't think that's right. I need to reread the paragraph to make sure that I understand what is happening. Now I see that Dad isn't unhappy with Marta, he's concerned that she had too much to do. That's why he says they'll try to use fewer dishes.

❸ Confirming Predictions

Remember to confirm predictions you've made as we read.

Student Sample

My prediction came true. Marta did a great job of washing the dishes. She even washed the pets' food dishes.

HOMEWORK TIP

Have students look through magazine or newspaper articles at home for examples of cause-and-effect relationships.

Marta Helps at Home

by Chris Murray
illustrated by Kate Flanagan

"This is great soup," said Marta. "It is <u>unusual</u>. I would like more, please. Who made it?"

Mom gave Dad a smile and said, "Well, we made it together."

Marta ate some more soup. After a while she said, "I know what. If I do the dishes, then everyone will have helped ❶ with dinner! We will be just like a team."

36

VOCABULARY

Remind students that some words are spelled the same but have different meanings. Tell them that the context of the story helps determine the meaning of these words. For a review lesson on multiple-meaning words, use *Language Arts* page T22.

After dinner Mom and Dad went to sit in the backyard. Marta started to wash the dishes. Later, when her dad came inside, she was hard at work. "Still not done?" he asked. "In the <u>future</u> we will try to use fewer dishes."

"I won't <u>argue</u> with that," Marta said. "I'm almost done, Dad." She picked the pets' dishes out of the water and set them in the window. As she let the water out, Marta said, "Now every dish in the house is clean!"

37

Second Read

Text Comprehension

Cause and Effect

Remind students that writers use cause-and-effect relationships in their writing to help readers understand what makes things happen the way they do.

- Ask them to identify the causes for these effects in the story:

  Marta agreed to do the dishes. *(Her parents made great soup for dinner.)*

  It took Marta a long time to wash the dishes. *(Her parents used a lot of dishes to make dinner.)*

- Use **Transparency** 21 to record their responses.
- For additional practice with Cause and Effect, have students complete **Decodable Stories and Comprehension Skills** page 85.

Discussing the Selection

After you have read the story, discuss it with students. Use prompts such as:

- *What did you like about this story?*
- *What did you learn from the story about kindness?*
- *How does this selection relate to the unit theme, Kindness?*
- *How did the reading strategies and skills that you've learned help you understand it?*

QUICK CHECK

Quickly review with students the other comprehension skills that they've used so far.

GRAMMAR

Tell students that *possessive nouns* show who or what owns or has something. Explain that to make most singular nouns possessive, add an *apostrophe (')* and *-s,* and to make most plural nouns possessive, just add an apostrophe *(').* For a lesson on possessive nouns, use **Language Arts** page T21.

23

SELECTION E • **Marta Helps at Home**

OBJECTIVES

- Identify and segment initial consonant sounds in words.
- Blend and break apart sounds in words.
- Participate in Word Play activity.
- Develop fluency by reading aloud.
- Apply decoding skills by reading *Unit 2, Decodable Story 10.*
- Develop writing skills by writing a caption.

MATERIALS

Sound/Spelling Card:
35—Long O
Decodable Stories and Comprehension Skills, p. 22
High-Frequency Word Cards

Phonemic Awareness

Segmentation: Initial Consonant Sounds

- Tell students they are going to play the Initial Consonant Sounds game again. Remind them that you will say a word and repeat the beginning consonant. Then you will ask them to repeat the word and to say what sounds were left off. Use this example:

Teacher:	hat . . . /h/
Teacher:	What's the word? What sounds were left off?
Students:	hat . . . /a/ /t/

- Continue the activity using the following words:

no	map	note
ride	row	fine
leap	hide	toad
sip	tap	rip
side	load	mine

TEACHER TIP

Segmentation Remember to move quickly through these activities. Do not hold the class back waiting on all students to catch on. Return to the same activity often. Frequent repetition is very beneficial and allows students additional opportunities to catch on.

Word Study

Word Play

Provide each student with a newspaper page. Tell students to look for and circle words on the page that contain any of the spellings for /ī/ that they have learned. Call on individuals to read and spell the words they find.

Phonics—Blending: Set 2

/ō/ spelled o, oa_, _oe, _ow

You will need the following *Sound/Spelling Card* for blending the words in Set 2. 35—Long O

- Point out and discuss the *Sound/Spelling Card.* Ask students what they know about it.

Blending Exercise

- Write the following words and sentences on the board.
- Have students blend the words and sentences using the whole-word procedure described in Unit 1 on page 12F.

Line 1:	so	go	woe	toe	hoe
Line 2:	low	slow	owner	snow	rowboat
Line 3:	float	goat	coat	load	oboe
Line 4:	grown	groan	toad	towed	
Sentence 1:	It will be <u>great</u> to <u>buy</u> the yellow sailboat!				
Sentence 2:	<u>Have</u> Joe and Joan driven on the coast roads?				

- Before reading a sentence, point to and read the underlined sight words.
- Discuss with students that each sentence begins with a capital letter and ends with a punctuation mark.
- Have students reread the sentences to encourage fluency and comprehension.

WRITING

Have students select a word from the word lines and create an illustration and a short caption using the word. Ask students to share their drawings and captions with the class.

SELECTION E • **Marta Helps at Home**

About the Words and Sentences

- Have students identify the spelling for /ō/ in each word.
- For Line 3, have students identify the rhyming words. *(float, goat, coat)*
- For Line 4, have students notice that the words on the lines are pairs of homophones. Have them use the words in sentences to show their different meanings.
- For the sentences, have students identify each kind of sentence. *(exclamation, question)*

Oral Language

Have students take turns choosing a word, reading it, using it in a sentence, and calling on a classmate to extend the sentence.

Dictation

For the dictation exercise, have students use writing paper. Dictate the words and sentence for them to write. Use the following procedure:

- Say the first word in each word line. Use the word in a sentence, then say the word again. Have students say the word.
- Tell students to think about how to segment the word into sounds. Then have them write the spelling for each sound.

- After each word line, write (or have a student write) the words on the board. Have students proofread their words. Tell them to circle any incorrect words and to correct them.
- Next dictate the sentence. Dictate one word at a time, following the sounds-in-sequence or whole-word dictation procedure, depending on your students. Remind students to start the sentence with a capital letter and to use correct end punctuation.
- Write (or have a student write) the sentence on the board. Have students proofread their work and correct any incorrect words.

Line 1:	blow	soap	over
Line 2:	post	throw	oboe
Sentence:	We got soaked at the boat show.		

TEACHER TIP

Multiple Spellings For sounds that have multiple spellings, remind students to ask *Which spelling?* when they are unsure which one to use in a given word. Remind them to use the *Sound/Spelling Cards* and to ask for help when they need it.

Building Fluency

Decodable Story: Unit 2, Story 10

- This story reviews the sound/spellings /ō/ spelled *o, oa_, _oe, _ow.*
- Have students silently read ***Decodable Stories and Comprehension Skills*** page 22.
- Call on volunteers to read each paragraph aloud.
- For those students who need help, divide sentences according to natural phrases. Mark these phrases with diagonal slash marks on their worksheets.
- After students have read the story aloud, ask them questions and have them point to and read the answers in the story.
- Have students reread the story aloud with a partner.

HOMEWORK TIP

To help students build fluency, have them take home the *Decodable Stories and Comprehension Skills* stories to read with their families.

Selection E • **Marta Helps at Home**

OBJECTIVES

- Develop reading skills as the story is reread to them.
- Gain knowledge of the comprehension skill Cause and Effect.
- Develop vocabulary by listening to and discussing a selection.
- Develop writing skills by writing a list.
- Identify possessive nouns.

MATERIALS

Transparencies 3, 21, 22
Decodable Stories and Comprehension Skills, p. 85
Student Reader, pp. 36–37
Listening Library Audiocassette/CD
Language Arts, p. T21

Rereading the Selection

Comprehension Skills

Revisiting or rereading a selection allows students to learn and apply skills that give them a more complete understanding of a selection. For today's lesson, reread the selection to students. During the second reading, students will apply the following comprehension skill:

Cause and Effect: Good readers look for relationships between events in what they read. This helps them to anticipate what will happen next.

After Reading

Independent Reading

- Have students choose books from the ***Classroom Library*** or other available books to take home and read. Encourage students to read at least one book each week on their own.
- Set aside time for students to talk in class about the independent reading that they are doing.
- Encourage students to use the comprehension strategies and skills they are learning as they read independently.
- Encourage students to record the titles of the books they are reading on the copy of ***Transparency*** 3.

TEACHER TIP

Have students listen to the selection recording on the *Listening Library Audiocassette/CD* for a proficient, fluent model of oral reading.

WRITING

Have students think about how Marta helped at home. Then have them write a list of three ways they can help at home. Encourage students to put their lists into practice by helping out at home.

SELECTION E • **Marta Helps at Home**

Assessment

Formal

At the conclusion of the lesson, have students complete the assessment Unit 2: Marta Helps at Home. The Lesson Assessments are found in the *Assessment Guide*.

For all the items in this assessment, you should read both the question and answer choices out loud while students follow along silently. Be sure students know they can ask you for help if they don't understand a question. You may also want to have them share their answers with you before they record them.

Have students refer to the Unit Assessment selection "A Place for Cats." Review the story briefly with students and then read Question 2 out loud. The answer to the question is obvious in the story, but you should encourage students to phrase the answer in their own words and to write complete sentences.

Informal

Review with students that some words have more than one meaning. Ask students to identify the different meanings of the following words from the story "Marta Helps at Home": *great (large, wonderful), still (yet, unmoving), set (place, group)*. Use the sentences from the story to help students understand one meaning of each word, then write another sentence on the board to demonstrate the other meanings.

Ending the Lesson

Point out how the family in the story shared in the chores. Have students discuss the various chores they do. You might want to share with them the way your family shares chores and how you and the students share chores in the classroom.

OBJECTIVES

- Complete lesson assessment.
- Rephrase details from a story.
- Review multiple-meaning words.
- Relate story events to their own life.

MATERIALS

Assessment Guide
Student Reader, pp. 36–37

SELECTION F • **Special Ears for Susan**

Support Materials

LESSON 26

- Sound/Spelling Card 36
- Decodable Stories and Comprehension Skills, p. 23
- Home Connection, p. 27
- High-Frequency Word Cards

HOME CONNECTIONS

Distribute **Home Connection** page 27, which describes this week's classwork and suggests activities for families to do at home. This letter is available in English and Spanish.

LESSON 27

- Student Reader, pp. 38–41
- Language Arts, p. T24

LESSON 28

- Sound/Spelling Cards
- Decodable Stories and Comprehension Skills, p. 24
- High-Frequency Word Cards

LESSON 29

- Student Reader, pp. 38–41, 42–43
- Transparencies 3, 23, 24
- Decodable Stories and Comprehension Skills, p. 86
- Listening Library Audiocassette/CD
- Language Arts, p. T23

LESSON 30

- Assessment Guide
- Student Reader, pp. 38–41

Teacher Focus	**Student Participation**
• Conduct Listening Game. • Conduct Word Play. • Introduce Sight Words and Set 1 blending words and sentences. • Conduct Oral Language activity. • Dictate word lines. • Assist students with decodable text. • Assign writing activity.	• Take part in Listening Game. • Take part in Word Play. • Read Sight Words. • Blend words and sentences. • Create sentences. • Write dictated words and sentences. • Read a decodable story. • Complete writing activity.
• Activate Prior Knowledge and provide background information. • Introduce and discuss selection vocabulary. • Preview selection. • Review Comprehension Strategies—Summarizing and Asking Questions. • Read the selection to students. • Introduce vocabulary skill. • Assign writing activity.	• Contribute to class discussion. • Read and discuss vocabulary words. Complete selection vocabulary activity. • Browse the selection. • Follow along as selection is read. • Complete vocabulary skill activity. • Complete writing activity.
• Conduct Initial Consonant Sounds game. • Conduct Word Play. • Introduce Set 2 blending words and sentences. • Conduct Oral Language activity. • Dictate word lines. • Assist students with decodable text. • Assign writing activity.	• Participate in Initial Consonant Sounds game. • Take part in Word Play. • Blend words and sentences. • Identify synonyms. • Write dictated words and sentences. • Read a decodable story. • Complete writing activity.
• Review Comprehension Skill—Drawing Conclusions. • Reread and discuss the selection with students. • Discuss Independent Reading. • Assign writing activity. • Introduce grammar skill. • Discuss Reading Reflections.	• Follow along as selection is read again. • Discuss the selection. • Select a book to take home and read. • Complete writing activity. • Complete grammar skill activity. • Discuss Reading Reflections.
• Administer weekly assessments. • Assess students' progress.	• Complete lesson and unit assessments.

SELECTION F • **Special Ears for Susan**

- Identify and blend initial consonant sounds in words.
- Blend and break apart sounds in words.
- Read sight words.
- Participate in Word Play activity.
- Develop fluency by reading aloud.
- Apply decoding skills by reading *Unit 2, Decodable Story 11.*
- Develop writing skills by writing words and identifying sound/spellings.

Sound/Spelling Card:
36—Long U
Decodable Stories and Comprehension Skills, p. 23
Home Connection, p. 27
High-Frequency Word Cards

Phonemic Awareness

The basic purpose of providing structured practice in phonemic awareness is to help students hear and understand the sounds from which words are made. Before students can be expected to understand the sound/symbol correspondence that forms the base of written English, they need to have a strong working knowledge of the sound relationships that make up the spoken language. This understanding of spoken language lays the foundation for the transition to written language. Phonemic awareness activities provide students with easy practice in discriminating the sounds that make up words. Once students begin reading and writing, this experience with manipulating sounds will help them use what they know about sounds and letters to sound out and spell unfamiliar words.

The two main formats for teaching phonemic awareness are oral blending and segmentation. These are supported by occasional discrimination activities and general word play. From these playful activities, students derive serious knowledge about language.

Oral Blending

In oral blending, students are led through a progression of activities designed to help them hear how sounds are put together to make words. The tone of the activities should be playful and informal and should move quickly. Although these activities will provide information about student progress, they are not diagnostic tools. Do not expect mastery.

Listening Game: Initial Consonant Sounds

Have students continue to replace the initial consonant sounds in words to make nonsense words. Remember, the idea of the activity is to focus attention on sounds in words and not their meanings.

Say a common word, then have students replace its initial consonant sound to make nonsense words.

> **Teacher:** [Write *melt* on the board.] *This word is* melt. *What's the word?*
>
> **Students:** *melt*
>
> **Teacher:** *I'm going to change the word.* [Erase *m*.] *It now starts with* /l/. *What's the new word?*
>
> **Students:** *lelt*
>
> Continue with these new sounds /t/, /g/, /j/, /k/.

TEACHER TIP

Listening Game Remember not to write the replacement consonant until after students have responded.

Unit 2 • LESSON

26

SELECTION F • **Special Ears for Susan**

Word Study

In this section of the lesson, students work on phonics, fluency, blending, and spelling. Increasing students' ability to work smoothly with printed words is one of the primary goals of the *Kaleidoscope* program.

Word Play

Provide each student with a newspaper page. Tell students to look for and circle words on the page that contain any of the spellings for /ō/ that they have learned. Call on individuals to read and spell the words they find.

Sight Words

This week's sight words:

> color   come   door

Use the following procedure for teaching sight words:

- Write this week's sight words on the board.
- Read the words to students, and then have them read the words.
- Pronounce any words with which students have difficulty.
- Have students use each sight word in a sentence.

Phonics—Blending: Set 1

> /ū/ spelled *u, _ue, _ew*

This section of the phonics lesson provides practice in building sounds and spellings into words.

- Point out and discuss the *Sound/Spelling Card.* Ask students what they know about it.

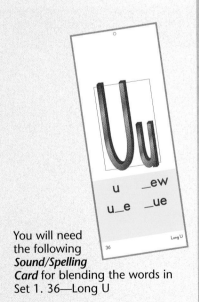

You will need the following *Sound/Spelling Card* for blending the words in Set 1. 36—Long U

Blending Exercise

- The words in the lines provide practice with the Set 1 sound/spellings. Write the following words and sentences on the board.

- Have students blend the words and sentences using the whole-word procedure described in Unit 1 on page 12F.

Line 1:	unit	few	amusing
Line 2:	cue	hue	hew
Line 3:	nephew	unity	rescue
Sentence 1:	Matthew opened the music teacher's <u>door</u>.		
Sentence 2:	We chose the <u>color</u> for my nephew's car.		
Sentence 3:	<u>Come</u> see the amusement park's unusual rides.		

About the Words and Sentences

- Have students identify the spelling for /ū/ in each word.
- For Line 2, have students find the words that are homophones. *(hue, hew)* Have them use dictionaries to find the meanings of the words, and then use the words in sentences to show their meanings.
- Have students identify the words that contain more than one syllable. *(unit, unity, amusing, nephew, rescue)*
- Before reading a sentence, point to and read the underlined sight words. Have students reread the sentences to encourage fluency and comprehension.
- For the sentences, have students identify the possessive nouns. *(teacher's, nephew's, park's)*

Oral Language

Have students take turns choosing a word from the lines, reading it, using it in a sentence, and calling on a classmate to extend the sentence.

WRITING

Tell students to write the words on Line 3. Have them circle the sound/spelling for /ū/ in each word.

SELECTION F • **Special Ears for Susan**

Dictation

Dictation gives students an opportunity to spell words by using the sound/spellings that they have learned. For this dictation exercise, have students use writing paper. Dictate the words and sentence for them to write. Use the following procedure:

● Say the first word in each word line. Use the word in a sentence, then say the word again. Have students say the word.

● Tell students to think about how to segment the word into sounds. Then have them write the spelling for each sound. Encourage them to check the ***Sound/Spelling Cards.***

● After each word line, write (or have a student write) the words on the board. Have students proofread their words. Tell them to circle any incorrect words and to correct them.

● Next, dictate the sentence. Dictate one word at a time, following the sounds-in-sequence or whole-word dictation procedure, depending on your students. Remind students to start the sentence with a capital letter and to use correct end punctuation.

● Write (or have a student write) the sentence on the board. Have students proofread their work and correct any incorrect words.

Line 1:	menu use music
Line 2:	cue unit few
Sentence:	My nephew rescued the cat.

Building Fluency

Decodable Story: Unit 2, Story 11

● This story reviews the sound/spellings /ū/ spelled *u, _ue, _ew.*

● Have students silently read *Decodable Stories and Comprehension Skills* page 23.

● Call on volunteers to read each paragraph aloud.

● For those students who need help, divide sentences according to natural phrases. Mark these phrases with diagonal slash marks on their worksheets.

● After students have read the story aloud, ask them questions and have them point to and read the answers in the story.

● Have students reread the story aloud with a partner. Rereading builds automaticity and fluency.

● Over the next few days, listen to each student reread the story.

Building Fluency To help students build fluency, have them share with the class books, stories, and magazines that they have brought from home and read previously with their families.

 QUICK CHECK

As a quick review of today's sound/spellings, say some sentences, and ask students to suggest words to fill the blanks. Sentences you might read aloud include the following:

I need to buy a _____ items from the store. *(few)*
The band members wore their new _____. *(uniforms)*
The firefighters _____ the kitten from the tree. *(rescued)*

SELECTION F • **Special Ears for Susan**

Before Reading

Build Background

Activate Prior Knowledge

● Remind students that this unit is about kindness. Review what they have learned so far about kindness from each selection they have read.

● Ask students if they know anyone who has a Seeing Eye dog. If anyone does, have them tell what kinds of things the dog does for its owner. If no one volunteers, ask if anyone has seen a Seeing Eye dog helping its owner.

Background Information

Use the following information to help students understand the selection you are about to read:

● Tell students that in addition to helping people with vision problems, dogs can also be trained to help people with hearing difficulties. Explain that these "hearing ear" dogs go through a long period of training before they are placed with a hearing impaired person.

● Also note that these dogs, as well as Seeing Eye dogs, are working dogs, and that they should never be distracted. Tell students always to ask the owner before approaching or petting such a dog.

Selection Vocabulary

Write the following vocabulary words on the board. Before browsing the selection, introduce and discuss these words and their meanings.

lucky: having good luck; fortunate

special: not ordinary

flash: an instant

Then have students read the words, stopping to blend any words that they have trouble reading. Demonstrate how to decode multisyllabic words by breaking the words into syllables and blending the syllables. Then have students try. If they still have trouble, refer them to the *Sound/Spelling Cards.* If the word is not decodable, give students the pronunciation.

As students study vocabulary, they will use a variety of skills to determine the meaning of a word. These skills include context clues, word structure, and apposition. In this unit, students will be learning about apposition. Write the following example on the board: *The fire engines were at the fire in a flash, or an instant.* Explain to students that they are going to use apposition to help them decipher the meaning of the word *flash.* Tell students that when they use apposition, they are looking for a word or group of words in the sentence that help define the word in question. Guide students until they can give a reasonable definition of the word.

OBJECTIVES

● Discuss vocabulary words and their meanings.
● Develop reading skills as the story is read to them.
● Gain knowledge of the comprehension strategies Asking Questions and Summarizing.
● Build vocabulary by expanding their knowledge of antonyms and synonyms.
● Develop writing skills by writing a summary.

MATERIALS

Student Reader, pp. 38–41
Language Arts, p. T24

Vocabulary Activity: Have students create an illustration of a person or an object that they think is special. Tell students to write the person's name or a short caption on their drawing. Ask students to share their drawings with the class.

Preview and Prepare

Before you read, use modeling and prompts such as:

- *Let's browse the title and the first page.*
- *What does the title tell you? What are special ears? Who is Susan? As we read, see if you can discover what the title means.*

During Reading

Read Aloud

For this lesson, read the entire selection aloud. As you read, stop at the points that are marked with numbers in magenta circles on the reduced student pages, and model for them how to use the indicated strategy. Encourage students to stop at any point in their reading if they don't understand something or want to talk about the meaning of a passage or word.

Comprehension Strategies

During the reading of "Special Ears for Susan" on pages 38–41, you will model the following reading comprehension strategies:

Asking Questions: As they read, good readers ask themselves questions to see if they are making sense of what they are reading.

Summarizing: Good readers often pause during reading to summarize. After reading, they may make a mental summary of the entire selection. Summarizing helps them to make sense of what they read.

TEACHER TIP

Asking Questions Students should be encouraged to stop to ask questions. Have students take time to reflect on the text from time to time to see if it makes sense.

First Read

Text Comprehension *Strategies*

As you read the selection, use modeling and prompts such as:

❶ Asking Questions

Asking yourself questions is a good way to be sure you understand what you're reading. My question here is, how is Susan lucky? From what we've read, it sounds as if her life is a bit difficult. Let's read on to see if we can answer my question.

❷ Answering Questions

Well, my question is answered. Susan is lucky because she has a dog, Buttons, who serves as her "special ears."

Encourage students to find out information about dogs that have been trained to help people. They might talk to family members or neighbors or use reference books and approved Web sites. Allow time in class for them to share what they have learned.

Special Ears for Susan

by Sally Lee
illustrated by Gerardo Suzán

Susan can't hear. How does she know when the doorbell rings? How does she know when her alarm clock sounds? How does she know when the bell on her oven rings?

38

VOCABULARY

Remind students that *antonyms* are words that are opposite in meaning, and *synonyms* are words that have the same or nearly the same meaning. For a review lesson on antonyms and synonyms, use *Language Arts* page T24.

Susan is <u>lucky</u>. She found someone with good ears to live with her. That someone is a dog named Buttons. Buttons is a <u>special</u> animal.

39

Text Comprehension

Drawing Conclusions

Remind students that authors do not always provide complete and clear information about a topic, character, thing, or event. They do, however, provide clues or suggestions that readers can use to "read between the lines" by drawing conclusions that are based on the information in the selection.

● Ask students to draw conclusions about Buttons. *(Possible answers: Buttons is smart; Buttons likes Susan; Buttons is well trained.)*

● Use **Transparency** 23 to record their responses.

GRAMMAR

Remind students that they have learned about common and proper nouns, regular and irregular plural nouns, and possessive nouns. For a review lesson on nouns, use **Language Arts** page T23.

27

Text Comprehension *strategies*

❸ Summarizing

Good readers stop now and then as they read so that they can summarize what they've read and make sure they're following what's happening. I'm going to summarize what we've read so far: Susan can't hear, but she is lucky because she has a dog, Buttons, who helps. When he hears the alarm clock, he jumps on Susan to wake her up. When he hears the doorbell, he runs to find her and takes her to the door.

❹ Summarizing

At the end of a selection, good readers often summarize what they've read to make sure they understand it. Who would like to summarize the story?

Student Sample

The selection tells about Susan and the special dog who helps her—her "special ears." But it also tells how Susan takes care of the dog. She gives him rewards to let him know that she appreciates what he does.

Student Sample The student sample is only one example of many possible student responses. Accept other responses that are reasonable and appropriate.

Buttons helps Susan in many ways. When the alarm clock sounds, Buttons jumps on Susan to get her up. Then they have their cereal.

When the doorbell rings, Buttons runs to find Susan in a <u>flash</u>. Then he takes ❸ her to the door.

40

WRITING

Ask students to think about how they would summarize the selection. Have them write a brief summary of the selection.

Susan likes to bake bread. The bell on the oven tells when the bread is ready. When Buttons hears the bell, he runs to get her. She gives him a little piece of bread for being such a good dog.

Susan takes good care of Buttons. And Buttons takes good care of Susan. ❹

41

Second Read

Text Comprehension

Drawing Conclusions

Drawing conclusions is an ongoing process. Readers draw conclusions as they gather additional information from a story.

- Ask students to draw conclusions about Susan. *(Possible answers: Susan is kind to Buttons; Susan likes Buttons; Susan is glad she has Buttons.)*
- Use **Transparency** 23 to record their responses.
- For additional practice with Drawing Conclusions, have students complete **Decodable Stories and Comprehension Skills** page 86.

Discussing the Selection

After you have read the story, discuss it with students. Use prompts such as:

- *What did you like about this story?*
- *What did you learn about "hearing ear" dogs?*
- *What did you learn about kindness from reading this selection?*
- *How does this selection relate to the unit theme, Kindness?*
- *How did the reading strategies and skills that you've learned help you understand it?*

QUICK CHECK

Quickly review with students the other comprehension skills that they've used so far.

SELECTION F • **Special Ears for Susan**

Phonemic Awareness

Segmentation: Initial Consonant Sounds

Play the Initial Consonant Sounds game again with students. Remind them that you will say a word and repeat the beginning consonant. Then you will ask them to repeat the word and to say what sounds were left off. Use the following words:

dust	bear	last
jet	fill	soap
must	list	met
dump	fast	rust
rice	care	bump
pet	pill	rope

Phonemic Awareness Remember that the phonemic awareness activities are purely oral and use many sounds whose spellings have not yet been introduced. In these sections you are not teaching phonics or sound-spelling correspondences. No writing is involved.

Word Study

Word Play

One by one, point to a spelling on each of the **Sound/Spelling Cards** that have been used in this unit—for example, the *ph* spelling for /f/, the *wr_* spelling for /r/, the *kn_* spelling for /n/, the *ai* spelling for /ā/, and so on. Ask students to say and spell a word for each sound/spelling that you indicate. Write their words on the board.

Phonics—Blending: Set 2

Discuss any **Sound/Spelling Cards** that you want students to review. Tell them that in this lesson, they will review the sound/spellings that they have learned so far.

Blending Exercise

- Write the following words and sentences on the board.
- Have students blend the words and sentences using the whole-word procedure described in Unit 1 on page 12F.

Line 1:	fish	phone	wring	road	kneel	night
Line 2:	ate	eight	sail	sale	sight	site
Line 3:	lady	three	write	show	use	my
Line 4:	scratch	think	wrong	when	knit	wish
Sentence 1:	Can Pete and Phil <u>come</u> to the play tonight?					
Sentence 2:	When will Jean <u>come</u> to see the peach tree?					
Sentence 3:	What <u>color</u> can we paint the <u>door</u>?					

- Before reading a sentence, point to and read the underlined sight words.
- Discuss with students that each sentence begins with a capital letter and ends with a punctuation mark.
- Have students reread the sentences to encourage fluency and comprehension.

28

SELECTION F • **Special Ears for Susan**

About the Words and Sentences

- For Line 1, have students identify the two spellings for each of the sounds /f/, /r/, and /n/.
- For Line 2, have students note that the words are pairs of homophones with long-vowel spellings. Have them use each word in a sentence.
- For Line 3, have students identify the long-vowel sound/spelling in each word.
- For Line 4, have students identify the initial and/or final sound/spelling in each word.
- For the sentences, have students identify the common and proper nouns.

Oral Language

Have students find, read, and erase words that are synonyms for the words *day (night), man (lady), right (wrong).*

Dictation

For the dictation exercise, have students use writing paper. Dictate the words and sentence for them to write. Use the following procedure:

- Say the first word in each word line. Use the word in a sentence, then say the word again. Have students say the word.
- Tell students to think about how to segment the word into sounds. Then have them write the spelling for each sound.
- After each word line, write (or have a student write) the words on the board. Have students proofread their words. Tell them to circle any incorrect words and to correct them.
- Next dictate the sentence. Dictate one word at a time, following the sounds-in-sequence or whole-word dictation procedure, depending on your students. Remind students to start the sentence with a capital letter and to use correct end punctuation.
- Write (or have a student write) the sentence on the board. Have students proofread their work and correct any incorrect words.

WRITING

Have students choose one word from the word lines and write a definition for it. Have volunteers read their definition aloud and have other students try to determine which word is being defined.

Line 1:	whale	while	switch
Line 2:	throat	shape	wrong
Line 3:	speech	knack	nephew
Sentence:	Jean sang a silly song at the show.		

Building Fluency

Decodable Story: Unit 2, Story 12

- This story reviews the sound/spellings introduced in the unit.
- Have students silently read *Decodable Stories and Comprehension Skills* page 24.
- Call on volunteers to read each paragraph aloud.
- For those students who need help, divide sentences according to natural phrases. Mark these phrases with diagonal slash marks on their worksheets.
- After students have read the story aloud, ask them questions and have them point to and read the answers in the story.
- Have students reread the story aloud with a partner.

HOMEWORK TIP

To help students build fluency, have them share with the class books, stories, and magazines that they have brought from home and read previously with their families.

SELECTION F • **Special Ears for Susan**

OBJECTIVES

- Develop reading skills as the story is reread to them.
- Gain knowledge of the comprehension skill Drawing Conclusions.
- Develop vocabulary by listening to and discussing a selection.
- Develop writing skills by writing about the unit theme.
- Identify and correctly use nouns.

MATERIALS

Transparencies 3, 23, 24
Decodable Stories and Comprehension Skills, p. 86
Student Reader, pp. 38–41, 42–43
Listening Library Audiocassette/CD
Language Arts, p. T23

Rereading the Selection

Comprehension Skills

Revisiting or rereading a selection allows students to learn and apply skills that give them a more complete understanding of a selection. For today's lesson, reread the selection to students. During the second reading, students will apply the following comprehension skill:

Drawing Conclusions: Good readers often "read between the lines," using clues provided by the author to draw conclusions about a selection's meaning.

After Reading

Reading Reflections

Have students discuss with a partner the Reading Reflections questions on pages 42–43. After partner discussions, have students discuss the answers to the questions as a class.

Independent Reading

- Have students choose books from the **Classroom Library** or other available books to take home and read. Encourage students to read at least one book a week on their own.
- Set aside time to talk with students about the independent reading they are doing.
- Encourage students to use the comprehension strategies and skills they are learning as they read independently.
- Encourage students to record the titles of the books they are reading on the copy of **Transparency** 3.

Have students listen to the selection recording on the *Listening Library Audiocassette/CD* for a proficient, fluent model of oral reading.

WRITING

Tell students to think about the selections in this unit. Have them write a list of three words that reflect ideas about kindness. Have students share their lists with the class.

SELECTION F • **Special Ears for Susan**

Assessment

Formal

At the conclusion of the lesson, have students complete the assessment Unit 2: Special Ears for Susan. The Lesson Assessments are found in the *Assessment Guide.*

For all the items in this assessment, you should read both the question and answer choices out loud while students follow along silently. Remind students that this is the last lesson in the unit and congratulate them for their hard work.

Ask students to refer to Question 3 of the Unit Assessment. Have them think of several different cats and then choose the one they want to draw. Before students start working, have them describe the cat with you in as much detail as they can remember. Encourage students to include these details in their drawing. They may even want to draw the cat playing or doing something that it likes. Have students complete the rest of the Unit Assessment questions. Review the answers as a group activity and give students an opportunity to share the performance items with the rest of the group.

Informal

Be sure students have the story "Special Ears for Susan" in front of them. Ask students questions that will point out the details in the story. Then ask them questions that will extend the meaning of the story, such as "Where do you think Susan got Buttons?" or "How old do you think Susan is?" Encourage students to ask questions on their own.

Ending the Lesson

Ask students to talk about dogs they know. It can be their own dog or the dog of a friend or family member. Discuss some of the common and unusual behaviors of the dog. Encourage them to remember specific details of the dog's behavior.

OBJECTIVES

- Complete lesson and unit assessments.
- Visualize a character.
- Review details in a story.
- Discuss a familiar pet.

MATERIALS

Assessment Guide
Student Reader, pp. 38–41

Reading Reflections

Focus on the Characters

- She agrees to help Mike's mom. Pat uses the extra money to buy a ball for Mike's dog instead of spending it all on herself.

- Tyler was very upset that he had broken his brother's bike chain. He was even more upset when he thought the bike had been stolen. However, Mr. Chang not only had the bike, but he had also fixed the chain. Thus, Tyler's day turned from bad to good.

- Possible Answer: At first the lion laughs and is amused by the idea of a mouse helping a lion. After the mouse saves his life, the lion is not only surprised but also relieved and grateful for the mouse's help.

Focus on the Stories

- "A Nature Adventure," "Special Ears for Susan"
- "Helping Others," "Marta Helps at Home"
- "Helping Others," "Marta Helps at Home," and "Tyler's Bad Day"

Reading Reflections

These questions can help you think about the stories you just read. After you write your responses, discuss them with a partner.

Focus on the Characters

- In "Helping Others," how does Pat show that she is an unselfish person?
- In "Tyler's Bad Day," how does Mr. Chang's act of kindness affect Tyler's day?
- In "The Lion and the Mouse," how does the lion feel when the mouse first suggests that the mouse can help him? How do his feelings change after the mouse actually saves him?

Focus on the Stories

- In "The Lion and the Mouse," the mouse rescues the lion by gnawing the strings of the net. Name another story in this unit where a character's kindness saves

42

Kindness

another from injury or death.

- As seen in "Tyler's Bad Day," adults often provide the helping hand to children. However, this is not the case in all the stories in this unit. Name a story that has a youth providing aid to an adult.

- Some stories in this unit showed people helping others that were injured or disabled. Name a story in this unit where a character helped someone in order to just be helpful.

Focus on the Theme

- Considering the stories in this unit, how does an act of kindness change the events of a story?

- Which story showed the helper getting something in return? Explain your choice.

- List three ways that you have helped a family member or friend.

43

Focus on the Theme

- Possible Answers: In "A Nature Adventure" and "The Lion and the Mouse," kindness saves an animal's life. In "Helping Others," "Marta Helps at Home," and "Special Ears for Susan," kindness allows others to complete a job and have more time to relax. In "Tyler's Bad Day," an act of kindness turns a bad day into a good one.

- Possible Answer: In "Special Ears for Susan," Buttons helps Susan with everyday tasks; in return, Buttons gets special treats and a nice home.

- Answers will vary.

UNIT 3

Overview

HOME CONNECTIONS

Distribute *Home Connection* page 29, which describes the unit theme and suggests activities for families to do at home. This letter is available in English and Spanish.

Unit Goals

Throughout the **Kaleidoscope** program, students will be introduced to a variety of reading and writing skills. In this unit students will

- develop phonemic awareness skills through oral blending and segmentation activities—initial and final consonants.

- learn to decode by introducing and reviewing the phonic elements *tion, ion;* /oo/ spelled *oo;* /o͞o/ spelled *oo, u, u_e, _ew, _ue;* /ow/ spelled *ow, ou_;* /aw/ spelled *au_, aw, augh, ough, al, all;* /oi/ spelled *_oy, oi.*

- increase their proficiency in decoding and word-attack skills through practice with decodable text highlighting introduced phonic elements.

- build reading fluency through repeated reading of decodable text.

- expand their vocabulary through instruction and practice in using prefixes.

- acquire an understanding of basic English grammar through work with pronouns and verbs.

- improve reading comprehension by working with the comprehension strategies Making Connections, Asking Questions, Monitoring and Clarifying, Monitoring and Adjusting Reading Speed, Visualizing, and Summarizing; and the comprehension skills Main Idea and Details, Cause and Effect, Classifying and Categorizing, Author's Purpose, and Drawing Conclusions, and Compare and Contrast.

- engage in daily writing activities related to the phonics and reading lessons.

Theme

Children love animals. They have a natural curiosity about them. This unit draws on that curiosity and offers students the opportunity to learn about an important characteristic of animals: camouflage. Because camouflage depends on the nature of an animal's environment, this unit also allows students to deepen their understanding of the relationship between an animal and the environment.

In this unit, students will read and talk about animals and their camouflage. They will examine different kinds of camouflage and how and why animals use it.

Introducing the Unit

- Tell students that in this unit they will be talking and reading about animals and their camouflage.
- Explain that *camouflage* is the name for the disguises that animals sometimes use to hide themselves. For example, some animals have colors or patterns of color that let them blend in with trees and rocks.
- Ask students why animals need to be able to hide.
- Ask them if they know of any animals that use camouflage to hide.
- Invite them to talk about any books or stories or magazine articles about animal camouflage that they have read.

Selection	Overview of Selection	Link to Theme
A Opossums	This nonfiction selection describes opossums and how they stay safe.	Opossums have a unique way to stay safe from their enemies.
B A Tricky Spider	The trapdoor spider and its hidden home are described in this nonfiction selection.	Some animals use their homes to hide themselves.
C Colors That Hide	Several animals and the special ways they stay safe are described in this nonfiction selection.	Animals are often hard to spot because their color, shape, and movements match their surroundings.
D Night Lights in the Ocean	This nonfiction selection tells of the flashlight fish and the way it uses its lights.	Fish and other sea creatures use camouflage.
E Insects Stay Safe	The camouflage of the walking stick and the moth are explained in this nonfiction selection.	Many insects are hard to spot because of their camouflage.
F Hide-and-Seek Animals	This nonfiction selection describes how the colors of some animals help them hide from their enemies.	The shapes and colors of some animals help them hide from their enemies.

CLASSROOM LIBRARY

The Big, Brown Box
by David Drew. Nelson Thomson Learning, 1994.

When insects escape from a big, brown box, their colors help them hide in their surroundings.

Who's Hiding Here?
by Yoshi. Simon & Schuster Books for Young Readers, 1987.
The illustrations and rhyming text provide insight into the camouflaged world of animals.

Worms, Wonderful Worms
By Kathie Atkinson. Nelson Thomson Learning, 1994.

Worms and their different methods of camouflage are explored in this informative book.

SELECTION A • **Opossums**

Support Materials

LESSON 1
- Decodable Stories and Comprehension Skills, p. 25
- Home Connection, p. 31
- High-Frequency Word Cards

HOME CONNECTIONS

Distribute *Home Connection* page 31, which describes this week's classwork and suggests activities for families to do at home. This letter is available in English and Spanish.

LESSON 2
- Student Reader, pp. 44–47
- Language Arts, p. T26

LESSON 3
- Sound/Spelling Card 42
- Decodable Stories and Comprehension Skills, p. 26
- High-Frequency Word Cards
- Sound/Spelling Card Stories Audiocassette/CD

LESSON 4
- Student Reader, pp. 44–47
- Transparencies 3, 11, 25
- Decodable Stories and Comprehension Skills, p. 87
- Language Arts, p. T25
- Listening Library Audiocassette/CD

LESSON 5
- Assessment Guide
- Student Reader, pp. 44–47

Teacher Focus	Student Participation
• Conduct Listening Game. • Conduct Word Play. • Introduce Sight Words and Set 1 blending words and sentences. • Provide riddle clues. • Dictate word lines. • Assist students with decodable text. • Assign writing activity.	• Take part in Listening Game. • Take part in Word Play. • Read Sight Words. • Blend words and sentences. • Solve riddles. • Write dictated words and sentences. • Read a decodable story. • Complete writing activity.
• Activate Prior Knowledge and provide background information. • Introduce and discuss selection vocabulary. • Preview selection. • Review Comprehension Strategies—Asking Questions and Making Connections. • Read the selection to students. • Assign writing activity. • Introduce vocabulary skill.	• Contribute to class discussion. • Read and discuss vocabulary words. Complete selection vocabulary activity. • Browse the selection. • Follow along as selection is read. • Complete writing activity. • Complete vocabulary skill activity.
• Conduct Restoring Final Consonants game. • Conduct Word Play. • Introduce Set 2 blending words and sentences. • Conduct Oral Language activity. • Dictate word lines. • Assist students with decodable text. • Assign writing activity.	• Participate in Restoring Final Consonants game. • Take part in Word Play. • Blend words and sentences. • Create sentences. • Write dictated words and sentences. • Read a decodable story. • Complete writing activity.
• Review Comprehension Skill—Main Idea and Details. • Reread and discuss the selection with students. • Discuss Independent Reading. • Assign writing activity. • Introduce writing activity. • Introduce grammar skill.	• Follow along as selection is read again. • Discuss the selection. • Select a book to take home and read. • Complete writing activity. • Complete grammar skill activity.
• Administer weekly assessments. • Assess students' progress.	• Complete lesson assessment.

Unit 3 • LESSON

1

OBJECTIVES

- Identify and blend initial consonant sounds in words.
- Blend and break apart sounds in words.
- Read sight words.
- Participate in Word Play activity.
- Develop fluency by reading aloud.
- Apply decoding skills by reading *Unit 3, Decodable Story 1.*
- Develop writing skills by writing a definition.

MATERIALS

Decodable Stories and Comprehension Skills, p. 25
Home Connection, p. 31
High-Frequency Word Cards

Phonemic Awareness

The basic purpose of providing structured practice in phonemic awareness is to help students hear and understand the sounds from which words are made. Before students can be expected to understand the sound/symbol correspondence that forms the base of written English, they need to have a strong working knowledge of the sound relationships that make up the spoken language. This understanding of spoken language lays the foundation for the transition to written language. Phonemic awareness activities provide students with easy practice in discriminating the sounds that make up words. Once students begin reading and writing, this experience with manipulating sounds will help them use what they know about sounds and letters to sound out and spell unfamiliar words.

The two main formats for teaching phonemic awareness are oral blending and segmentation. These are supported by occasional discrimination activities and general word play. From these playful activities, students derive serious knowledge about language.

Oral Blending

Oral blending prepares students for phonics instruction by developing an awareness of the separate sounds that make up speech. Because these activities involve simply listening to and reproducing sounds, oral blending need not be restricted to the sounds students have been taught in phonics. The oral blending activities should be playful and informal and should move quickly.

Listening Game: Initial Consonant Sounds

Have students continue to replace the initial consonant sounds in words to make new words. In this lesson, you will use easy, one-syllable words, and some of the words produced may be actual words. Point out to students when a nonsense word is produced and when an actual word is produced. Say a common word, then have students replace its initial consonant sound to make new words.

Begin by writing the word *tent* on the board. Touch the word, and tell students that this word is *tent*. Have them say the word. Erase the initial *t*. Tell students that now the word begins with /s/. Ask them to say the new word *(sent)*. Use any single initial consonants in any order. Try the following words:

ban	rain	tip
mail	had	song
tag	seen	tight

TEACHER TIP

Listening Game Remember not to write the replacement consonant until after students have responded.

SELECTION A • **Opossums**

Word Study

In this section of the lesson, students work on phonics, fluency, blending, and spelling. Increasing students' ability to work smoothly with printed words is one of the primary goals of the *Kaleidoscope* program.

Word Play

Have students make a Word Search puzzle. On the board, write at least ten words that contain sound/spellings from Unit 1. Review the words with students, asking them to identify and say the target sound/spelling. Help students to make word-search puzzles. If they are not familiar with word searches, create a puzzle on the board. Draw a chart with five columns and five rows. Choose three words from the board and write them, one letter per square, on the chart, with one word running across a row, one running down a column, and one running up a column. Fill in the empty squares with random letters. Explain to students that they can choose any of the words on the board, and that they can place them anywhere on their charts. When they have finished, have them exchange puzzles. Tell them to circle the words as they find them.

Sight Words

This week's sight words:

could   **should**   **would**

Use the following procedure for teaching sight words:

- Write this week's sight words on the board.
- Read the words to students, and then have them read the words.
- Pronounce any words with which students have difficulty.
- Have students use each sight word in a sentence.

Phonics—Blending: Set 1

This section of the phonics lesson provides practice in building sounds and spellings into words.

- Point out and discuss any *Sound/Spelling Cards* that you want students to review. Tell them that in this lesson, they will work with sound/spelling patterns rather than individual sound/spellings.
- Write the spelling patterns *-ion* and *-tion* on the board and pronounce each one: /ən/ and /shən/. Explain that these sound/spelling patterns come at the end of words.

TEACHER TIP

Sight Words Use the *High-Frequency Word Cards* to assess and review students' knowledge of sight words.

Blending Exercise

- The words in the lines provide practice with the Set 1 sound/spellings. Write the following words and sentences on the board.
- Have students blend the words and sentences using the whole-word procedure described in Unit 1 on page 12F.

Line 1:	champion companion expression discussion
Line 2:	motion vacation definition addition
Sentence 1:	The teacher should have the class's complete attention.
Sentence 2:	I would need to ask for permission to go to the celebration.
Sentence 3:	Could Sam complete the subtraction problems?

About the Words and Sentences

- Have students say the words, emphasizing the sound/spellings at the end of the words.
- Have students count the syllables in each word.
- Before reading a sentence, point to and read the underlined sight words. Have students reread the sentences to encourage fluency and comprehension.
- For Sentence 1, have students find the possessive noun (*class's*). Ask them to explain what a possessive noun does. (*It shows who or what owns or has something.*)

Oral Language

Give clues for words on the lines for students to find and read. Use clues such as the following:

Which word is a synonym for *winner*? (*champion*)

Which word is an antonym for *stillness*? (*motion*)

Which word is a synonym for *friend*? (*companion*)

TEACHER TIP

As you read the words with the endings -tion and -ion, pronounce the endings for students and tell them the vowel sound in the endings is called a *schwa* sound. Students should be able to blend the words once you pronounce the endings for them.

WRITING

Have students choose one word from the word lines and write a definition for it. Have volunteers read their definition aloud and have other students try to determine which word is being defined.

Unit 3 • LESSON

Dictation

Dictation gives students an opportunity to spell words by using the sound/spellings that they have learned. For this dictation exercise, have students use writing paper. Dictate the words and sentence for them to write. Use the following procedure to have students practice whole-word and sentence dictation:

● Say the first word in each word line. Use the word in a sentence, then say the word again. Have students say the word.

● Tell students to think about how to segment the word into sounds. Then have them write the spelling for each sound. Encourage them to check the *Sound/Spelling Cards.*

● After each word line, write (or have a student write) the words on the board. Have students proofread their words. Tell them to circle any incorrect words and to correct them.

● Next, dictate the sentence. Dictate one word at a time, following the sounds-in-sequence or whole-word dictation procedure, depending on your students. Remind students to start the sentence with a capital letter and to use correct end punctuation.

● Write (or have a student write) the sentence on the board. Have students proofread their work and correct any incorrect words.

Line 1:	action	attention	portion
Line 2:	session	condition	permission
Sentence:	What is the location of the old mission?		

Building Fluency

Decodable Story: Unit 3, Story 1

- This story reviews the sound/spellings *-tion, -ion.*
- Have students silently read *Decodable Stories and Comprehension Skills* page 25.
- Call on volunteers to read each paragraph aloud.
- For those students who need help, divide sentences according to natural phrases. Mark these phrases with diagonal slash marks on their worksheets.
- After students have read the story aloud, ask them questions and have them point to and read the answers in the story.
- Have students reread the story aloud with a partner. Rereading builds automaticity and fluency.
- Over the next few days, listen to each student reread the story.

Develop Fluency Model fluent reading frequently for students, showing them how pausing in the right places and adding expression can make a passage easier to understand.

QUICK CHECK

As a quick review of today's sound/spellings, say some sentences, and ask students to suggest words to fill the blanks. Sentences you might read aloud include:

We went to Florida on our summer _____. *(vacation)*
Derek's dog is his constant _____. *(companion)*
Use the dictionary to find the _____ of any hard word. *(definition)*

SELECTION A • **Opossums**

Before Reading

Build Background

Activate Prior Knowledge

- Remind students that this unit is about animals and animal camouflage.
- Ask students if anyone has ever seen an opossum. If so, have students describe what the animal looks like. If not, find and show them a picture of an opossum.
- Write the word *opossum* on the board. Explain that the word *possum* is a shortened form of *opossum,* which is the name of an animal.

Background Information

Use the following information to help students understand the selection you are about to read:

- Tell students that this selection is nonfiction. Remind them that nonfiction is different from fiction, or made-up stories, because it is true. Explain that nonfiction is written to inform, explain, describe, and sometimes to persuade.
- Ask students if they know the expression *to play possum.* If no one does, tell them that the expression means to pretend to be dead.

Selection Vocabulary

Write the following vocabulary words on the board. Before reading the selection, introduce and discuss the words and their meanings.

tiptoes: to walk on the tips of one's toes

enemy: someone who wishes to do harm to another

fascinating: very interesting

Then have students read the words, stopping to blend any words that they have trouble reading. Demonstrate how to decode multisyllabic words by breaking the words into syllables and blending the syllables. Then have students try. If they still have trouble, refer them to the **Sound/Spelling Cards.** If the word is not decodable, give students the pronunciation.

As students study vocabulary, they will use a variety of skills to determine the meaning of a word. These skills include context clues, word structure, and apposition. In this lesson, students will be learning about word structure. Write the following example on the board: *Steve tiptoes quietly when he goes into the woods.*

OBJECTIVES

- Discuss vocabulary words and their meanings.
- Develop reading skills as the story is read to them.
- Gain knowledge of the comprehension strategies Asking Questions and Making Connections.
- Build vocabulary by learning about prefixes.
- Develop writing skills by writing a list.

MATERIALS

Student Reader, pp. 44–47
Language Arts, p. T26

Explain to students that they are going to use word structure to help them decipher the meaning of the word *tiptoes*. Tell students that when they use word structure, they should break the word down into smaller words to determine the word's meaning. Guide students until they can give a reasonable definition of the word.

Vocabulary Activity: Have students use the letters from the word *fascinating* to make as many new words as possible. Write the new words on the board as students suggest them. Some words they may make include *as, in, cat, fat, sat, at, it.*

Preview and Prepare

Before you read, use modeling and prompts such as:

● *Because this selection is nonfiction, we can browse all of it.*
● *As you browse, look for key words that will help you understand what the selection is explaining.*

During Reading

Read Aloud

For this lesson, read the entire selection aloud. If you feel your students are ready to read the selection orally, have them do so. As you read, stop at the points that are marked with numbers in magenta circles on the reduced student pages, and model for them how to use the indicated strategy. Encourage students to stop at any point in their reading if they don't understand something or want to talk about the meaning of a passage or word.

Comprehension Strategies

During the reading of "Opossums" on pages 44–47, you will model the following reading comprehension strategies:

Asking Questions: As they read, good readers ask themselves questions to see if they are making sense of what they are reading.

Making Connections: Readers improve their understanding of a selection by making connections between what they already know and what they are reading.

TEACHER TIP

Comprehension Strategies Encourage students to ask any questions they have about things in the story that they do not understand. Remind them that readers often stop to clarify things that are not clear.

2

First Read

Text Comprehension *Strategies*

As you read the selection, use modeling and prompts such as:

❶ Asking Questions

Asking yourself questions is a good way to be sure you understand what you're reading. Why is Steve tiptoeing? No one can hear him in the woods, so why does he need to be quiet? If I continue reading, maybe I will find the answer to my question. I see. He's being quiet so he can watch the opossums. They would probably run away if they heard him.

❷ Making Connections

Good readers relate what they already know to what they read to improve their understanding of the selection. I know about cats, so it helps to know that opossums are about the same size.

Opossums

by Rosalie Koskimaki
illustrated by Pat Paris

Steve goes to the woods often. He
❶ tiptoes quietly. Then he hides behind a tree. He watches the opossums play.

44

WRITING

Tell students to think about some of the things that Steve will see in the woods as he is watching the opossums. Have them write a list of three things they think Steve will see.

VOCABULARY

Tell students that a *prefix* is a word part that comes at the beginning of a base word, and that adding a prefix to a word changes the meaning of the word. Explain that the prefix *re-* usually means "again." For a lesson on the prefix *re-*, use *Language Arts* page T26.

The opossums are as big as cats. They
are blue-gray with white faces. They have
black eyes and ears. They have long,
pointed noses. They have sharp teeth to
chew with.

45

Text Comprehension

Main Idea and Details

Explain to students that finding the main idea of a
paragraph or passage helps them to see how the
author organized the ideas in the selection and
lets them better understand what those ideas are.

● For page 45, ask students to identify the main
idea and three details to support that idea.
*(Possible answers: Main Idea – What do opossums
look like? Supporting Details – Opossums are as big
as cats; opossums are blue-gray with white faces;
opossums have black eyes and ears; opossums have
long, pointed noses; opossums have sharp teeth.)*

● Use **Transparency** 11 to record their responses.

GRAMMAR

Tell students that *pronouns* are words that replace
nouns. Discuss some pronouns from the selection
and point out the nouns that they replace (page
44— *he* replaces *Steve,* page 45—*they* replace
opossums). For a lesson on pronouns, use **Language
Arts** page T25.

First
Read

Text Comprehension *Strategies*

3 **Making Connections**

I've got a pretty good picture of what opossums look like and how they live in the wild. They do things that I know other wild animals do—climb trees, use their tails to hold things, and use their feet like hands.

4 **Asking Questions**

I wonder why the author told us that few animals will eat a dead opossum. That sounds strange. Let's read on to see if there's a reason. Of course, the opossum plays dead, and the other animals leave it alone. Opossums know how to hide in plain sight, don't they? What great camouflage!

HOMEWORK TIP

Encourage students to use computers at home or on their own time to find out more about opossums. Invite them to share their new information with the class.

Steve watches them climb. Climbing is easy for opossums. Their feet have five toes. One toe is like a thumb. They use their feet like hands. Their tails help, too. Their tails are long and thin. Opossums can hold things in their tails and climb
3 with their tails.

46

Some animals eat opossums. But very few will bother a dead opossum. So, when an <u>enemy</u> comes along, opossums play dead. They lie down. They shut their eyes. They don't move. They look dead. Soon the enemy goes away. That is how opossums stay safe.

Opossums are truly <u>fascinating</u> animals.

47

Second Read

Text Comprehension *skills*

Main Idea and Details

- Have students identify the main idea for the first paragraph on each page. *(Possible answers: page 46—climbing is easy for opossums; page 47—opossums "play dead" to stay safe from their enemies.)*
- For additional practice with Main Idea and Details, have students complete **Decodable Stories and Comprehension Skills** page 87.

Discussing the Selection

After you have read the selection, discuss it with students. Use prompts such as:

- *What did you learn about opossums?*
- *Did anything surprise you? If so, what was it and why was it a surprise?*
- *What did you learn about animal camouflage from this selection?*
- *Explain what it means to "play possum."*

QUICK CHECK

Ask students to identify a sentence in the selection that identifies the main idea of the story. *(Opossums are truly fascinating animals.)*

Unit 3 • LESSON

3

OBJECTIVES

- Identify and restore final consonant sounds in words.
- Blend and break apart sounds in words.
- Participate in Word Play activity.
- Develop fluency by reading aloud.
- Apply decoding skills by reading **Unit 3, Decodable Story 2.**
- Develop writing skills by writing rhyming words.

MATERIALS

Sound/Spelling Card:
42—Foot
Decodable Stories and Comprehension Skills, p. 26
High-Frequency Word Cards
Sound/Spelling Card Stories Audiocassette/CD

Phonemic Awareness

Segmentation: Restoring Final Consonants

● Tell students you are going to say a word, then you will repeat the word but leave off the ending sound. Then you will ask them to repeat the word and say what sound was left off. Use this example:

Teacher:	soon . . . soo
Teacher:	What's the word? What sound did I leave off?
Students:	soon, /n/

● Continue with the following words:

soup	bike	beep
bake	leap	lake
loop	like	moon

TEACHER TIP

Segmentation Remember to move quickly through these activities. Do not hold the class back waiting on all students to catch on. Return to the same activity often. Frequent repetition is very beneficial and allows students additional opportunities to catch on.

Word Study

Word Play

Have students work in pairs to look through old magazines or newspapers for words with the *-ion* or *-tion* spelling pattern. Have them circle each word that they find. Call on each pair to read their words to the class.

Phonics—Blending: Set 2

> /oo/ spelled *oo*

Point out and discuss the new **Sound/Spelling Card.** Ask students what they know about it.

Blending Exercise

- Write the following words and sentences on the board.
- Have students blend the words and sentences using the whole-word procedure described in Unit 1 on page 12F.

Line 1:	hook cook shook took look
Line 2:	wood good stood wool brook
Line 3:	footpath workbook bookmark
Sentence 1:	Could I use Brooke's notebook?
Sentence 2:	Sam said he would meet us by the woodshed.

- Before reading a sentence, point to and read the underlined sight words.
- Discuss with students that each sentence begins with a capital letter and ends with a punctuation mark.
- Have students reread the sentences to encourage fluency and comprehension.

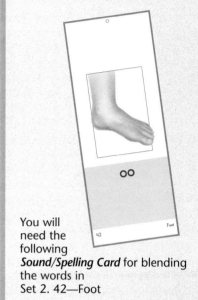

You will need the following **Sound/Spelling Card** for blending the words in Set 2. 42—Foot

WRITING

Tell students to look at the words in Line 2 and write the words that rhyme (*wood, good, stood*). Then have them circle the sound/spelling for /oo/ in each word.

3

SELECTION A • **Opossums**

About the Words and Sentences

- For Line 2, have students find the word that is a homophone for a sight word. *(wood)*
- For Line 3, have students notice that all the words are compound words. Ask if knowing the meaning of each small word helps them figure out the meaning of the compound word.
- For the sentences, have students find the nouns and tell if they are common or proper.

Oral Language

Have students take turns choosing a word, reading it, using it in a sentence, and calling on a classmate to extend the sentence.

Dictation

For the dictation exercise, have students use writing paper. Dictate the words and sentence for them to write. Use the following procedure:

- Say the first word in each word line. Use the word in a sentence, then say the word again. Have students say the word.
- Tell students to think about how to segment the word into sounds. Then have them write the spelling for each sound.
- After each word line, write (or have a student write) the words on the board. Have students proofread their words. Tell them to circle any incorrect words and to correct them.
- Next dictate the sentence. Dictate one word at a time, following the sounds-in-sequence or whole-word dictation procedure, depending on your students. Remind students to start the sentence with a capital letter and to use correct end punctuation.
- Write (or have a student write) the sentence on the board. Have students proofread their work and correct any incorrect words.

Line 1:	stood	cookie	good
Line 2:	hoof	brook	foot
Sentence:	Do not overlook the steps in the cookbook.		

Building Fluency

Decodable Story: Unit 3, Story 2

● This story reviews the sound/spellings /oo/ spelled *oo*.

● Have students silently read ***Decodable Stories and Comprehension Skills*** page 26.

● Call on volunteers to read each paragraph aloud.

● For those students who need help, divide sentences according to natural phrases. Mark these phrases with diagonal slash marks on their worksheets.

● After students have read the story aloud, ask them questions and have them point to and read the answers in the story.

● Have students reread the story aloud with a partner.

HOMEWORK TIP

To help students build fluency, have them take home the *Decodable Stories and Comprehension Skills* stories to read with their families.

TEACHER TIP

Sound/Spelling Card Stories Review today's sounds by using the *Sound/Spelling Card Stories.* Listening to the stories will help students understand how they can use the pictures on the *Sound/Spelling Cards* to remember the sounds associated with them. The stories are provided in the appendix and are also available on the *Sound/Spelling Card Stories Audiocassette/CD.*

SELECTION A • **Opossums**

Rereading the Selection

Comprehension Skills

Revisiting or rereading a selection allows students to learn and apply skills that give them a more complete understanding of a selection. For today's lesson, reread the selection to students. During the second reading, students will apply the following comprehension skill:

Main Idea and Details: Good readers identify the most important points, or main ideas, in the selections that they read. This helps them organize information and better understand the selection.

After Reading

Independent Reading

- Have students choose books from the *Classroom Library* or other available books to take home and read. Encourage students to read at least one book each week on their own.
- Set aside a few minutes each day for students to meet one-on-one with you to discuss their reading.
- Encourage students to record the titles of the books they are reading on the copy of *Transparency* 3.

OBJECTIVES

- Develop reading skills as the story is reread to them.
- Gain knowledge of the comprehension skill Main Idea and Details.
- Develop vocabulary by listening to and discussing a selection.
- Create and label a drawing of an animal.
- Identify and correctly use pronouns.

MATERIALS

Transparencies 3, 11, 25
Decodable Stories and Comprehension Skills, p. 87
Student Reader, pp. 44–47
Listening Library Audiocassette/CD
Language Arts, p. T25

TEACHER TIP

Have students listen to the selection recording on the *Listening Library Audiocassette/CD* for a proficient, fluent model of oral reading.

WRITING

Write the following words on the board: *wolf, coyote, fox, owl,* and *hawk.* Discuss with students that these are some of the enemies of opossums. Have students draw one of these animals and write the animal's name below their drawing.

Assessment

Formal

At the conclusion of the lesson, have students complete the assessment Unit 3: Opossums. The Lesson Assessments are found in the ***Assessment Guide.***

For all the items in this assessment, you should read both the question and answer choices out loud while students follow along silently. You may find it helpful to walk around the room while students are completing the assessment to provide them with any help they need to understand the questions.

Students should have the lesson selection in front of them when they answer the questions. Ask students to explain how they will answer the questions. Ask them to show you the portions of the selection that will help them find the answers.

Informal

Review pronouns with the students. Give them sample sentences such as *My sisters like to ski* and ask volunteers to name the pronoun that should take the place of *my sisters.*

Ending the Lesson

Have volunteers summarize the selection "Opossums." Ask students what new information they learned from the selection and what they already knew. Ask students if anyone knows any additional facts about opossums or have them do research using the library or the Internet to find out additional information about opossums.

OBJECTIVES

- Complete lesson assessment.
- Review pronouns.
- Summarize a selection.
- Extend the information in a selection.

MATERIALS

Assessment Guide
Student Reader, pp. 44–47

SELECTION B • **A Tricky Spider**

Support Materials

LESSON 6
- Sound/Spelling Card 41
- Decodable Stories and Comprehension Skills, p. 27
- Home Connection, p. 33
- High-Frequency Word Cards
- Sound/Spelling Card Stories Audiocassette/CD

LESSON 7
- Student Reader, pp. 48–51
- Language Arts, p. T28

LESSON 8
- Sound/Spelling Card 41
- Decodable Stories and Comprehension Skills, p. 28
- High-Frequency Word Cards
- Sound/Spelling Card Stories Audiocassette/CD

LESSON 9
- Language Arts, p. T27
- Transparencies 3, 26, 27
- Decodable Stories and Comprehension Skills, p. 88
- Student Reader, pp. 48–51
- Listening Library Audiocassette/CD

LESSON 10
- Assessment Guide
- Student Reader, pp. 48–51

HOME CONNECTIONS

Distribute *Home Connection* page 33, which describes this week's classwork and suggests activities for families to do at home. This letter is available in English and Spanish.

Teacher Focus	Student Participation
• Conduct Listening Game. • Conduct Word Play. • Introduce Sight Words and Set 1 blending words and sentences. • Conduct Oral Language activity. • Dictate word lines. • Assist students with decodable text. • Assign writing activity.	• Take part in Listening Game. • Take part in Word Play. • Read Sight Words. • Blend words and sentences. • Create sentences. • Write dictated words and sentences. • Read a decodable story. • Complete writing activity.
• Activate Prior Knowledge and provide background information. • Introduce and discuss selection vocabulary. • Preview selection. • Review Comprehension Strategies—Monitoring and Clarifying and Monitoring and Adjusting Reading Speed. • Read the selection to students. • Assign writing activity. • Introduce vocabulary skill.	• Contribute to class discussion. • Read and discuss vocabulary words. Complete selection vocabulary activity. • Browse the selection. • Follow along as the selection is read. • Complete writing activity. • Complete vocabulary skill activity.
• Conduct Restoring Final Consonants game. • Conduct Word Play. • Introduce Set 2 blending words and sentences. • Conduct Oral Language activity. • Dictate word lines. • Assist students with decodable text. • Assign writing activity.	• Participate in Restoring Final Consonants game. • Take part in Word Play. • Blend words and sentences. • Create sentences. • Write dictated words and sentences. • Read a decodable story. • Complete writing activity.
• Review Comprehension Skill—Cause and Effect. • Reread and discuss the selection with students. • Discuss Independent Reading. • Assign writing activity. • Introduce grammar skill.	• Follow along as the selection is read again. • Discuss the selection. • Select a book to take home and read. • Complete writing activity. • Complete grammar skill activity.
• Administer weekly assessments. • Assess students' progress.	• Complete lesson assessment.

SELECTION B • **A Tricky Spider**

Phonemic Awareness

The basic purpose of providing structured practice in phonemic awareness is to help students hear and understand the sounds from which words are made. Before students can be expected to understand the sound/symbol correspondence that forms the base of written English, they need to have a strong working knowledge of the sound relationships that make up the spoken language. This understanding of spoken language lays the foundation for the transition to written language. Phonemic awareness activities provide students with easy practice in discriminating the sounds that make up words. Once students begin reading and writing, this experience with manipulating sounds will help them use what they know about sounds and letters to sound out and spell unfamiliar words.

The two main formats for teaching phonemic awareness are oral blending and segmentation. These are supported by occasional discrimination activities and general word play. From these playful activities, students derive serious knowledge about language.

Oral Blending

Oral blending prepares students for phonics instruction by developing an awareness of the separate sounds that make up speech. Because these activities involve simply listening to and reproducing sounds, oral blending need not be restricted to the sounds students have been taught in phonics. The oral blending activities should be playful and informal and should move quickly.

OBJECTIVES

- Identify and blend initial consonant sounds in words.
- Blend and break apart sounds in words.
- Read sight words.
- Participate in Word Play activity.
- Develop fluency by reading aloud.
- Apply decoding skills by reading *Unit 3, Decodable Story 3.*
- Develop writing skills by writing words and identifying sound/spellings.

MATERIALS

Sound/Spelling Card:
41—Goo
Decodable Stories and Comprehension Skills, p. 27
Home Connection, p. 33
High-Frequency Word Cards
Sound/Spelling Card Stories Audiocassette/CD

Listening Game: Initial Consonant Sounds

Have students continue to replace the initial consonant sounds in words to make new words.

Continue erasing and changing the initial letter, using any consonant. Pronounce the sound of the new letter and ask students to identify the new word. Use words such as:

gap	eat	line
soon	sun	make
had	mean	rode

TEACHER TIP

Wait Time Allow ample time for students to respond.

Unit 3 • LESSON

6

Word Study

In this section of the lesson, students work on phonics, fluency, blending, and spelling. Increasing students' ability to work smoothly with printed words is one of the primary goals of the *Kaleidoscope* program.

Word Play

Have students work in teams of three or four. On the board, write the spelling *oo* and have the students say the /oo/ sound several times. Give the teams about five minutes to write as many words as they can that contain this spelling. Have each team read its list as you write the words on the board. Award a point for each correct word. The team with the most points wins.

TEACHER TIP

Sight Words Use the *High-Frequency Word Cards* to assess and review students' knowledge of sight words.

Sight Words

This week's sight words:

| learn | move | other |

Use the following procedure for teaching sight words:

- Write this week's sight words on the board.
- Read the words to students, and then have them read the words.
- Pronounce any words with which students have difficulty.
- Have students use each sight word in a sentence.

Phonics—Blending: Set 1

/ōō/ spelled *oo, u, u_e*

This section of the phonics lesson provides practice in building sounds and spellings into words.

- Point out the new *Sound/Spelling Card.* Ask students what they know about it.
- Quickly go over any of the previously introduced *Sound/Spelling Cards* that you think the students need to review.

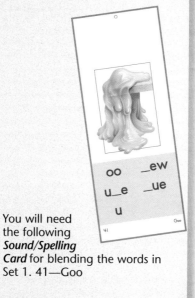

oo   _ew
u_e   _ue
u

41   Goo

You will need the following *Sound/Spelling Card* for blending the words in Set 1. 41—Goo

Blending Exercise

- The words in the lines provide practice with the Set 1 sound/spellings. Write the following words and sentences on the board.
- Have students blend the words and sentences using the whole-word procedure described in Unit 1 on page 12F.

Line 1:	chute	flu	tune	shoot
Line 2:	noon	trooper	broom	ruler
Line 3:	tube	ruby	truth	soon
Sentence 1:	We want to <u>learn</u> to play the tune on the flute.			
Sentence 2:	Did he <u>move</u> the <u>other</u> bamboo tree by the pool?			

About the Words and Sentences

- For Line 1, ask students to find the pair of words that are homophones *(chute, shoot)*. Have them use each word in a sentence.
- For Line 3, have students find antonyms for the words *later* and *lie*. *(soon, truth)*
- Have students find the words on the lines that contain more than one syllable *(trooper, ruler, ruby)*.
- Before reading a sentence, point to and read the underlined sight words. Have students reread the sentences to encourage fluency and comprehension.
- For the sentences, have students identify the pronouns. *(we, he)*

Oral Language

Have students take turns coming to the board, touching a word, and using it in a sentence. Encourage them to extend their sentences by asking *when, where, how,* and *why* questions.

WRITING

Have students write the words on Line 1 and circle the sound/spelling for /o͞o/ in each word.

SELECTION B • **A Tricky Spider**

Dictation

Dictation gives students an opportunity to spell words by using the sound/spellings that they have learned. For this dictation exercise, have students use writing paper. Dictate the words and sentence for them to write. Use the following procedure to have students practice whole-word and sentence dictation:

- Say each word in the word lines. Use the word in a sentence, then say the word again. Have students say the word.

- Tell students to think about how to segment the word into sounds. Then have them write the spelling for each sound. Encourage them to check the **Sound/Spelling Cards.**

- After each word line, write (or have a student write) the words on the board. Have students proofread their words. Tell them to circle any incorrect words and to correct them.

- Next, dictate the sentence. Dictate one word at a time, following the sounds-in-sequence or whole-word dictation procedure, depending on your students. Remind students to start the sentence with a capital letter and to use correct end punctuation.

- Write (or have a student write) the sentence on the board. Have students proofread their work and correct any incorrect words.

Line 1:	rule truth June
Line 2:	super mood duty
Sentence:	Is it too cool to go to the pool?

Building Fluency

Decodable Story: Unit 3, Story 3

● This story reviews the sound/spellings /oo̅/ spelled *oo, u, u_e.*
● Have students silently read *Decodable Stories and Comprehension Skills* page 27.
● Call on volunteers to read each paragraph aloud.
● For those students who need help, divide sentences according to natural phrases. Mark these phrases with diagonal slash marks on their worksheets.
● After students have read the story aloud, ask them questions and have them point to and read the answers in the story.
● Have students reread the story aloud with a partner. Rereading builds automaticity and fluency.
● Over the next few days, listen to each student reread the story.

Sound/Spelling Card Stories
Review today's sounds by using the *Sound/Spelling Card Stories.* Listening to the stories will help students understand how they can use the pictures on the *Sound/Spelling Cards* to remember the sounds associated with them. The stories are provided in the appendix and are also available on the *Sound/Spelling Card Stories Audiocassette/CD.*

 QUICK CHECK

As a quick review of today's sound/spellings, say some sentences, and ask students to suggest words to fill the blanks. Sentences you might read aloud include:

Use this _____ to sweep the floor. *(broom)*
Who can play a _____ on the tuba? *(tune)*
I like watching the monkeys at the _____. *(zoo)*

Unit 3 • LESSON

7

OBJECTIVES

- Discuss vocabulary words and their meanings.
- Develop reading skills as the story is read to them.
- Gain knowledge of the comprehension strategies Monitoring and Adjusting Reading Speed and Monitoring and Clarifying.
- Build vocabulary by learning about prefixes.
- Develop writing skills by writing a prediction.

MATERIALS

Student Reader, pp. 48–51
Language Arts, p. T28

Before Reading

Build Background

Activate Prior Knowledge

- Remind students that this unit is about animals and animal camouflage. Review with them what they know about animal camouflage.
- Ask students to talk about spiders. What kind of spiders have they seen? How many legs do spiders have? What do they eat? How do they catch their food?
- Invite them to talk about any stories or articles they may have read about animals that play "tricks."

Background Information

Use the following information to help students understand the selection you are about to read:

- Tell students that this selection is nonfiction. Remind them that nonfiction is different from fiction, or made-up stories, because it is true. Explain that nonfiction is written to inform, explain, describe, and sometimes to persuade.
- Help students understand that a *trap door* is a kind of door that is difficult to see. Trap doors can hide dangers of all kinds for people and animals who do not see them.

Selection Vocabulary

Write the following vocabulary words on the board. Before reading the selection, introduce and discuss the following words and their meanings.

careless: not paying enough attention

silk: something that looks like the soft, shiny fiber spun by silkworms

useful: helpful

Then have students read the words, stopping to blend any words that they have trouble reading. Demonstrate how to decode multisyllabic words by breaking the words into syllables and blending the syllables. Then have students try. If they still have trouble, refer them to the **Sound/Spelling Cards.** If the word is not decodable, give students the pronunciation.

As students study vocabulary, they will use a variety of skills to determine the meaning of a word. These skills include context clues, word structure, and apposition. In this lesson, students will be learning about apposition. Write the following example on the board: *A cookbook provides useful, or helpful, tips on cooking.*

Explain to students that they are going to use apposition to help them decipher the meaning of the word *useful*. Tell students that when they use apposition, they are looking for a word or group of words in the sentence that help define the word in question. Guide students until they can give a reasonable definition of the word.

Vocabulary Activity: Using the vocabulary words, create riddles for students to solve. You can use the following examples: *I rhyme with milk. I can be used to make blouses and scarves. What am I? (silk) My friend crossed the street without looking for cars. What was she? (careless)*

Preview and Prepare

Before you read, use modeling and prompts such as:

● *This is another nonfiction selection. This one describes something.*

● *As you browse, look for key words that will help you understand what the selection is describing.*

During Reading

Read Aloud

For this lesson, read the entire selection aloud. As you read, stop at the points that are marked with numbers in magenta circles on the reduced student pages, and model for them how to use the indicated strategy. Encourage students to stop at any point in their reading if they don't understand something or want to talk about the meaning of a passage or word.

Comprehension Strategies

During the reading of "A Tricky Spider" on pages 48–51, you will model the following reading comprehension strategies:

Monitoring and Adjusting Reading Speed: If they notice that they are having trouble understanding what they read, good readers slow down. They also may reread passages.

Monitoring and Clarifying: Good readers pay attention to how well they understand what they are reading. They stop to clarify the meanings of new words and to think about unfamiliar or difficult passages.

WRITING

After browsing the selection, have students write a word or phrase that describes what they think the selection will be about.

First Read

Text Comprehension *strategies*

As you read the selection, use modeling and prompts such as:

❶ Monitoring and Adjusting Reading Speed

When they don't understand what they're reading, good readers go back and reread part of a selection. They read slower until they understand what is happening. I need to stop and reread to make sure that I have a clear idea of what has happened so far. A bug was walking along, then disappeared. It was captured by a spider that was hiding. The spider is called a trap-door spider. I can picture it hiding under the door, then jumping out when the bug walked by. I understand, so I can read on.

❷ Monitoring and Clarifying

The word silk is confusing. Maybe if I reread this sentence, I can figure out what it means. OK, I understand now. Silk must be another name for the material that spiders make.

A Tricky Spider

by Pam Bliss

A tiny bug walks along the ground in the woods. Then the bug is gone! What happened?

The bug walked by the home of a trapdoor spider. The bug was <u>careless</u> and did not see the spider. The spider ❶ was hiding in its home.

48

VOCABULARY

Remind students that a *prefix* is a word part that comes at the beginning of a base word, and that adding a prefix to a word changes the meaning of the word. Explain that the prefix *dis-* usually means "opposite of" or "not." For a lesson on the prefix *dis-*, use *Language Arts* page T28.

A trapdoor spider digs a hole in the ground to live in. It lines the hole with <u>silk</u> it spins from its body. Next, it covers 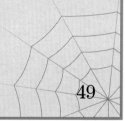 the hole with a lid. The lid looks like a roof but opens just like a door. It is very <u>useful</u>.

49

Text Comprehension

Cause and Effect

Remind students that writers use cause-and-effect relationships in their writing to help readers understand what makes things happen the way they do.

- Ask them to identify the causes that led to these effects:

    the bug being caught by the spider
    (*The spider was hiding in its home.*)

    the spider's trap door being useful
    (*The trap door looks like a roof but opens like a door.*)

- Use **Transparency** 26 to record their responses.

Cause and Effect For students who are confused about cause-and-effect relationships, suggest some obvious examples. For example, place a paper on a desk so half of it hangs off the edge. Hit the suspended end and watch the paper fall. Ask, "What happened to the paper?" (*effect*) Then ask, "Why did the paper fall from the desk?" (*cause*)

GRAMMAR

Tell students that *possessive pronouns* show who or what owns or has something. Explain that unlike possessive nouns, possessive pronouns have special spellings, and they do not use apostrophes. For a lesson on possessive pronouns, use *Language Arts* page T27.

7

First
Read

Text Comprehension *Strategies*

③ Monitoring and Adjusting Reading Speed

These pages have a lot of information on them, and I'm not sure I understand it all. I must have read too fast. I'm going to reread the pages slower to see if I can follow what is happening. I know the spider caught the bug. But how did it do that? Let's see, it waited in its hole, it felt the bug come by, it opened the trap-door lid, grabbed the bug, and dragged it back into the hole. But now I also see that the spider uses the trap door for something else—it closes it to keep other animals out! Trap-door spiders are very tricky!

HOMEWORK
TIP

Encourage students to use computers at home or on their own time to find out more about trap-door spiders. Invite them to share their new information with the class.

The spider waits in its hole for a bug to come along. Bugs are food for the spider. When a bug comes by, the spider opens the lid. It grabs the bug and drags it back into the hole. The spider also uses the hole to keep safe. The spider can hold the lid shut if an animal tries to get in.

50

Would you like to see a trapdoor spider?
That may be hard. You can look and look.
But unless you are a bug walking by, you
may never get to see one. **3**

51

Second Read

Text Comprehension

Cause and Effect

- Ask students to find causes for these effects:

 The spider opens the trap door.
 (A bug comes along.)

 The spider keeps safe from other animals.
 (The spider holds the trap door shut.)

- For additional practice with Cause and Effect,
have students complete **Decodable Stories and
Comprehension Skills** page 88.

Discussing the Selection

After you have read the selection, discuss it with
students. Use prompts such as:

- *What did you learn about trap-door spiders?*
- *Why is the selection title "A Tricky Spider" a good
one?*
- *Did anything surprise you in the selection? If so,
what was it and why was it a surprise?*
- *What did you learn about animal camouflage from
this selection?*

QUICK CHECK

Reread small sections of the story and ask
students to identify the causes for various
effects.

OBJECTIVES

- Identify and restore final consonant sounds in words.
- Blend and break apart sounds in words.
- Participate in Word Play activity.
- Develop fluency by reading aloud.
- Apply decoding skills by reading *Unit 3, Decodable Story 4.*
- Develop writing skills by writing a sentence.

MATERIALS

Sound/Spelling Card:
41—Goo
Decodable Stories and Comprehension Skills, p. 28
High-Frequency Word Cards
Sound/Spelling Card Stories Audiocassette/CD

SELECTION B • **A Tricky Spider**

Segmentation: Restoring Final Consonants

● Continue the game of Restoring Final Consonants. Remind students that you will say a word, and then you will repeat the word but leave off the ending sound. Then you will ask them to repeat the word and say what sound was left off. Use the following example:

Teacher:	much . . . mu
Teacher:	What's the word? What sound did I leave off?
Students:	much, /ch/

● Continue with the following words:

teen	greet	broom
train	steam	tweak
braid	bean	trace
street	take	bruise
beach	greed	tweet

Word Study

Word Play

Play the game Go Fish. On the backs of several "fish," write the spellings for /oo/ that students have learned—*oo, u, u_e* (use each spelling more than once). One by one, give students the fishing pole and tell them to "go fish." When a student catches a fish, have him or her read the spelling, say the sound, and then say and write on the board a word that contains the sound/spelling.

Phonics—Blending: Set 2

> /oo/ spelled *_ew, _ue*

Point out and discuss the **Sound/Spelling Card.** Ask students what they know about it. Focus attention on the target spellings and ask students what the blank means. *(The spelling comes at the end of a syllable or word.)*

Blending Exercise

● Write the following words and sentences on the board.
● Have students blend the words and sentences using the whole-word procedure described in Unit 1 on page 12F.

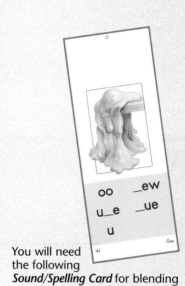

You will need the following **Sound/Spelling Card** for blending the words in Set 2. 41—Goo

Line 1:	blue	blew	flew	flu
Line 2:	dew	due	glue	stew
Sentence 1:	The crew and I will <u>move</u> the new hoop.			
Sentence 2:	Drew gave them the <u>other</u> team's clues.			

● Before reading a sentence, point to and read the underlined sight words.
● Discuss with students that each sentence begins with a capital letter and ends with a punctuation mark.
● Have students reread the sentences to encourage fluency and comprehension.

WRITING

Have students choose a word on the word lines and write a sentence using the word. Remind students to start their sentence with a capital letter and to use correct end punctuation. Ask students to share their sentences with the class.

SELECTION B • **A Tricky Spider**

About the Words and Sentences

- Have students identify the sound/spelling for /o͞o/ in each word.
- Have students find pairs of words on the lines that are homophones. *(blue, blew; flew, flu; dew, due)*
- For the sentences, have students identify the pronouns. *(I, them)*
- For Sentence 2, have students identify the possessive noun. *(team's)*

Oral Language

Have students take turns choosing a word, reading it, using it in a sentence, and calling on a classmate to extend the sentence.

Dictation

For the dictation exercise, have students use writing paper. Dictate the words and sentence for them to write. Use the following procedure:

- Say the first word in each word line. Use the word in a sentence, then say the word again. Have students say the word.
- Tell students to think about how to segment the word into sounds. Then have them write the spelling for each sound.
- After each word line, write (or have a student write) the words on the board. Have students proofread their words. Tell them to circle any incorrect words and to correct them.
- Next dictate the sentence. Dictate one word at a time, following the sounds-in-sequence or whole-word dictation procedure, depending on your students. Remind students to start the sentence with a capital letter and to use correct end punctuation.
- Write (or have a student write) the sentence on the board. Have students proofread their work and correct any incorrect words.

Line 1:	due	drew	blue
Line 2:	threw	grew	true
Sentence:	Stewart knew the clue.		

Building Fluency

Decodable Story: Unit 3, Story 4

- This story reviews the sound/spellings /o͞o/ spelled _ew, _ue._
- Have students silently read **Decodable Stories and Comprehension Skills** page 28.
- Call on volunteers to read each paragraph aloud.
- For those students who need help, divide sentences according to natural phrases. Mark these phrases with diagonal slash marks on their worksheets.
- After students have read the story aloud, ask them questions and have them point to and read the answers in the story.
- Have students reread the story aloud with a partner.

HOMEWORK TIP

Tell students to look for words with the /o͞o/ sound and to make separate lists of words for each spelling that they have learned for that sound. Allow time for them to share their lists with the class.

9

SELECTION B • **A Tricky Spider**

OBJECTIVES

- Develop reading skills as the story is reread to them.
- Gain knowledge of the comprehension skill Cause and Effect.
- Develop vocabulary by listening to and discussing a selection.
- Develop writing skills by writing a description.
- Identify and correctly use possessive pronouns.

MATERIALS

Transparencies 3, 26, 27
Decodable Stories and Comprehension Skills, p. 88
Student Reader, pp. 48–51
Listening Library Audiocassette/CD
Language Arts, p. T27

Rereading the Selection

Comprehension Skills

Revisiting or rereading a selection allows students to learn and apply skills that give them a more complete understanding of a selection. For today's lesson, reread the selection to students. During the second reading, students will apply the following comprehension skill:

Cause and Effect: Good readers look for relationships between events in what they read. This helps them to make accurate predictions about what will happen.

After Reading

Independent Reading

- Have students choose books from the *Classroom Library* or other available books to take home and read. Encourage students to read at least one book a week on their own.
- Set aside time for students to talk in class about their independent reading.
- Encourage students to use the comprehension strategies and skills they are learning as they read independently.
- Encourage students to record the titles of the books they are reading on the copy of *Transparency* 3.

Have students listen to the selection recording on the *Listening Library Audiocassette/CD* for a proficient, fluent model of oral reading.

WRITING

Have students think about the selection and what they learned about trapdoor spiders. Ask them to write a brief description of trapdoor spiders.

SELECTION B • **A Tricky Spider**

Assessment

Formal

At the conclusion of the lesson, have students complete the assessment Unit 3: A Tricky Spider. The Lesson Assessments are found in the *Assessment Guide.*

For all the items in this assessment, you should read both the question and answer choices out loud while students follow along silently. You may find it helpful to walk around the room while students are completing the assessment to provide them with any help they need to understand the questions.

After completing the lesson assessment, discuss the answers with students. Help them correct any mistakes and revise the extended response questions. Remain positive while correcting students' mistakes in order to reduce the anxiety they may feel about assessment.

Informal

Review possessive pronouns with students. Write a possessive pronoun on the board and have a volunteer think of a sentence using the possessive pronoun. Write the sentence on the board and then have students name a noun or nouns to which the pronoun might correspond.

Ending the Lesson

Have volunteers clarify information in the selection by responding to questions you raise. For example, you might ask, "Does the spider dig a hole or use the hole of another animal?" Students can refer to the selection or a reference source to answer the question, but they should try to do so in their own words.

OBJECTIVES

- Complete lesson assessment.
- Revise incorrect answers.
- Review possessive pronouns.
- Clarify information in a story.

MATERIALS

Assessment Guide
Student Reader, pp. 48–51

SELECTION C • **Colors That Hide**

Support Materials

LESSON 11
- Sound/Spelling Card 39
- Decodable Stories and Comprehension Skills, p. 29
- Home Connection, p. 35
- High-Frequency Word Cards
- Sound/Spelling Card Stories Audiocassette/CD

LESSON 12
- Student Reader, pp. 52–57
- Language Arts, p. T30
- Transparency 28

LESSON 13
- Sound/Spelling Cards
- Decodable Stories and Comprehension Skills, p. 30
- High-Frequency Word Cards
- Sound/Spelling Card Stories Audiocassette/CD

LESSON 14
- Student Reader, pp. 52–57
- Transparencies 3, 29
- Decodable Stories and Comprehension Skills, p. 89
- Language Arts, p. T29
- Listening Library Audiocassette/CD

LESSON 15
- Assessment Guide
- Student Reader, pp. 52–57

HOME CONNECTIONS

Distribute *Home Connection* page 35, which describes this week's classwork and suggests activities for families to do at home. This letter is available in English and Spanish.

Teacher Focus	Student Participation
<ul><li>Conduct Listening Game.</li><li>Conduct Word Play.</li><li>Introduce Sight Words and Set 1 blending words and sentences.</li><li>Provide riddle clues.</li><li>Dictate word lines.</li><li>Assist students with decodable text.</li><li>Assign writing activity.</li></ul>	<ul><li>Take part in Listening Game.</li><li>Take part in Word Play.</li><li>Read Sight Words.</li><li>Blend words and sentences.</li><li>Solve riddles.</li><li>Write dictated words and sentences.</li><li>Read a decodable story.</li><li>Complete writing activity.</li></ul>
<ul><li>Activate Prior Knowledge and provide background information.</li><li>Introduce and discuss selection vocabulary.</li><li>Preview selection.</li><li>Review Comprehension Strategies—Visualizing and Monitoring and Clarifying.</li><li>Read the selection to students.</li><li>Assign writing activity.</li><li>Introduce vocabulary skill.</li></ul>	<ul><li>Contribute to class discussion.</li><li>Read and discuss vocabulary words. Complete selection vocabulary activity.</li><li>Browse the selection.</li><li>Follow along as the selection is read.</li><li>Complete writing activity.</li><li>Complete vocabulary skill activity.</li></ul>
<ul><li>Conduct Restoring Final Consonants game.</li><li>Conduct Word Play.</li><li>Introduce Set 2 blending words and sentences.</li><li>Conduct Oral Language activity.</li><li>Dictate word lines.</li><li>Assist students with decodable text.</li><li>Assign writing activity.</li></ul>	<ul><li>Participate in Restoring Final Consonants game.</li><li>Take part in Word Play.</li><li>Blend words and sentences.</li><li>Create sentences.</li><li>Write dictated words and sentences.</li><li>Read a decodable story.</li><li>Complete writing activity.</li></ul>
<ul><li>Introduce Comprehension Skill—Classifying and Categorizing.</li><li>Reread and discuss the selection with students.</li><li>Discuss Independent Reading.</li><li>Assign writing activity.</li><li>Introduce grammar skill.</li></ul>	<ul><li>Follow along as selection is read again.</li><li>Discuss the selection.</li><li>Select a book to take home and read.</li><li>Complete writing activity.</li><li>Complete grammar skill activity.</li></ul>
<ul><li>Administer weekly assessments.</li><li>Assess students' progress.</li></ul>	<ul><li>Complete lesson assessment.</li></ul>

OBJECTIVES

- Identify and blend one-syllable words.
- Blend and break apart sounds in words.
- Read sight words.
- Participate in Word Play activity.
- Develop fluency by reading aloud.
- Apply decoding skills by reading *Unit 3, Decodable Story 5.*
- Develop writing skills by writing rhyming words.

MATERIALS

Sound/Spelling Card:
39—Cow
Decodable Stories and Comprehension Skills, p. 29
Home Connection, p. 35
High-Frequency Word Cards
Sound/Spelling Card Stories Audiocassette/CD

SELECTION C • **Colors That Hide**

Phonemic Awareness

The basic purpose of providing structured practice in phonemic awareness is to help students hear and understand the sounds from which words are made. Before students can be expected to understand the sound/symbol correspondence that forms the base of written English, they need to have a strong working knowledge of the sound relationships that make up the spoken language. This understanding of spoken language lays the foundation for the transition to written language. Phonemic awareness activities provide students with easy practice in discriminating the sounds that make up words. Once students begin reading and writing, this experience with manipulating sounds will help them use what they know about sounds and letters to sound out and spell unfamiliar words.

The two main formats for teaching phonemic awareness are oral blending and segmentation. These are supported by occasional discrimination activities and general word play. From these playful activities, students derive serious knowledge about language.

Oral Blending

Oral blending prepares students for phonics instruction by developing an awareness of the separate sounds that make up speech. Because these activities involve simply listening to and reproducing sounds, oral blending need not be restricted to the sounds students have been taught in phonics. The oral blending activities should be playful and informal and should move quickly.

Listening Game: One-Syllable Words

The final step in oral blending is being able to blend individual phonemes into words. Success with this activity will help students master what is for many the most difficult step in learning to read. To ease the task, the phonemes to be blended in these activities are presented in story context, which aids students in identifying the word to be blended. In addition, the first words chosen for these activities are made of sounds that are easy for students to blend.

Explain to students that you are going to tell them a story and you need their help. Use the following story and questions:

Old brown Frog sat in the /s/ /u/ /n/.

Where did Frog sit? *(sun)*

His pal Toad hid under a /r/ /o/ /k/.

Under what did Toad hide? *(rock)*

Toad told Frog that the sun would turn him into /m/ /u/ /sh/.

What would Frog turn into? *(mush)*

Frog told Toad that he looked like a gopher's next /s/ /n/ /a/ /k/.

What did Toad look like? *(snack)*

Suddenly it began to /r/ /ā/ /n/.

What did it start to do? *(rain)*

Frog and Toad played together in the /m/ /u/ /d/.

In what did they play? *(mud)*

Oral Blending Take students through a quick review of oral blending in which they identify initial consonant sounds in words.

11

SELECTION C • **Colors That Hide**

Word Study

In this section of the lesson, students work on phonics, fluency, blending, and spelling. Increasing students' ability to work smoothly with printed words is one of the primary goals of the *Kaleidoscope* program.

Word Play

Play the game Go Fish again. On the backs of several "fish," write the additional spellings for /o͞o/ that students have learned and add them to fish made in Lesson 8 (use each spelling more than once). One by one, give students the fishing pole and tell them to "go fish." When a student catches a fish, have him or her read the spelling, say the sound, and then say and write on the board a word that contains the sound/spelling.

Sight Words

This week's sight words:

| measure | only | people |

Use the following procedure for teaching sight words:
- Write this week's sight words on the board.
- Read the words to students, and then have them read the words.
- Pronounce any words with which students have difficulty.
- Have students use each sight word in a sentence.

Phonics—Blending: Set 1

> /ow/ spelled *ou_* , *ow*

This section of the phonics lesson provides practice in building sounds and spellings into words.
- Point out the new **Sound/Spelling Card.** Ask students what they know about it.
- Discuss any other **Sound/Spelling Cards** that you think students need to review.

ow

ou_

You will need the following **Sound/Spelling Card** for blending the words in Set 1. 39—Cow

Building Fluency

Decodable Story: Unit 3, Story 5

- This story reviews the sound/spellings /ow/ spelled *ou_, ow.*
- Have students silently read **Decodable Stories and Comprehension Skills** page 29.
- Call on volunteers to read each paragraph aloud.
- For those students who need help, divide sentences according to natural phrases. Mark these phrases with diagonal slash marks on their worksheets.
- After students have read the story aloud, ask them questions and have them point to and read the answers in the story.
- Have students reread the story aloud with a partner. Rereading builds automaticity and fluency.
- Over the next few days, listen to each student reread the story.

Develop Fluency Model fluent reading frequently for students, showing them how pausing in the right places and adding expression can make a passage easier to understand.

QUICK CHECK

As a quick review of today's sound/spellings, say some sentences, and ask students to suggest words to fill the blanks. Sentences you might read aloud include:

The _____ sat on the tree branch. *(owl)*
The farmer had to _____ his field. *(plow)*
I bought a _____ at the department store. *(blouse)*

SELECTION C • **Colors That Hide**

Before Reading

Build Background

Activate Prior Knowledge

- Remind students that this unit is about animals and animal camouflage. Review with them what they have learned so far.
- If possible, bring to class a piece of camouflage clothing—a shirt, hat, jacket, and so on. If such clothing is not available, show students pictures of military personnel wearing camouflage. Explain that members of the military often wear clothing that will help them blend in with rocks, trees, or grass and hide them from enemies.

Background Information

Use the following information to help students understand the selection you are about to read:

- Explain to students that this selection is nonfiction. Remind them that nonfiction is different from fiction, or made-up stories, because it is true.
- Explain that this selection was written to inform and explain.

Selection Vocabulary

Write the following vocabulary words on the board. Before reading the selection, introduce and discuss the following words and their meanings.

glowed: shone

vanish: to go out of sight

disappear: to pass from sight

surroundings: environment

motionless: not moving

Then have students read the words, stopping to blend any words that they have trouble reading. Demonstrate how to decode multisyllabic words by breaking the words into syllables and blending the syllables. Then have students try. If they still have trouble, refer them to the **Sound/Spelling Cards.** If the word is not decodable, give students the pronunciation.

As students study vocabulary, they will use a variety of skills to determine the meaning of a word. These skills include context clues, word structure, and apposition. In this lesson, students will be learning about context clues. Write the following example on the board: *We watched the sun disappear behind the clouds.*

Explain to students that they are going to use context clues, or other words in the sentence, to help them decipher the meaning of the word *disappear*. Guide students until they can give a reasonable definition of the word.

Vocabulary Activity: Write the word *glowed* on the board and have students give examples of objects that glow (such as *the sun, a light, a candle*). Write their suggestions on the board and discuss the list as a class.

Preview and Prepare

Before you read, use modeling and prompts such as:

● *Let's browse this selection before we read it. Since it's nonfiction, we can look at the entire selection without spoiling any surprise.*

● *As you browse, look for key words that will help you organize and understand the information in the selection.*

WRITING

Remind students that the title of this selection is "Colors That Hide." Have students write three colors that they noticed as they were browsing the selection.

During Reading

Read Aloud

For this lesson, read the entire selection aloud. As you read, stop at the points that are marked with numbers in magenta circles on the reduced student pages, and model for them how to use the indicated strategy. Encourage students to stop at any point in their reading if they don't understand something or want to talk about the meaning of a passage or word.

Comprehension Strategies

During the reading of "Colors That Hide" on pages 52–57, you will model the following reading comprehension strategies:

Monitoring and Clarifying: Good readers pay attention to how well they understand what they read. They stop to clarify the meanings of new words and to think about unfamiliar or difficult passages.

Visualizing: Readers often make pictures in their minds of the characters, events, and settings in a selection to help them better understand what they're reading.

First Read

Text Comprehension *Strategies*

As you read the selection, use modeling and prompts such as:

❶ Visualizing

Readers make mental pictures, or visualize, as they read to help them better understand a story. I've made a picture here. I see a blazing red setting sun lighting up a large field of grass. I can see a zebra standing there, with its ears twitching, listening for lions. What do you visualize?

❷ Monitoring and Clarifying

Readers stop to clarify, or figure out, words and passages that confuse them. I'm not sure how a zebra can vanish. I'll reread a few sentences to see if I can figure it out. OK, I understand now. The zebra ran into the grass, and its stripes blended with the tall grass blades, so the zebra was hard to see. Now I understand how a zebra can vanish.

HOMEWORK TIP

Encourage students to use computers at home or on their own time to find out more about animals who change colors to camouflage themselves. Invite them to share their new information with the class.

Colors That Hide

by Joshua Young

The setting sun glowed red. Soon night would fall over the African grasslands. A zebra stood still. It listened. This was a dangerous time of day. This was the time ❶ when lions liked to hunt.

52

The zebra knew what to do. It ran into the tall grass. Then it stopped. It stood still. The zebra seemed to <u>vanish</u>. And for **2** a while it was safe. The grass and its lack of movement made it <u>disappear</u>.

Why was it safe there? Because of its stripes. They looked a lot like the tall grass and shadows. They made the zebra hard to see.

53

Second Read

Text Comprehension

Classifying and Categorizing

Explain to students that by classifying pieces of information and putting the pieces into categories, they can get a better understanding of a selection.

Explain that many things can be classified and put into categories. We can classify food as vegetables, fruits, and meats. Then put the different foods into categories such as things to eat for breakfast, lunch, and dinner.

- Tell students that on these pages, the animals can be classified as "Animals Who Hunt" and "Animals Who Are Hunted." Ask them how they would categorize the zebra and the lion. Ask them to name other animals that fit into these categories.

- Use *Transparency* 29 to record their responses.

TEACHER TIP

Classifying and Categorizing If some students are not clear about the concept, give them a collection of objects such as buttons to classify and categorize. Help them see that the buttons can be classified by color or size and then placed into categories such as the number of holes in each or their purpose.

First Read

Text Comprehension *Strategies*

③ Monitoring and Clarifying

I haven't seen the expression protective coloring *before. I'll read on to see if I can find some information that will help me understand what the expression means. Yes, the next sentence gives a definition: "looks like its surroundings." Now I understand what that expression means.*

④ Visualizing

I can see the baby deer. Can you? They're brown with speckles of white. I'll bet when they're lying on the ground, they do look just like patches of sunlight.

⑤ Visualizing

Wow! I can see the alligator in the water, with just its back and eyes showing. Its bumpy skin makes it look just like a log floating in the water. I imagine that it fools a lot of frogs that way.

③   A zebra has "protective coloring." It looks like its surroundings. And that helps keep it safe. But the zebra isn't the only animal whose color protects it. There are many others.

Baby deer are not strong. They can't run from danger. But their color helps hide them. Their brown fur has patches of white. These look like patches of
④ sunlight on the ground.

54

VOCABULARY

Remind students that a *prefix* is a word part that comes at the beginning of a base word, and that adding a prefix to a word changes the meaning of the word. Explain that the prefix *pre-* usually means "before" and the prefix *un-* usually means "not." For a lesson on the prefixes *pre-* and *un-,* use *Language Arts* page T30.

Some rabbits grow white fur in winter. This makes them hard to see in the snow.

And then there's the alligator. When it lies <u>motionless</u>, what does it look like? A log. Why? The alligator's bumpy skin gives it a likeness to a log. **5**

55

Text Comprehension *skills*

Classifying and Categorizing

- Continue to classify the animals as "Animals Who Hunt" and "Animals Who Are Hunted." Ask students into which category they would place the baby deer. Ask them what animals might hunt the baby deer *(wildcats, coyotes, wolves)*.

- Ask students into which category they would place the rabbit and the alligator.

- Continue using *Transparency* 29 to record their responses.

GRAMMAR

Explain to students that pronouns must agree with the nouns that they replace. That means, if the noun is plural, the pronoun that replaces it has to be plural as well. If the noun is possessive, the pronoun must also be possessive. For a lesson on pronoun-antecedent agreement, use *Language Arts* page T29.

12

Text Comprehension Strategies

❻ Monitoring and Clarifying

Have you ever seen a real owl? What clues give you an idea of what an owl looks like?

Student Sample

I've never seen a real owl. But the selection says that owls have bright eyes and they shine like little moons. This helps me picture what owl eyes might look like at night.

> **Student Sample** The student sample is only one example of many possible student responses. Accept other responses that are reasonable and appropriate.

At night you can see a brown owl as it peeps from a hole in a tree. The owl's bright eyes give it away. They shine like ❻ little moons. But what if it keeps them almost closed? Then the owl is hidden. It seems to be part of the tree.

56

Can you name other creatures whose color hides them? What about white polar bears? What about striped tigers? What about little green frogs? What about snakes?

57

Text Comprehension

Classifying and Categorizing

● Ask students to continue to classify and categorize the animals on these pages according to "Animals Who Hunt" and "Animals Who Are Hunted." Ask students into which category they would place owls, polar bears, tigers, frogs, and snakes.

● Continue using **Transparency** 29 to record their responses.

● For additional practice with Classifying and Categorizing, have students complete **Decodable Stories and Comprehension Skills** page 89.

Discussing the Selection

After you have read the selection, discuss it with students. Use prompts such as:

● *What did you learn about different kinds of animal camouflage?*

● *Did anything surprise you in the selection? If so, what was it and why was it a surprise?*

● *How does this selection relate to the unit theme, Look Again?*

QUICK CHECK

Quickly review with students the other comprehension skills that they've used so far.

OBJECTIVES

- Identify and restore final consonant sounds in words.
- Blend and break apart sounds in words.
- Participate in Word Play activity.
- Review the sound/spellings introduced in this unit.
- Develop fluency by reading aloud.
- Apply decoding skills by reading **Unit 3, Decodable Story 6.**
- Develop writing skills by writing compound words.

MATERIALS

Sound/Spelling Cards
Decodable Stories and Comprehension Skills, p. 30
High-Frequency Word Cards
Sound/Spelling Card Stories Audiocassette/CD

Phonemic Awareness The phonemic awareness activities may contain sounds for spellings that have not yet been introduced. Remember, these activities are for practice with listening for sounds. They are not phonics lessons.

SELECTION C • **Colors That Hide**

Phonemic Awareness

Segmentation: Restoring Final Consonants

Continue the game of Restoring Final Consonants. Use the following example to remind students how the game is played.

Teacher:	seed . . . see
Teacher:	What's the word? What sound did I leave off?
Students:	seed, /d/

- Continue with the following words:

cloud	steam	sneer
train	teach	reach
lane	seem	brain
treat	beach	make

Word Study

Word Play

Have students work in teams of three or four. On the board, write the spellings *ow* and *ou_*. Give the teams five or so minutes to write as many words as they can that contain one of these spellings for /ow/. Have each team read its list as you write the words on the board. Award a point for each correct word. The team with the most points wins.

Phonics—Blending: Set 2

Point out and discuss any *Sound/Spelling Cards* that you particularly want students to review. Tell them that in this lesson, they will review the sound/spellings that they have learned so far in this unit.

Blending Exercise

● Write the following words and sentences on the board.

● Have students blend the words and sentences using the whole-word procedure described in Unit 1 on page 12F.

Line 1:	broom	round	glue	bookmark	action
Line 2:	choose	chews	session	flowerpot	cookie
Line 3:	lotion	due	sound	powder	lookout
Sentence 1:	They saw <u>only</u> three clouds in the blue sky.				
Sentence 2:	You must <u>measure</u> the correct amount of stew.				
Sentence 3:	How many <u>people</u> will be at our cookout?				

● Before reading a sentence, point to and read the underlined sight words.

● Discuss with students that each sentence begins with a capital letter and ends with a punctuation mark.

● Have students reread the sentences to encourage fluency and comprehension.

TEACHER TIP

Sound/Spelling Card Stories Review sounds by using the *Sound/Spelling Card Stories.* Listening to the stories will help students understand how they can use the pictures on the *Sound/Spelling Cards* to remember the sounds associated with them. The stories are provided in the appendix and are also available on the *Sound/Spelling Card Stories Audiocassette/CD.*

SELECTION C • **Colors That Hide**

WRITING

Have students identify and write the compound words on the lines *(bookmark, flowerpot, lookout)*. Then have them write the two smaller words that make up each compound word. Discuss the meanings of the compound words as a class.

About the Words and Sentences

- For the lines, have students identify the target sound/spelling in each word.
- For Line 2, have students find two words that are homophones *(choose, chews)*. Have them use each word in a sentence to show its meaning.
- Ask students to find words on the lines that have multiple meanings and to give at least two meanings of each word (for example, *round, glue, due, sound*).
- Have students identify the pronouns in each sentence. *(They, You, our)*

Oral Language

Have students take turns coming to the board, touching a word, and using it in a sentence. Encourage them to extend their sentences by asking *When? Where? How?* and *Why?* questions.

Dictation

For the dictation exercise, have students use writing paper. Dictate the words and sentence for them to write. Use the following procedure:

- Say the first word in each word line. Use the word in a sentence, then say the word again. Have students say the word.
- Tell students to think about how to segment the word into sounds. Then have them write the spelling for each sound.
- After each word line, write (or have a student write) the words on the board. Have students proofread their words. Tell them to circle any incorrect words and to correct them.
- Next dictate the sentence. Dictate one word at a time, following the sounds-in-sequence or whole-word dictation procedure, depending on your students. Remind students to start the sentence with a capital letter and to use correct end punctuation.
- Write (or have a student write) the sentence on the board. Have students proofread their work and correct any incorrect words.

Line 1:	clown good blue
Line 2:	flew soon count
Sentence:	Look at the brown cloud over the town.

Building Fluency

Decodable Story: Unit 3, Story 6

- This story reviews the sound/spellings introduced in this unit.
- Have students silently read *Decodable Stories and Comprehension Skills* page 30.
- Call on volunteers to read each paragraph aloud.
- For those students who need help, divide sentences according to natural phrases. Mark these phrases with diagonal slash marks on their worksheets.
- After students have read the story aloud, ask them questions and have them point to and read the answers in the story.
- Have students reread the story aloud with a partner.

HOMEWORK TIP

Ask students to think about the names of friends and family members. Ask them to make a list of the names and to circle the vowel sounds in each. Have them share their lists with the class.

SELECTION C • **Colors That Hide**

OBJECTIVES

- Develop reading skills as the story is reread to them.
- Gain knowledge of the comprehension skill Classifying and Categorizing.
- Develop vocabulary by listening to and discussing the selection.
- Create and label a drawing of an animal.
- Learn about pronoun-antecedent agreement.

MATERIALS

Transparencies 3, 29
Decodable Stories and Comprehension Skills, p. 89
Student Reader, pp. 52–57
Listening Library Audiocassette/CD
Language Arts, p. T29

Rereading the Selection

Comprehension Skills

Revisiting or rereading a selection allows students to learn and apply skills that give them a more complete understanding of a selection. For today's lesson, reread the selection to students. During the second reading, students will apply the following comprehension skill:

Classifying and Categorizing: Good readers find ways to put pieces of information together to help them better understand what they are reading.

After Reading

Independent Reading

- Have students choose books from the *Classroom Library* or other available books to take home and read. Encourage students to read at least one book a week on their own.
- Set aside time for students to talk in class about the independent reading that they are doing.
- Encourage students to use the comprehension strategies and skills they are learning as they read independently.
- Encourage students to record the titles of the books they are reading on the copy of *Transparency* 3.

TEACHER TIP

Have students listen to the selection recording on the *Listening Library Audiocassette/CD* for a proficient, fluent model of oral reading.

WRITING

Have students draw one of the animals described in the selection. Tell them to write the animal's name and two words that describe the animal beneath their drawing.

15

SELECTION C • **Colors That Hide**

Assessment

Formal

At the conclusion of the lesson, have students complete the assessment Unit 3: Colors That Hide. The Lesson Assessments are found in the *Assessment Guide.*

For all the items in this assessment, you should read both the question and answer choices out loud while students follow along silently. If students appear confused by a question, clarify it for them.

In the Unit Assessment, students will answer reading and language arts questions about a new selection, "Bat-Eared Foxes." We recommend reading the story out loud several times in advance while students follow along silently. If you start this process now, students should be familiar with the story when the unit assessment takes place.

Informal

Choose words from the selection "Colors That Hide" that have regular consonant endings. Say the words out loud, then repeat the words without the final consonants. Have students replace the missing final consonants. As an option, you may have students challenge one another with the exercise.

Ending the Lesson

Have students explain in their own words how camouflage works and what purposes it serves. Raise questions such as "How do zebras' stripes help them hide?" Encourage students to respond in complete sentences with information from the story or other information they already know.

OBJECTIVES

- Complete lesson assessment.
- Preview the unit assessment selection.
- Replace final consonants.
- Clarify information in a selection.

MATERIALS

Assessment Guide
Student Reader, pp. 52–57

SELECTION D • **Night Lights in the Ocean**

Support Materials

LESSON 16

- Sound/Spelling Card 40
- Decodable Stories and Comprehension Skills, p. 31
- Home Connection, p. 37
- High-Frequency Word Cards
- Sound/Spelling Card Stories Audiocassette/CD

LESSON 17

- Student Reader, pp. 58–59
- Language Arts, p. T32

LESSON 18

- Sound/Spelling Card 40
- Decodable Stories and Comprehension Skills, p. 32
- High-Frequency Word Cards
- Sound/Spelling Card Stories Audiocassette/CD

LESSON 19

- Student Reader, pp. 58–59
- Transparencies 3, 5, 30
- Decodable Stories and Comprehension Skills, p. 90
- Language Arts, p. T31
- Listening Library Audiocassette/CD

LESSON 20

- Assessment Guide
- Student Reader, pp. 58–59

HOME CONNECTIONS

Distribute *Home Connection* page 37, which describes this week's classwork and suggests activities for families to do at home. This letter is available in English and Spanish.

Teacher Focus	Student Participation
• Conduct Listening Game. • Conduct Word Play. • Introduce Sight Words and Set 1 blending words and sentences. • Conduct Oral Language activity. • Dictate word lines. • Assist students with decodable text. • Assign writing activity.	• Take part in Listening Game. • Take part in Word Play. • Read Sight Words. • Blend words and sentences. • Identify spellings for /aw/. • Write dictated words and sentences. • Read a decodable story. • Complete writing activity.
• Activate Prior Knowledge and provide background information. • Introduce and discuss selection vocabulary. • Preview selection. • Review Comprehension Strategies—Asking Questions and Summarizing. • Read the selection to students. • Assign writing activity. • Introduce vocabulary skill.	• Contribute to class discussion. • Read and discuss vocabulary words. Complete selection vocabulary activity. • Browse the selection. • Follow along as the selection is read. • Complete writing activity. • Complete vocabulary skill activity.
• Conduct Restoring Final Consonants game. • Conduct Word Play. • Introduce Set 2 blending words and sentences. • Conduct Oral Language activity. • Dictate word lines. • Assist students with decodable text. • Assign writing activity.	• Participate in Restoring Final Consonants game. • Take part in Word Play. • Blend words and sentences. • Create sentences. • Write dictated words and sentences. • Read a decodable story. • Complete writing activity.
• Review Comprehension Skill—Author's Purpose. • Reread and discuss the selection with students. • Discuss Independent Reading. • Assign writing activity. • Introduce grammar skill.	• Follow along as selection is read again. • Discuss the selection. • Select a book to take home and read. • Complete writing activity. • Complete grammar skill activity.
• Administer weekly assessments. • Assess students' progress.	• Complete lesson assessment.

SELECTION D • **Night Lights in the Ocean**

- Identify and blend one-syllable words.
- Blend and break apart sounds in words.
- Read sight words.
- Participate in Word Play activity.
- Develop fluency by reading aloud.
- Apply decoding skills by reading **Unit 3, Decodable Story 7.**
- Develop writing skills by writing a caption.

Sound/Spelling Card:
40—Hawk
Decodable Stories and Comprehension Skills, p. 31
Home Connection, p. 37
High-Frequency Word Cards
Sound/Spelling Card Stories
Audiocassette/CD

Phonemic Awareness

The basic purpose of providing structured practice in phonemic awareness is to help students hear and understand the sounds from which words are made. Before students can be expected to understand the sound/symbol correspondence that forms the base of written English, they need to have a strong working knowledge of the sound relationships that make up the spoken language. This understanding of spoken language lays the foundation for the transition to written language. Phonemic awareness activities provide students with easy practice in discriminating the sounds that make up words. Once students begin reading and writing, this experience with manipulating sounds will help them use what they know about sounds and letters to sound out and spell unfamiliar words.

The two main formats for teaching phonemic awareness are oral blending and segmentation. These are supported by occasional discrimination activities and general word play. From these playful activities, students derive serious knowledge about language.

Oral Blending

Oral blending prepares students for phonics instruction by developing an awareness of the separate sounds that make up speech. Because these activities involve simply listening to and reproducing sounds, oral blending need not be restricted to the sounds students have been taught in phonics. The oral blending activities should be playful and informal and should move quickly.

Listening Game: One-Syllable Words

Explain to students that you are going to tell them a story and that you need their help. Use the following story and questions:

There once was a little red /h/ /e/ /n/.

There was a little red what? *(hen)*

She asked her friends if they would help her plant some wheat.

"Not I," said the /k/ /a/ /t/.

Who wouldn't help her? *(cat)*

"Not I," said the /d/ /o/ /g/.

Who else wouldn't help her? *(dog)*

"Not I," said the /p/ /i/ /g/.

And who else wouldn't help her? *(pig)*

So she planted it herself.

When it was time to harvest the wheat,

her lazy friends would not help her /k/ /u/ /t/ it.

What wouldn't they help her do? *(cut)*

So she cut it herself.

After the wheat had been ground into flour, they would not help her /b/ /ā/ /k/ the bread.

What else wouldn't they help her do? *(bake)*

So she baked it herself.

When the delicious-smelling bread came out of the oven, the lazy cat, dog, and pig began to /b/ /e/ /g/ for some.

What did they do? *(beg)*

But the little red hen said, "You didn't help me with all the hard work, so you will not help me eat the /b/ /r/ /e/ /d/."

What won't she let the other animals eat? *(bread)*

So she ate it herself.

Phonemic Awareness Success with the phoneme-blending activities will help students master what is for many the most difficult step in learning to read. To ease the task, the phonemes to be blended in these activities are presented in story context, which aids students in identifying the word to be blended.

Unit 3 • LESSON

16

Word Study

In this section of the lesson, students work on phonics, fluency, blending, and spelling. Increasing students' ability to work smoothly with printed words is one of the primary goals of the *Kaleidoscope* program.

Word Play

On the board, write all of the spellings for /oo/, /o͞o/, and /ow/, and the spelling patterns *-ion* and *-tion*. Review each spelling with students. Hand out newspaper pages and tell students to look for and circle words on their pages that contain any of these spellings. Call on individuals to read and spell the words they find.

Sight Words

This week's sight words:

become	country	off

TEACHER TIP

Sight Words Use *High-Frequency Word Cards* to assess and review students' knowledge of sight words.

Use the following procedure for teaching sight words:

- Write this week's sight words on the board.
- Read the words to students, and then have them read the words.
- Pronounce any words with which students have difficulty.
- Have students use each sight word in a sentence.

Phonics—Blending: Set 1

> /aw/ spelled *au_, aw*

This section of the phonics lesson provides practice in building sounds and spellings into words.

- Point out the new *Sound/Spelling Card.* Ask students what they know about it.
- Discuss any other *Sound/Spelling Cards* that you think students need to review.

aw
au_

40   Hawk

You will need the following *Sound/Spelling Card* for blending the words in Set 1. 40—Hawk

Blending Exercise

● The words in the lines provide practice with the Set 1 sound/spellings Write the following words and sentences on the board.

● Have students blend the words and sentences using the whole-word procedure described in Unit 1 on page 12F.

Line 1:	law	paw	jaw	claw
Line 2:	sawdust	crawlspace	lawn	hawk
Line 3:	cause	haul	fault	auto
Line 4:	caution	auburn	author	because
Sentence 1:	The <u>country</u> will <u>become</u> awfully hot this August.			
Sentence 2:	Paul will turn <u>off</u> the faucet in the laundry room.			

About the Words and Sentences

● Have students identify the words on the lines that have more than one syllable. *(sawdust, crawlspace, auto, caution, auburn, author, because)*

● For Line 2, have students identify the compound words. *(sawdust, crawlspace)*

● Before reading a sentence, point to and read the underlined sight words. Have students reread the sentences to encourage fluency and comprehension.

● For each sentence, have students identify the proper nouns. *(August, Paul)*

Oral Language

Have students take turns choosing a word and asking each other to identify the spelling for /aw/.

WRITING

Have students create an illustration and write a short caption using the word *hawk* as the main idea. Ask students to share their drawings and captions with the class.

SELECTION D • **Night Lights in the Ocean**

Dictation

Dictation gives students an opportunity to spell words by using the sound/spellings that they have learned. For this dictation exercise, have students use writing paper. Dictate the words and sentence for them to write. Use the following procedure to have students practice whole-word and sentence dictation:

● Say the first word in the Dictation word lines. Use the word in a sentence, then say the word again. Have students say the word.

● Tell students to think about how to segment the word into sounds. Then have them write the spelling for each sound. Encourage them to check the *Sound/Spelling Cards.*

● After each word line, write (or have a student write) the words on the board. Have students proofread their words. Tell them to circle any incorrect words and to correct them.

● Next, dictate the sentence. Dictate one word at a time, following the sounds-in-sequence or whole-word dictation procedure, depending on your students. Remind students to start the sentence with a capital letter and to use correct end punctuation.

● Write (or have a student write) the sentence on the board. Have students proofread their work and correct any incorrect words.

Line 1:	raw thaw because
Line 2:	sauce auto seesaw
Sentence:	The hawk squawked at the applause.

TEACHER TIP

Sound/Spelling Card Stories Review today's sounds by using the *Sound/ Spelling Card Stories.* Listening to the stories will help students understand how they can use the pictures on the *Sound/Spelling Cards* to remember the sounds associated with them. The stories are provided in the appendix and are also available on the *Sound/ Spelling Card Stories Audiocassette/CD.*

Building Fluency

Decodable Story: Unit 3, Story 7

- This story reviews the sound/spellings /aw/ spelled *aw, au_*.
- Have students silently read **Decodable Stories and Comprehension Skills** page 31.
- Call on volunteers to read each paragraph aloud.
- For those students who need help, divide sentences according to natural phrases. Mark these phrases with diagonal slash marks on their worksheets.
- After students have read the story aloud, ask them questions and have them point to and read the answers in the story.
- Have students reread the story aloud with a partner. Rereading builds automaticity and fluency.
- Over the next few days, listen to each student reread the story.

Applying Reading Skills As students read a story, make sure that they are using their knowledge of sound/spellings to read and understand unfamiliar words.

QUICK CHECK

As a quick review of today's sound/spellings, say some sentences, and ask students to suggest words to fill the blanks. Sentences you might read aloud include:

The _____ has written many books. *(author)*
The _____ sat quietly during the recital. *(audience)*
The dog has a thorn stuck in its _____. *(paw)*

SELECTION D • **Night Lights in the Ocean**

OBJECTIVES

- Discuss vocabulary words and their meanings.
- Develop reading skills as the story is read to them.
- Gain knowledge of the comprehension strategies Asking Questions and Summarizing.
- Build vocabulary by learning about prefixes.
- Develop writing skills by writing a prediction.

MATERIALS

Student Reader, pp. 58–59
Language Arts, p. T32

Before Reading

Build Background

Activate Prior Knowledge

- Review with students the previous selections and ask them what they have learned so far about animals and animal camouflage.
- Ask students what animals they know that live in the ocean, or sea. Then ask, *If you lived in the ocean, what kind of camouflage would you need in order to hide from danger?*

Background Information

Use the following information to help students understand the selection you are about to read:

- If possible, bring in pictures of flashlight fish. Let students know that the name for the kind of camouflage used by the flashlight fish is *bioluminescence*—meaning the ability of a creature to make itself light up, or glow.
- Explain to students that this selection is nonfiction. Remind them that nonfiction is different from fiction, or made-up stories, because it is true.
- Explain that this selection was written to inform and describe.

Selection Vocabulary

Write the following vocabulary words on the board. Before reading the selection, introduce and discuss the following words and their meanings.

dawdle: to waste time

champion: the best in an activity

luring: attracting

Then have students read the words, stopping to blend any words that they have trouble reading. Demonstrate how to decode multisyllabic words by breaking the words into syllables and blending the syllables. Then have students try. If they still have trouble, refer them to the **Sound/Spelling Cards.** If the word is not decodable, give students the pronunciation.

As students study vocabulary, they will use a variety of skills to determine the meaning of a word. These skills include context clues, word structure, and apposition. In this lesson, students will be learning about apposition. Write the following example on the board: *The flashlight fish is good at luring, or attracting, other fish.*

Explain to students that they are going to use apposition to help them decipher the meaning of the word *luring*. Remind students that when they use apposition, they are looking for a word or group of words in the sentence that help define the word in question. Guide students until they can give a reasonable definition of the word.

Vocabulary Activity: Have students look through magazines or newspapers and cut out examples of the word *champion*. For example, students might find pictures of sports stars, Olympic athletes, spelling bee winners, or blue ribbon winners at a county fair.

Preview and Prepare

Before you read, use modeling and prompts such as:

● *Let's browse. Since it's nonfiction, we can look at the entire selection without spoiling any surprise.*

● *As you browse, look for words or ideas that you think might be difficult or need clarifying.*

WRITING

Dictate the following sentence to students: *This selection looks like it might be about _____.* Have students write their ideas about the selection's content based on their browsing.

During Reading

Read Aloud

For this session, read the entire selection aloud. As you read, stop at the points that are marked with numbers in magenta circles on the reduced student pages, and model for them how to use the indicated strategy. Encourage students to stop at any point in their reading if they don't understand something or want to talk about the meaning of a passage or word.

Comprehension Strategies

During the reading of "Night Lights in the Ocean" on pages 58–59, you will model the following reading comprehension strategies:

Asking Questions: As they read, good readers ask themselves questions to see if they are making sense of what they are reading.

Summarizing: Readers often pause during reading to summarize. After reading, they may make a mental summary of the entire selection. Summarizing helps readers to make sense of what they read.

Text Comprehension *Strategies*

As you read the selection, use modeling and prompts such as:

1 Asking Questions

Asking yourself questions is a good way to be sure you understand what you're reading. I'm wondering what kind of lights a fish can possibly have. It's called a flashlight fish. Does that mean it carries a flashlight? Let's read on to see if my questions are answered. Yes, the answer to the first question is that the fish has a way of lighting up, like car lights. The answer to the second question is, of course, no!

2 Summarizing

At the end of a selection, good readers often summarize what they've read to make sure they understand it. The selection tells about flashlight fish and how they use a system of lights both to attract other fish they want to eat and to fool bigger fish and keep themselves safe.

Encourage students to use computers at home or on their own time to find out more about bioluminescent fish. Invite them to share their new information with the class.

Night Lights in the Ocean

by Nina Smiley
illustrated by Barbara Kiwak

All fish can swim at night. But one kind really likes to swim in the dark. It is called the flashlight fish. And it has its
1 own lights!

The flashlight fish has a spot under each eye. These spots give off light. The lights are like a car's lights. They turn on and off.

58

VOCABULARY

Remind students that a *prefix* is a word part that comes at the beginning of a base word, and that adding a *prefix* to a word changes the meaning of the word. Explain that the prefix *il-* usually means "not" and the prefix *mis-* usually means "bad" or "wrong." For a lesson on the prefixes *il-* and *mis-*, use *Language Arts* page T32.

When the fish gets hungry, the lights come on. Smaller fish see them. They swim to the lights almost as if they were called. Here comes dinner! It isn't safe to dawdle in the lights. The flashlight fish is a champion at luring other fish.

Sometimes bigger fish follow the flashlight fish. But it tricks them. It turns the lights off. The flashlight fish swims away and doesn't get caught. Its lights keep it safe. ❷

59

Text Comprehension *skills*

Author's Purpose

Remind students that authors always have a purpose for writing. Sometimes the purpose is to give information, other times it is to persuade, and still other times it is to entertain.

● Ask students what they think the author's purpose was for writing "Night Lights in the Ocean." *(to give information)*

● Ask them how they know, and have them find specific information from the selection to support their answers.

● Use **Transparency** 5 to record their responses.

● For additional practice with Author's Purpose, have students complete **Decodable Stories and Comprehension Skills** page 90.

Discussing the Selection

After you have read the story, discuss it with students. Use prompts such as:

● *What new information did you learn about animal camouflage?*

● *How is the camouflage described in this selection different from other types that you've read about?*

● *Did anything surprise you in the selection? If so, what was it and why was it a surprise?*

QUICK CHECK

Quickly review with students the other comprehension skills that they've used so far.

GRAMMAR

Tell students that verbs are words that show action or link parts of a sentence. Explain that *action verbs* tell what is happening in a sentence. For a lesson on action verbs, use *Language Arts* page T31.

OBJECTIVES

- Identify and segment final consonant sounds in words.
- Blend and break apart sounds in words.
- Participate in Word Play activity.
- Develop fluency by reading aloud.
- Apply decoding skills by reading **Unit 3, Decodable Story 8.**
- Develop writing skills by identifying and writing words.

MATERIALS

Sound/Spelling Card:
40—Hawk
Decodable Stories and Comprehension Skills, p. 32
High-Frequency Word Cards
Sound/Spelling Card Stories
Audiocassette/CD

Phonemic Awareness

Segmentation: Restoring Final Consonants

This segmentation activity is a variation of those activities in the three previous lessons, in which the final consonant sound was left off. Tell students that you want to have lunch. Ask them to listen and to tell you what you want to eat. Then they should repeat the sound that was left off.

a peanut butter sandwi . . .

chicken noodle sou . . .

vanilla ice crea . . .

chocolate mil . . .

a cupca . . .

fruit jui . . .

some crackers and chee . . .

Word Study

Word Play

Provide each student with a newspaper page. Tell students to look for and circle words on the page that contain the *aw* or *au_* spellings for /aw/. Call on individuals to read and spell the words they find.

Phonics—Blending: Set 2

> /aw/ spelled *augh, ough*

- Review the previously introduced sound/spellings for /aw/.
- Discuss the sound/spellings that are the focus of this set.

Blending Exercise

- Write the following words and sentences on the board.
- Have students blend the words and sentences using the whole-word procedure described in Unit 1 on page 12F.

Line 1:	daughter	uncaught	taught
Line 2:	ought	bought	brought
Sentence 1:	She thought her granddaughter had turned <u>off</u> the light.		
Sentence 2:	Dawn bought a <u>country</u> music CD.		

- Before reading a sentence, point to and read the underlined sight words.
- Discuss with students that each sentence begins with a capital letter and ends with a punctuation mark.
- Have students reread the sentences to encourage fluency and comprehension.

You will need the following **Sound/Spelling Card** for blending the words in Set 1. 40—Hawk

WRITING

Have students identify and write the words from the lines with the sound/spelling *ough* for /aw/. *(ought, bought, brought)*

SELECTION D • **Night Lights in the Ocean**

About the Words and Sentences

- Have students identify the sound/spelling for /aw/ in each word.
- For Line 1, point out the word *uncaught*. Ask students what the prefix is and what the word means.
- For the sentences, have students identify each spelling for /aw/.

Oral Language

Have students take turns coming to the board, touching a word, and using it in a sentence. Encourage them to extend their sentences by asking *When? Where? How?* and *Why?* questions.

Dictation

For the dictation exercise, have students use writing paper. Dictate the words and sentence for them to write. Use the following procedure:

Line 1:	taught caught
Line 2:	thought ought
Sentence:	We bought red roses.

- Say the first word in each word line. Use the word in a sentence, then say the word again. Have students say the word.
- Tell students to think about how to segment the word into sounds. Then have them write the spelling for each sound.
- After each word line, write (or have a student write) the words on the board. Have students proofread their words. Tell them to circle any incorrect words and to correct them.
- Next dictate the sentence. Dictate one word at a time, following the sounds-in-sequence or whole-word dictation procedure, depending on your students. Remind students to start the sentence with a capital letter and to use correct end punctuation.
- Write (or have a student write) the sentence on the board. Have students proofread their work and correct any incorrect words.

TEACHER TIP

Multiple Spellings For sounds that have multiple spellings, remind students to ask *Which spelling?* when they are unsure which one to use in a given word. Remind them to use the *Sound/Spelling Cards* and to ask for help when they need it.

Building Fluency

Decodable Story: Unit 3, Story 8

- This story reviews the sound/spellings /aw/ spelled *augh, ough.*
- Have students silently read *Decodable Stories and Comprehension Skills* page 32.
- Call on volunteers to read each paragraph aloud.
- For those students who need help, divide sentences according to natural phrases. Mark these phrases with diagonal slash marks on their worksheets.
- After students have read the story aloud, ask them questions and have them point to and read the answers in the story.
- Have students reread the story aloud with a partner.

HOMEWORK TIP

To help students build fluency, have them take home the *Decodable Stories and Comprehension Skills* stories to read with their families.

19

SELECTION D • **Night Lights in the Ocean**

Rereading the Selection

Comprehension Skills

Revisiting or rereading a selection allows students to learn and apply skills that give them a more complete understanding of a selection. For today's lesson, reread the selection to students. During the second reading, students will apply the following comprehension skill:

Author's Purpose: Good readers recognize that authors have a reason for writing—to entertain, to inform, to persuade, and so on—and they use this knowledge to help them better understand a selection.

After Reading

Independent Reading

- Have students choose books from the **Classroom Library** or other available books to take home and read. Encourage students to read at least one book a week on their own.
- Set aside a few minutes each day for students to meet one-on-one with you to discuss their reading.
- Encourage students to record the titles of the books they are reading on the copy of **Transparency** 3.

OBJECTIVES

- Develop reading skills as the story is reread to them.
- Gain knowledge of the comprehension skill Author's Purpose.
- Develop vocabulary by listening to and discussing a selection.
- Develop writing skills by writing the author's purpose.
- Identify and correctly use action verbs.

MATERIALS

Transparencies 3, 5, 30
Decodable Stories and
  Comprehension Skills, p. 90
Student Reader, pp. 58–59
Listening Library
  Audiocassette/CD
Language Arts, p. T31

Have students listen to the selection recording on the *Listening Library Audiocassette/CD* for a proficient, fluent model of oral reading.

WRITING

Have students write whether the author's purpose for writing "Night Lights in the Ocean" was *to entertain, to inform,* or *to persuade.* Then have them write one fact about flashlight fish that they learned from the selection.

SELECTION D • **Night Lights in the Ocean**

Assessment

Formal

At the conclusion of the lesson, have students complete the assessment Unit 3: Night Lights in the Ocean. The Lesson Assessments are found in the *Assessment Guide.*

For all the items in this assessment, you should read both the question and answer choices out loud while students follow along silently. For the extended response items, have students draft their answers on scratch paper before they write them on the assessment page.

By now, students should be familiar with the Unit Assessment selection "Bat-Eared Foxes." Read Question 1 to students. Tell them that they should choose information from the selection that they find interesting and then explain the information in their own words. You may have students compose their answer orally and discuss it with you before writing it. They will share their completed answers with other students during the Unit Assessment.

Informal

Be sure students have the lesson selection in front of them. Choose decodable one-syllable words from the story (such as *fish, it, lights, safe*), say the words out loud, and ask volunteers to find them in the story. Ask the volunteers to point to the words in the story, and then ask other students if the word appears in another part of the story.

Ending the Lesson

Have students discuss the reason the author wrote this selection. You may prompt them with questions such as "Is this a funny or exciting story?" or "Does this story tell you how to do something, like a set of directions?" Encourage students to conclude that the selection is intended to inform. Be sure they understand what this means.

SELECTION E • **Insects Stay Safe**

Support Materials

HOME CONNECTIONS

Distribute *Home Connection* page 39, which describes this week's classwork and suggests activities for families to do at home. This letter is available in English and Spanish.

LESSON 21

- Sound/Spelling Card 43
- Decodable Stories and Comprehension Skills, p. 33
- Home Connection, p. 39
- High-Frequency Word Cards
- Sound/Spelling Card Stories Audiocassette/CD

LESSON 22

- Student Reader, pp. 60–63
- Language Arts, p. T34
- Transparency 31

LESSON 23

- Sound/Spelling Card 40
- Decodable Stories and Comprehension Skills, p. 34
- High-Frequency Word Cards
- Sound/Spelling Card Stories Audiocassette/CD

LESSON 24

- Student Reader, pp. 60–63
- Transparencies 3, 32
- Decodable Stories and Comprehension Skills, p. 91
- Language Arts, p. T33
- Listening Library Audiocassette/CD

LESSON 25

- Assessment Guide
- Student Reader, pp. 60–63

Teacher Focus

- Conduct Listening Game.
- Conduct Word Play.
- Introduce Sight Words and Set 1 blending words and sentences.
- Conduct Oral Language activity.
- Dictate word lines.
- Assist students with decodable text.
- Assign writing activity.

- Activate Prior Knowledge and provide background information.
- Introduce and discuss selection vocabulary.
- Preview selection.
- Review Comprehension Strategies— Summarizing and Monitoring and Adjusting Reading Speed.
- Read the selection to students.
- Assign writing activity.
- Introduce vocabulary skill.

- Conduct Rhyming Words game.
- Conduct Word Play.
- Introduce Set 2 blending words and sentences.
- Conduct Oral Language activity.
- Dictate word lines.
- Assist students with decodable text.
- Assign writing activity.

- Review Comprehension Skill— Drawing Conclusions.
- Reread and discuss the selection with students.
- Discuss Independent Reading.
- Assign writing activity.
- Introduce grammar skill.

- Administer weekly assessments.
- Assess students' progress.

Student Participation

- Take part in Listening Game.
- Take part in Word Play.
- Read Sight Words.
- Blend words and sentences.
- Identify synonyms.
- Write dictated words and sentences.
- Read a decodable story
- Complete writing activity.

- Contribute to class discussion.
- Read and discuss vocabulary words. Complete selection vocabulary activity.
- Browse the selection.
- Follow along as the selection is read.
- Complete writing activity.
- Complete vocabulary skill activity.

- Participate in Rhyming Words game.
- Take part in Word Play.
- Blend words and sentences.
- Create sentences.
- Write dictated words and sentences.
- Read a decodable story.
- Complete writing activity.

- Follow along as the selection is read again.
- Discuss the selection.
- Select a book to take home and read.
- Complete writing activity.
- Complete grammar skill activity.

- Complete lesson assessment.

SELECTION E • **Insects Stay Safe**

- Identify and blend one-syllable words.
- Blend and break apart sounds in words.
- Read sight words.
- Participate in Word Play activity.
- Develop fluency by reading aloud.
- Apply decoding skills by reading *Unit 3, Decodable Story 9.*
- Develop writing skills by writing words and their prefixes.

Sound/Spelling Card:
43—Coil
Decodable Stories and Comprehension Skills,
p. 33
Home Connection, p. 39
High-Frequency Word Cards
Sound/Spelling Card Stories Audiocassette/CD

Phonemic Awareness

The basic purpose of providing structured practice in phonemic awareness is to help students hear and understand the sounds from which words are made. Before students can be expected to understand the sound/symbol correspondence that forms the base of written English, they need to have a strong working knowledge of the sound relationships that make up the spoken language. This understanding of spoken language lays the foundation for the transition to written language. Phonemic awareness activities provide students with easy practice in discriminating the sounds that make up words. Once students begin reading and writing, this experience with manipulating sounds will help them use what they know about sounds and letters to sound out and spell unfamiliar words.

The two main formats for teaching phonemic awareness are oral blending and segmentation. These are supported by occasional discrimination activities and general word play. From these playful activities, students derive serious knowledge about language.

Oral Blending

Oral blending prepares students for phonics instruction by developing an awareness of the separate sounds that make up speech. Because these activities involve simply listening to and reproducing sounds, oral blending need not be restricted to the sounds students have been taught in phonics. The oral blending activities should be playful and informal and should move quickly.

Listening Game: One-Syllable Words

In this activity, phoneme blending is extended to include some four phoneme words that begin with consonant blends. Explain to students that you are going to tell them a story and you need their help. Use the following story and questions:

There once was a very good /d/ /o/ /g/.

What was good? *(dog)*

The dog was so good that his owner gave him a /b/ /ō/ /n/.

What did the master give the dog? *(bone)*

The dog /r/ /a/ /n/ away to hide his bone.

What did the dog do? *(ran)*

But he had to /s/ /t/ /o /p/ when he came to the end of the yard.

What did the dog have to do? *(stop)*

He looked across the yard and saw another /d/ /o/ /g/ who had another bone.

What did the dog see? *(dog)*

He thought he might /g/ /r/ /a/ /b/ the other dog's bone, and then he would have two.

What did he want to do? *(grab)*

The other dog opened her mouth to bark and her bone /f/ /e/ /l/ to the ground.

What did the bone do when she opened her mouth? *(fell)*

The first dog liked the sound of her bark and no longer wanted to grab the bone.

He thought it would be nice to share both bones.

So both dogs had plenty of /f/ /oo/ /d/ that day.

What did both dogs have? *(food)*

Consonant Blends It is often difficult for students to hear both consonant sounds in a blend. Make sure to pronounce each sound clearly as you say words with blends.

SELECTION E • **Insects Stay Safe**

Word Study

In this section of the lesson, students work on phonics, fluency, blending, and spelling. Increasing students' ability to work smoothly with printed words is one of the primary goals of the *Kaleidoscope* program.

Word Play

Have students work in teams of three or four. On the board, write the spellings for /aw/ that students have learned. Give the teams five minutes to write as many words as they can that contain one of these spellings. Have each team read its list as you write the words on the board. Award a point for each correct word. The team with the most points wins.

Sight Words

This week's sight words:

| heard | mountain | women |

Use the following procedure for teaching sight words:

- Write this week's sight words on the board.
- Read the words to students, and then have them read the words.
- Pronounce any words with which students have difficulty.
- Have students use each sight word in a sentence.

Phonics—Blending: Set 1

> /oi/ spelled _oy, oi

This section of the phonics lesson provides practice in building sounds and spellings into words.

- Point out the new *Sound/Spelling Card.* Ask students what they know about it.
- Discuss any other *Sound/Spelling Cards* that you think students need to review.

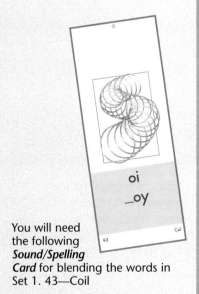

oi
_oy

43   Coil

You will need the following *Sound/Spelling Card* for blending the words in Set 1. 43—Coil

Blending Exercise

● The words in the lines provide practice with the Set 1 sound/spellings. Write the following words and sentences on the board.

● Have students blend the words and sentences using the whole-word procedure described in Unit 1 on page 12F.

Line 1:	boil	spoil	soil	point
Line 2:	coin	noise	joint	choice
Line 3:	joy	toy	royal	cowboy
Line 4:	uncoil	reemploy	disloyal	rejoin
Sentence 1:	The <u>women</u> rejoiced when they reached the <u>mountain</u>.			
Sentence 2:	Roy <u>heard</u> about soybeans from the farmer.			

About the Words and Sentences

● Have students identify the sound/spelling for /oi/ in each word.

● For Line 1, have students identify the rhyming words. *(boil, spoil, soil)*

● For Line 4, have students notice that all the words have prefixes. Ask them what each word means.

● Have students identify the words on the lines that have more than one syllable. *(royal, cowboy, uncoil, reemploy, disloyal, rejoin)*

● Before reading a sentence, point to and read the underlined sight words. Have students reread the sentences to encourage fluency and comprehension.

Oral Language

Have students find, read, and erase words that are synonyms for these words: *happiness (joy), dirt (soil), ruin (spoil), sound (noise).*

WRITING

Have students identify and write the prefixed words *(uncoil, reemploy, disloyal, rejoin)*. Then have them write the prefix next to each word. Discuss the meanings of the prefixes as a class.

SELECTION E • **Insects Stay Safe**

Dictation

Dictation gives students an opportunity to spell words by using the sound/spellings that they have learned. For this dictation exercise, have students use writing paper. Dictate the words and sentence for them to write. Use the following procedure to have students practice whole-word and sentence dictation:

● Say the first word in each word line. Use the word in a sentence, then say the word again. Have students say the word.

● Tell students to think about how to segment the word into sounds. Then have them write the spelling for each sound. Encourage them to check the ***Sound/Spelling Cards.***

● After each word line, write (or have a student write) the words on the board. Have students proofread their words. Tell them to circle any incorrect words and to correct them.

● Next, dictate the sentence. Dictate one word at a time, following the sounds-in-sequence or whole-word dictation procedure, depending on your students. Remind students to start the sentence with a capital letter and to use correct end punctuation.

● Write (or have a student write) the sentence on the board. Have students proofread their work and correct any incorrect words.

Line 1:	boy	employ	toyshop
Line 2:	broil	join	voice
Sentence:	Joyce enjoys digging in the soil.		

TEACHER TIP

Sound/Spelling Card Stories
Review today's sounds by using the ***Sound/Spelling Card Stories.*** Listening to the stories will help students understand how they can use the pictures on the ***Sound/Spelling Cards*** to remember the sounds associated with them. The stories are provided in the appendix and are also available on the ***Sound/Spelling Card Stories Audiocassette/CD.***

Building Fluency

Decodable Story: Unit 3, Story 9

- This story reviews the sound/spellings /oi/ spelled _oy, oi._
- Have students silently read **Decodable Stories and Comprehension Skills** page 33.
- Call on volunteers to read each paragraph aloud.
- For those students who need help, divide sentences according to natural phrases. Mark these phrases with diagonal slash marks on their worksheets.
- After students have read the story aloud, ask them questions and have them point to and read the answers in the story.
- Have students reread the story aloud with a partner. Rereading builds automaticity and fluency.
- Over the next few days, listen to each student reread the story.

Develop Fluency Some students may find it difficult to read with fluency because they do not recognize the importance of grouping words into natural meaning units, such as phrases, as they read. Model fluent reading frequently for students, showing them how pausing in the right places and adding expression can make a passage easier to understand.

QUICK CHECK

As a quick review of today's sound/spellings, say some sentences, and ask students to suggest words to fill the blanks. Sentences you might read aloud include:

The _____ wore a ten-gallon hat. *(cowboy)*
There are ten _____ and ten girls in the class. *(boys)*
The king and queen are part of the _____ family. *(royal)*

SELECTION E • **Insects Stay Safe**

Before Reading

Build Background

Activate Prior Knowledge

● Ask students to review what they have learned so far about animals and animal camouflage.

● Ask students to talk about the different ways that animals use camouflage.

● Ask them what they know about insects and how they think that insects might use camouflage to protect themselves from danger.

Background Information

Use the following information to help students understand the selection you are about to read:

● Tell students that the insects called "walking sticks" like warm, moist weather and live mostly in the tropics. Many varieties of moths have special color patterns that protect them from danger.

● Tell students that like all of the selections they have read in this unit, this one is nonfiction.

Selection Vocabulary

Write the following vocabulary words on the board. Before reading the selection, introduce and discuss the following words and their meanings.

avoid: to keep away from

afraid: frightened

Then have students read the words, stopping to blend any words that they have trouble reading. Demonstrate how to decode multisyllabic words by breaking the words into syllables and blending the syllables. Then have students try. If they still have trouble, refer them to the **Sound/Spelling Cards.** If the word is not decodable, give students the pronunciation.

As students study vocabulary, they will use a variety of skills to determine the meaning of a word. These skills include context clues, word structure, and apposition. In this lesson, students will be learning about context clues. Write the following example on the board: *We took a back road to avoid the heavy highway traffic.* Explain to students that they are going to use context clues, or other words in the sentence, to help them decipher the meaning of the word *avoid*. Guide students until they can give a reasonable definition of the word.

OBJECTIVES

• Discuss vocabulary words and their meanings.
• Develop reading skills as the story is read to them.
• Gain knowledge of the comprehension strategies Monitoring and Adjusting Reading Speed and Summarizing.
• Build vocabulary by learning about prefixes.
• Develop writing skills by writing a summary of the selection.

MATERIALS

Student Reader, pp. 60–63
Language Arts, p. T34
Transparency 31

Vocabulary Activity: Write the word *afraid* on the board and have students give examples of things that might frighten them (such as *snakes, the dark, or thunderstorms*). Write their suggestions on the board and discuss the list as a class.

Preview and Prepare

Before you read, use modeling and prompts such as:

- *Let's browse. Since it's nonfiction, we can look at the entire selection without spoiling any surprise.*
- *As you browse, look for words or ideas that you think might be difficult or need clarifying.*

During Reading

Read Aloud

For this lesson, read the entire selection aloud. As you read, stop at the points that are marked with numbers in magenta circles on the reduced student pages, and model for them how to use the indicated strategy. Encourage students to stop at any point in their reading if they don't understand something or want to talk about the meaning of a passage or word.

Comprehension Strategies

During the reading of "Insects Stay Safe" on pages 60–63, you will model the following reading comprehension strategies:

Monitoring and Adjusting Reading Speed: If they notice that they are having trouble understanding what they read, good readers slow down. They also may reread passages.

Summarizing: Readers often pause during reading to summarize. After reading, they may make a mental summary of the entire selection. Summarizing helps readers to make sense of what they read.

TEACHER TIP

Asking Questions Students should be encouraged to stop to ask questions. Have students take time to reflect on the text from time to time to see if it makes sense.

First Read

Text Comprehension *Strategies*

As you read the selection, use modeling and prompts such as:

❶ Monitoring and Adjusting Reading Speed

When they don't understand what they're reading, good readers go back and reread part of a selection. They read slower until they do understand what's happening. I'm not sure that I have a clear idea of what this selection is about, so I'm going to go back and read this page again, but slower this time. Now I understand. I was confused because of the name "walking stick." I read so fast, I didn't realize that's the name of an insect. Rereading helped me to get back on track.

❷ Summarizing

Good readers stop now and then as they read so that they can summarize what they've read and make sure they're following what's happening. Can anyone summarize what we've read so far?

Student Sample

Walking sticks are a kind of insect that looks like a stick. Birds like to eat them, so they have learned a trick: they stay still for a very long time and the birds think they are just part of a tree or bush.

Insects Stay Safe

by Helen Squires

Many insects can stay safe—even when they are out in the open.

Have you heard about the tiny stick that walks? It's not made of wood. It is a small animal. It is called a walking stick.

Most walking sticks are as long as your finger. But they're not as wide. They have ❶ long, thin legs. They look like small sticks!

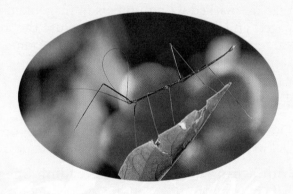

60

VOCABULARY

Explain to students that some prefixes represent numbers and amounts. For example, the prefix *bi-* usually means "two" and the prefix *tri-* usually means "three." For a lesson on number prefixes, use ***Language Arts*** page T34.

Birds like to eat the walking stick. But it tricks them. It sits still for a long time to <u>avoid</u> getting caught. The birds think it's a stick. So the birds do not eat it.

That's the trick of the walking stick. ❷

61

Text Comprehension

Drawing Conclusions

Remind students that authors do not always provide complete and clear information about a topic, character, thing, or event. They do, however, provide clues or suggestions that readers can use to "read between the lines" by drawing conclusions that are based on the information in the selection.

● For these pages, ask students to use clues from "Insects Stay Safe" to draw conclusions about the following:

What does a walking stick look like?

What happens when a walking stick knows that a bird is nearby?

● Use *Transparency* 32 to record their responses.

GRAMMAR

Remind students that verbs are words that show action or link parts of a sentence. Explain that *linking verbs* join, or connect, the parts of a sentence. Some common linking verbs are *am, be, is, are, was, were*. For a lesson on linking verbs, use *Language Arts* page T33.

Unit 3 • LESSON

22

First
Read

Text Comprehension *Strategies*

❸ Monitoring and Adjusting Reading Speed

Remember that good readers are aware when they do not understand what they are reading and stop to reread more slowly. Tell us about it when you do this too.

Student Sample

I was reading about walking sticks, and this page seems to be about some other kind of insect. I think I need to reread this page more slowly to see what I missed. Well, I missed the change in the topic. Now the selection is telling about another insect—moths—and a trick some of them have.

❹ Summarizing

I've read the whole selection, and now I'm going to summarize it to see if I understand what it is about. The title is "Insects Stay Safe," so I know the selection is about insects. The first type of insect discussed is the walking stick, which blends with tree branches to keep from being eaten by birds. The second insect discussed is moths. Some moths have special color patterns on their wings that look like big owl eyes. When one of its enemies comes near, a moth lifts its wings and frightens the enemy away. So I've learned two more ways that animals use camouflage to stay safe.

HOMEWORK
TIP

Encourage students to use computers at home or on their own time to find out more about walking sticks and other insects that use tricks to stay safe. Invite them to share their new information with the class.

Another tricky insect is the moth. Some moths have special "eyes" for staying safe. They have large spots on their wings. These spots look like owl eyes. When an enemy comes near, the moth lifts its front wings and shows its "eyes." The enemy is <u>afraid</u> and leaves the ❸ moth alone.

62

WRITING

Ask students to think about how they would summarize the selection. Have them write a brief summary of the selection.

Would you enjoy seeing a moth show its "eyes" to you?

Now that you know some of their tricks, maybe you can spot these insects. But you'll have to look hard. **4**

63

Text Comprehension

Drawing Conclusions

- For these pages, have students use clues from the selection to draw conclusions about the following:

  What do the spots on moths' wings look like?

  What happens when a moth lifts its wings to show an enemy? What does the enemy think?

- For additional practice with Drawing Conclusions, have students complete *Decodable Stories and Comprehension Skills* page 91.

Discussing the Selection

After you have read the selection, discuss it with students. Use prompts such as:

- *What new information did you learn from this selection about animal camouflage?*
- *How is the camouflage described in this selection different from other types that you've read about?*
- *Did anything surprise you in the selection? If so, what was it and why was it a surprise?*

QUICK CHECK

Reread sections of the selection and then have students summarize what you read.

23

OBJECTIVES

- Identify and say rhyming words.
- Blend and break apart sounds in words.
- Participate in Word Play activity.
- Develop fluency by reading aloud.
- Apply decoding skills by reading **Unit 3, Decodable Story 10.**
- Develop writing skills by identifying and writing words.

MATERIALS

Sound/Spelling Card:
40—Hawk
Decodable Stories and Comprehension Skills, p. 34
High-Frequency Word Cards
Sound/Spelling Card Stories Audiocassette/CD

Phonemic Awareness

Rhyming Words

Ask students to think of words that rhyme with the following /a/ words:

cat	back	man
map	Sam	bad

Have students generate as many rhymes for each word as they can. In addition to group responses, call on individual students to say words so that everyone participates. Allow nonsense words as well.

TEACHER TIP

Rhyming Games Playing rhyming games can be both fun and helpful in building students' ability to hear sounds in spoken language. Have students play a familiar rhyming game such as "One Potato, Two Potato."

Word Study

Word Play

Provide each student with a newspaper page. Tell students to look for and circle words on the page that contain any of the spellings for /oi/ that they have learned. Call on individuals to read and spell the words they find.

Phonics—Blending: Set 2

> /aw/ spelled *al, all*

Point out and review the **Sound/Spelling Card.** Ask students what they know about it. Explain that in addition to the spellings on the card, /aw/ may also be spelled *al,* as in *walnut,* and *all,* as in *call.*

Blending Exercise

- Write the following words and sentences on the board.
- Have students blend the words and sentences using the whole-word procedure described in Unit 1 on page 12F.

Line 1:	chalk	talk	salt	also	walk
Line 2:	call	stall	ball	fall	overall
Sentence 1:	I saw in the almanac that the fall will be cold on the <u>mountain</u>.				
Sentence 2:	Shawn <u>heard</u> that the <u>women</u> wanted to play baseball.				

- Before reading a sentence, point to and read the underlined sight words.
- Discuss with students that each sentence begins with a capital letter and ends with a punctuation mark.
- Have students reread the sentences to encourage fluency and comprehension.

You will need the following **Sound/Spelling Card** for blending the words in Set 2.
40—Hawk

TEACHER TIP

Sight Words Use the *High-Frequency Word Cards* to assess and review students' knowledge of sight words.

23

SELECTION E • **Insects Stay Safe**

About the Words and Sentences

- For Line 1, have students identify the rhyming words. *(chalk, talk, walk)*
- For Line 2, have students find the words that have multiple meanings. *(call, stall, ball, fall)*
- For the sentences, have students identify each spelling for /aw/.

Oral Language

Have students take turns choosing a word, reading it, using it in a sentence, and calling on a classmate to extend the sentence.

Dictation

For the dictation exercise, have students use writing paper. Dictate the words and sentence for them to write. Use the following procedure:

- Say the first word in each word line. Use the word in a sentence, then say the word again. Have students say the word.
- Tell students to think about how to segment the word into sounds. Then have them write the spelling for each sound.
- After each word line, write (or have a student write) the words on the board. Have students proofread their words. Tell them to circle any incorrect words and to correct them.
- Next dictate the sentence. Dictate one word at a time, following the sounds-in-sequence or whole-word dictation procedure, depending on your students. Remind students to start the sentence with a capital letter and to use correct end punctuation.
- Write (or have a student write) the sentence on the board. Have students proofread their work and correct any incorrect words.

WRITING

Give clues about words from the word lines and have students find and write the word. Clues you might use include:
It is used to write on the board. *(chalk)*
It is a seasoning for food. *(salt)*
It is a round object used in sports. *(ball)*

Line 1:	false	recall	wallpaper
Line 2:	always	tall	hallway
Sentence:	We saw many flowers as we walked.		

Building Fluency

Decodable Story: Unit 3, Story 10

● This story reviews the sound/spellings /aw/ spelled *al, all.*

● Have students silently read *Decodable Stories and Comprehension Skills* page 34.

● Call on volunteers to read each paragraph aloud.

● For those students who need help, divide sentences according to natural phrases. Mark these phrases with diagonal slash marks on their worksheets.

● After students have read the story aloud, ask them questions and have them point to and read the answers in the story.

● Have students reread the story aloud with a partner.

HOMEWORK TIP

Tell students to have family members help them write silly poems and rhymes that use words with the /aw/ sound/spellings. Allow time for sharing with the class.

SELECTION E • **Insects Stay Safe**

OBJECTIVES

- Develop reading skills as the story is reread to them.
- Gain knowledge of the comprehension skill Drawing Conclusions.
- Develop vocabulary by listening to and discussing a selection.
- Develop writing skills by drawing and writing conclusions.
- Identify and correctly use linking verbs.

MATERIALS

Transparencies 3, 32
Decodable Stories and Comprehension Skills, p. 91
Student Reader, pp. 60–63
Listening Library Audiocassette/CD
Language Arts, p. T33

Rereading the Selection

Comprehension Skills

Revisiting or rereading a selection allows students to learn and apply skills that give them a more complete understanding of a selection. For today's lesson, reread the selection to students. During the second reading, students will apply the following comprehension skill:

Drawing Conclusions: Good readers often "read between the lines," using clues provided by the author to draw conclusions about a selection's meaning.

After Reading

Independent Reading

- Have students choose books from the **Classroom Library** or other available books to take home and read. Encourage students to read at least one book a week on their own.
- Set aside time for students to talk in class about the independent reading that they are doing.
- Encourage students to use the comprehension strategies and skills they are learning as they read independently.
- Encourage students to record the titles of the books they are reading on the copy of **Transparency** 3.

TEACHER TIP

Have students listen to the selection recording on the *Listening Library Audiocassette/CD* for a proficient, fluent model of oral reading.

WRITING

Have students write their responses to the following statements. Tell them to use clues from the selection to complete the statements.
The color of walking sticks is _____.
The color of the spots on moths' wings is _____.

SELECTION E • **Insects Stay Safe**

Assessment

Formal

At the conclusion of the lesson, have students complete the assessment Unit 3: Insects Stay Safe. The Lesson Assessments are found in the ***Assessment Guide.***

For all the items in this assessment, you should read both the question and answer choices out loud while students follow along silently. Be sure students know they can ask you for help if they don't understand a question. You may have volunteers read a question or answer choice out loud after you have done so.

Have students refer to the Unit Assessment selection "Bat-Eared Foxes." Review the story briefly with students and then read Question 2 out loud. Be sure students use the last paragraph to answer the question, use their own words, and write in complete sentences.

Informal

Choose familiar words from the lesson selection and ask students to find words that rhyme with them. Write the rhyming word pairs on the board. Point out the spelling patterns that make the words rhyme. Pay special attention to the patterns that are spelled differently but sound the same.

Ending the Lesson

Ask students to point out the two ways that the animals in the story protect themselves. Encourage them to conclude that the walking stick hides and the moth imitates another animal that frightens its enemies. Have students discuss the advantages and disadvantages of each form of camouflage.

OBJECTIVES

- Complete lesson assessment.
- Identify rhyming words.
- Review spelling patterns.
- Draw conclusions from a selection.

MATERIALS

Assessment Guide
Student Reader, pp. 60–63

SELECTION F • **Hide-and-Seek Animals**

Support Materials

LESSON 26
- Sound/Spelling Cards 39, 41, 42
- Decodable Stories and Comprehension Skills, p. 35
- Home Connection, p. 41

HOME CONNECTIONS

Distribute *Home Connection* page 41, which describes this week's classwork and suggests activities for families to do at home. This letter is available in English and Spanish.

LESSON 27
- Student Reader, pp. 64–67
- Language Arts, p. T36

LESSON 28
- Sound/Spelling Cards 40, 43
- Decodable Stories and Comprehension Skills, p. 36
- High-Frequency Word Cards
- Sound/Spelling Card Stories Audiocassette/CD

LESSON 29
- Student Reader, pp. 64–67, 68–69
- Transparencies 3, 18, 33
- Decodable Stories and Comprehension Skills, p. 92
- Language Arts, p. T35
- Listening Library Audiocassette/CD

LESSON 30
- Assessment Guide
- Student Reader, pp. 64–67

Teacher Focus	Student Participation
• Conduct Listening Game. • Conduct Word Play. • Introduce Sight Words and Set 1 blending words and sentences. • Conduct Oral Language activity. • Dictate word lines. • Assist students with decodable text. • Assign writing activity.	• Take part in Listening Game. • Take part in Word Play. • Read Sight Words. • Blend words and sentences. • Create a story. • Write dictated words and sentences. • Read a decodable story. • Complete writing activity.
• Activate Prior Knowledge and provide background information. • Introduce and discuss selection vocabulary. • Preview selection. • Review Comprehension Strategies—Monitoring and Clarifying and Asking Questions. • Read the selection to students. • Assign writing activity. • Introduce vocabulary skill.	• Contribute to class discussion. • Read and discuss vocabulary words. Complete selection vocabulary activity. • Browse the selection. • Follow along as selection is read. • Complete writing activity. • Complete vocabulary skill activity.
• Conduct Repeating Final Consonants game. • Conduct Word Play. • Introduce Set 2 blending words and sentences. • Conduct Oral Language activity. • Dictate word lines. • Assist students with decodable text. • Assign writing activity.	• Participate in Repeating Final Consonants game. • Take part in Word Play. • Blend words and sentences. • Create sentences. • Write dictated words and sentences. • Read a decodable story. • Complete writing activity.
• Review Comprehension Skill—Compare and Contrast. • Reread and discuss the selection with students. • Discuss Independent Reading. • Assign writing activity. • Introduce grammar skill. • Discuss Reading Reflections.	• Follow along as the selection is read again. • Discuss the selection. • Select a book to take home and read. • Complete writing activity. • Complete grammar skill activity. • Discuss Reading Reflections.
• Administer weekly assessments. • Assess students' progress.	• Complete lesson and unit assessments.

26

OBJECTIVES

- Identify and blend one-syllable words.
- Blend and break apart sounds in words.
- Read sight words.
- Participate in Word Play activity.
- Review sound/spellings introduced in this unit.
- Develop fluency by reading aloud.
- Apply decoding skills by reading **Unit 3, Decodable Story 11.**
- Develop writing skills by writing a caption.

MATERIALS

Sound/Spelling Cards:
39—Cow
41—Goo
42—Foot
Decodable Stories and Comprehension Skills, p. 35
Home Connection, p. 41
High-Frequency Word Cards
Sound/Spelling Card Stories Audiocassette/CD

Phonemic Awareness

The basic purpose of providing structured practice in phonemic awareness is to help students hear and understand the sounds from which words are made. Before students can be expected to understand the sound/symbol correspondence that forms the base of written English, they need to have a strong working knowledge of the sound relationships that make up the spoken language. This understanding of spoken language lays the foundation for the transition to written language. Phonemic awareness activities provide students with easy practice in discriminating the sounds that make up words. Once students begin reading and writing, this experience with manipulating sounds will help them use what they know about sounds and letters to sound out and spell unfamiliar words.

The two main formats for teaching phonemic awareness are oral blending and segmentation. These are supported by occasional discrimination activities and general word play. From these playful activities, students derive serious knowledge about language.

Oral Blending

Oral blending prepares students for phonics instruction by developing an awareness of the separate sounds that make up speech. Because these activities involve simply listening to and reproducing sounds, oral blending need not be restricted to the sounds students have been taught in phonics. The oral blending activities should be playful and informal and should move quickly.

Listening Game: One-Syllable Words

In this activity, phoneme blending is extended to four-phoneme words that begin with consonant blends. Explain to students that you are going to tell them a story and you need their help. Use the following story and questions:

A crow flew to the top of a tree with a piece of /ch/ /ē/ /z/.

What did the crow have? *(cheese)*

A /f/ /o/ /ks/ saw the crow in the tree.

Who saw the crow? *(fox)*

The fox thought, "I shall have that cheese for my /l/ /u/ /n/ /ch/."

What does the fox want the cheese for? *(lunch)*

"How beautiful you are, Miss Crow," said the fox.

"Your feathers /sh/ /ī/ /n/ in the sun."

What did the fox say the crow's feathers did? *(shine)*

"Will you sing a song for me? You must also have a beautiful /v/ /oi/ /s/."

What did the fox say the crow must have? *(voice)*

The vain crow was so flattered that she opened her /b/ /ē/ /k/ to sing.

What did the crow open? *(beak)*

Down dropped the cheese! The fox gobbled it up, and the poor crow had /n/ /u/ /n/.

What did the crow have? *(none)*

Oral Blending In order to make sure that every student is thinking on every turn, switch unpredictably from asking for a whole group response to asking for individual responses.

SELECTION F • **Hide-and-Seek Animals**

Word Study

In this section of the lesson, students work on phonics, fluency, blending, and spelling. Increasing students' ability to work smoothly with printed words is one of the primary goals of the *Kaleidoscope* program.

Word Play

Play the game Go Fish again. On the backs of "fish," write the spellings students have learned for /aw/ (use each spelling more than once). One by one, give students the fishing pole and tell them to "go fish." When a student catches a fish, have him or her read the spelling, say the sound, and then say and write on the board a word that contains the sound/spelling.

Sight Words

This week's sight words:

> **earth**   **father**   **mother**

Use the following procedure for teaching sight words:

● Write this week's sight words on the board.
● Read the words to students, then have them read the words.
● Pronounce any words with which students have difficulty.
● Have students use each sight word in a sentence.

Phonics—Blending: Set 1

This section of the phonics lesson provides practice in building sounds and spellings into words.

/oo/ spelled *oo*	/o͞o/ spelled *oo, _ew, u_e, _ue, u*
/ow/ spelled *ow, ou_*	

Discuss the **Sound/Spelling Cards** for /oo/, /o͞o/, and /ow/. Tell students that these are the sounds and spellings they will review in this lesson.

You will need the following *Sound/Spelling Cards* for blending the words in Set 1. 39—Cow, 41—Goo, 42—Foot

Blending Exercise

● The words in the lines provide practice with the Set 1 sound/spellings. Write the following words and sentences on the board.

● Have students blend the words and sentences using the whole-word procedure described in Unit 1 on page 12F.

Line 1:	zoo	good	look	doghouse
Line 2:	blue	town	shower	knew
LIne 3:	bookmark	due	stood	pound
Sentence 1:	Stu's <u>father</u> and <u>mother</u> are proud of his woodwork.			
Sentence 2:	People have used wooden plows to till the <u>earth</u>.			

About the Words and Sentences

● Have students identify the target sound/spelling in each word.

● Have students identify the compound words. *(doghouse, bookmark)*

● For the sentences, have students identify each previously learned sight word. *(are, of, people, have, to, the)*

Oral Language

To review the words, have a volunteer choose a word from the word lines. Ask the student to use that word in a sentence to begin a simple story. Have another volunteer continue the story by supplying a sentence that uses another word from the lines. Continue until all words are used.

TEACHER TIP

The goal of the blending exercises is to have students read the words, stopping to blend only those words that are problematic. If they can read the words, let them. If they are having trouble, drop back to whole-word blending. If this is not working, drop back to sound-by-sound blending.

WRITING

Have students create an illustration and write a short caption using the word *zoo* as the main idea. Ask students to share their drawings and captions with the class.

SELECTION F • **Hide-and-Seek Animals**

Dictation

Dictation gives students an opportunity to spell words by using the sound/spellings that they have learned. For this dictation exercise, have students use writing paper. Dictate the words and sentence for them to write. Use the following procedure to have students practice whole-word and sentence dictation:

- Say the first word in each word line. Use the word in a sentence, then say the word again. Have students say the word.
- Tell students to think about how to segment the word into sounds. Then have them write the spelling for each sound. Encourage them to check the **Sound/Spelling Cards.**
- After each word line, write (or have a student write) the words on the board. Have students proofread their words. Tell them to circle any incorrect words and to correct them.
- Next, dictate the sentence. Dictate one word at a time, following the sounds-in-sequence or whole-word dictation procedure, depending on your students. Remind students to start the sentence with a capital letter and to use correct end punctuation.
- Write (or have a student write) the sentence on the board. Have students proofread their work and correct any incorrect words.

Line 1:	crew moon cookbook
Line 2:	clown June stood
Sentence:	The wind blew the football out of bounds.

Building Fluency

Decodable Story: Unit 3, Story 11

- This story reviews the sound/spellings introduced in this unit.
- Have students silently read **Decodable Stories and Comprehension Skills** page 35.
- Call on volunteers to read each paragraph aloud.
- For those students who need help, divide sentences according to natural phrases. Mark these phrases with diagonal slash marks on their worksheets.
- After students have read the story aloud, ask them questions and have them point to and read the answers in the story.
- Have students reread the story aloud with a partner. Rereading builds automaticity and fluency.
- Over the next few days, listen to each student reread the story.

Sound/Spelling Card Stories Review today's sounds by using the *Sound/Spelling Card Stories*. Listening to the stories will help students understand how they can use the pictures on the *Sound/Spelling Cards* to remember the sounds associated with them. The stories are provided in the appendix and are also available on the *Sound/Spelling Card Stories Audiocassette/CD*.

QUICK CHECK

As a quick review of today's sound/spellings, say some sentences, and ask students to suggest words to fill the blanks. Sentences you might read aloud include:

My favorite color is _____ . *(blue)*
Mother makes very good beef _____. *(stew)*
My grandmother's _____ is on Elm Street. *(house)*

Unit 3 • LESSON

27

OBJECTIVES

- Discuss vocabulary words and their meanings.
- Develop reading skills as the story is read.
- Gain knowledge of the comprehension strategies Asking Questions and Monitoring and Clarifying.
- Build vocabulary by learning about prefixes.
- Develop writing skills by writing a description.

MATERIALS

Student Reader, pp. 64–67
Language Arts, p. T36

Before Reading

Build Background

Activate Prior Knowledge

- Ask students to review what they have learned so far about animals and animal camouflage.
- With the students' help, create a list of animals that they have read about that use camouflage.

Background Information

Use the following information to help students understand the selection you are about to read:

- Ask students to review everything they now know about the different ways that animals use camouflage.
- Tell students that like all of the selections they have read in this unit, this selection is nonfiction.

Vocabulary

Write the following vocabulary words on the board. Before reading the selection, introduce and discuss the following words and their meanings.

camouflage: a disguise, appearance, or behavior that helps to conceal or deceive

shadows: dark areas that are sometimes made when light shines on a person or thing

Then have students read the words, stopping to blend any words that they have trouble reading. Demonstrate how to decode multisyllabic words by breaking the words into syllables and blending the syllables. Then have students try. If they still have trouble, refer them to the *Sound/Spelling Cards.* If the word is not decodable, give students the pronunciation.

As students study vocabulary, they will use a variety of skills to determine the meaning of a word. These skills include context clues, word structure, and apposition. In this lesson, students will be learning about apposition. Write the following example on the board: *The camouflage, or appearance, of zebras helps them hide from their enemies.* Explain to students that they are going to use apposition to help them decipher the meaning of the word *camouflage.* Remind students that when they use apposition, they are looking for a word or group of words in the sentence that help defines the word in question. Guide students until they can give a reasonable definition of the word.

Vocabulary Activity: Have students draw a picture that illustrates an animal that is camouflaged. Have them share their drawing with the class and discuss the way(s) that their animal uses camouflage.

Preview and Prepare

Before you read, use modeling and prompts such as:

- *Let's look at the title, "Hide-and-Seek Animals." Do you think this selection might be about animals playing games?*
- *As you browse, look at the words in dark print. These are headings. Writers use headings to organize their writing. See if the headings help you figure out what the selection is about.*

During Reading

Read Aloud

For this lesson, read the entire selection. As you read, stop at the points that are marked with numbers in magenta circles on the reduced student pages, and model for them how to use the indicated strategy. Encourage students to stop at any point in their reading if they don't understand something or want to talk about the meaning of a passage or word.

Comprehension Strategies

During the reading of "Hide-and-Seek Animals" on pages 64–67, you will model the following comprehension strategies:

Asking Questions: As they read, good readers ask themselves questions to see if they are making sense of what they are reading.

Monitoring and Clarifying: Good readers pay attention to how well they understand what they are reading. They stop to clarify the meanings of new words and to think about unfamiliar or difficult passages.

TEACHER TIP

Comprehension Strategies Encourage students to ask any questions they have about things in the story that they do not understand. Remind them that good readers often stop to clarify things that are not clear.

27

First Read

Text Comprehension *Strategies*

As you read the selection, use modeling and prompts such as:

❶ Monitoring and Clarifying

I'm not sure what this title means. I know about the game Hide-and-Seek, but I don't think animals play that game. I'll start reading to see what the author means by the title. Now the title makes sense—animals hide because other animals are seeking them for food! That's hardly a game, is it?

❷ Asking Questions

Asking yourself questions is a good way to be sure you understand what you're reading. The wild rabbits that I've seen are mostly brown. I don't know how that color would help a rabbit hide in the winter. Snow isn't brown. I'll read on to see if the selection answers this question. Now I see. The rabbit's fur turns white in the winter.

❶ Hide-and-Seek Animals

by Shirley Granahan

How Do Animals Stay Safe?

Animals try to be safe. Why? Other animals want to eat them. Some animals eat only plants. But many animals eat other animals. Owls eat mice. Bears eat fish. So animals have special ways to help them stay safe. They have camouflage to protect them from their enemies.

The way some animals look helps them stay safe. The shapes and colors of the animals help them hide from their enemies.

64

VOCABULARY

Remind students that a *prefix* is a word part that comes at the beginning of a base word, and that adding a prefix to a word changes the meaning of the word. For a review lesson on prefixes, use **Language Arts** page T36.

The Rabbit

This rabbit's color helps it hide. Its fur **❷** is brown most of the year. The rabbit hides in fields of dry grass. In winter, the rabbit's fur turns white. Then the animal can hide in fields of snow.

65

Text Comprehension

Compare and Contrast

Remind students that to *compare* is to tell how things are alike and to *contrast* is to say how they are different. Explain that as they read, good readers both compare and contrast characters, things, and events to get a better understanding of the story.

- Have students look at the two photographs on page 65. Have them compare and contrast the rabbit in each photo. *(Similarity—the rabbit blends into the surroundings; difference—the rabbit is white in one photo and brown in the other.)*
- Use **Transparency** 18 to record their responses.

G R A M M A R

Remind students that verbs are words that can show action or link parts of a sentence. Explain to them that verbs also tell *when* the action in a sentence takes place. For a lesson on past, present, and future tense of verbs, use *Language Arts* page T35.

Unit 3 • LESSON

27

First Read

Text Comprehension *Strategies*

❸ Monitoring and Clarifying

The heading lets me know that this section is about giraffes. From the pictures I've seen, I know that giraffes are very tall animals. I don't know how they can hide. Maybe I should reread this section to see if I can figure it out. Oh, I see. Giraffes blend in with tall trees.

HOMEWORK TIP

Encourage students to use computers at home or on their own time to find out more about giraffes and how they keep safe. Invite them to share their new information with the class.

The Giraffe

The giraffe is the same color as the grass and trees around it. Its spots look ❸ like <u>shadows</u> from tall trees. A giraffe eats only plants. But a lion eats only meat. So spots help the giraffe hide from the lion.

66

WRITING

Have students choose their favorite animal that they have read about in this unit. Then, have them write a brief description of how that animal uses camouflage.

Look for animals where you live. You may not see them right away, but keep looking. Animals could be hiding in all kinds of places.

67

Second Read

Text Comprehension *skills*

Compare and Contrast

● Choose several animals that have been discussed in the selections in this unit and have students compare and contrast them. For example, how are giraffes and zebras alike? How are they different? How are owls and walking sticks alike? How are they different?

● For additional practice with Compare and Contrast, have students complete **Decodable Stories and Comprehension Skills** page 92.

Discussing the Selection

After you have read the selection, discuss it with students. Use prompts such as:

● *What new information did you learn about animal camouflage?*

● *How is the camouflage described in this selection different from other types that you've read about?*

✓ QUICK CHECK

Reread each section of the selection and then ask students to summarize what you read.

28

OBJECTIVES

- Identify and repeat final consonant sounds.
- Blend and break apart sounds in words.
- Participate in Word Play activity.
- Review sound/spellings introduced in this unit.
- Develop fluency by reading aloud.
- Apply decoding skills by reading **Unit 3, Decodable Story 12.**
- Develop writing skills by writing rhyming words.

MATERIALS

Sound/Spelling Cards:
40—Hawk
43—Coil
Decodable Stories and Comprehension Skills, p. 36
High-Frequency Word Cards
Sound/Spelling Card Stories Audiocassette/CD

Phonemic Awareness

Segmentation: Repeating Final Consonants

This activity provides another opportunity for students to focus on final consonant sounds. Say a word, then ask students to repeat the final sound.

Teacher:	maze
Teacher:	What is the final sound?
Students:	/z/

Continue with the following words:

sleep	truck	please
tough	treat	teach
leak	place	leap

Word Study

Word Play

One by one, point to a spelling on each of the **Sound/Spelling Cards** that have been used in this unit—for example, the *ow* spelling for /ow/, the *oo* spelling for /oo/, the *au_* spelling for /aw/, and so on. Ask students to say and spell a word for each sound/spelling that you indicate. Write their words on the board.

Phonics—Blending: Set 2

/aw/ spelled *au_, aw, augh, ough, al, all*

/oi/ spelled *_oy, oi*

Point to the **Sound/Spelling Cards** and tell students that in this lesson, they will review the spellings for /aw/ and /oi/.

Blending Exercise

- Write the following words and sentences on the board.
- Have students blend the words and sentences using the whole-word procedure described in Unit 1 on page 12F.

Line 1:	small	bought	almost	also
Line 2:	fault	caught	jaw	draw
Line 3:	soil	boil	broil	boy
Line 4:	destroy	loyal	voice	choice
Sentence 1:	The earth spins like a ball on its voyage in space.			
Sentence 2:	Roy's father and mother have always enjoyed oysters with sauce.			

- Before reading a sentence, point to and read the underlined sight words.
- Discuss with students that each sentence begins with a capital letter and ends with a punctuation mark.
- Have students reread the sentences to encourage fluency and comprehension.

You will need the following **Sound/Spelling Cards** for blending the words in Set 2.
40—Hawk, 43—Coil

WRITING

Have students identify and write the rhyming words on Line 3 *(soil, boil, broil)*. As a class, ask students to suggest other words that rhyme with these words.

28

SELECTION F • **Hide-and-Seek Animals**

About the Words and Sentences

- For the lines, have students identify the target sound/spelling in each word.
- Have students identify the words with more than one syllable. *(almost, also, destroy, loyal)*
- For Sentence 1, have students identify the possessive pronoun. *(its)*
- For Sentence 2, have students identify the possessive noun. *(Roy's)*

Oral Language

Have students take turns coming to the board, touching a word, and using it in a sentence. Encourage them to extend their sentences by asking *When? Where? How?* and *Why?* questions.

Dictation

For the dictation exercise, have students use writing paper. Dictate the words and sentence for them to write. Use the following procedure:

- Say the first word in each word line. Use the word in a sentence, then say the word again. Have students say the word.
- Tell students to think about how to segment the word into sounds. Then have them write the spelling for each sound.
- After each word line, write (or have a student write) the words on the board. Have students proofread their words. Tell them to circle any incorrect words and to correct them.
- Next dictate the sentence. Dictate one word at a time, following the sounds-in-sequence or whole-word dictation procedure, depending on your students. Remind students to start the sentence with a capital letter and to use correct end punctuation.
- Write (or have a student write) the sentence on the board. Have students proofread their work and correct any incorrect words.

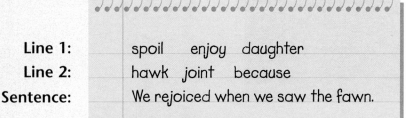

Line 1:	spoil enjoy daughter
Line 2:	hawk joint because
Sentence:	We rejoiced when we saw the fawn.

Building Fluency

Decobable Story: Unit 3, Story 12

- This story reviews the sound/spellings introduced in this unit.
- Have students silently read *Decodable Stories and Comprehension Skills* page 36.
- Call on volunteers to read each paragraph aloud.
- For those students who need help, divide sentences according to natural phrases. Mark these phrases with diagonal slash marks on their worksheets.
- After students have read the story aloud, ask them questions and have them point to and read the answers in the story.
- Have students reread the story aloud with a partner.

HOMEWORK TIP

To help students build fluency, have them take home and read with their families the *Decodable Stories and Comprehension Skills* stories.

29

SELECTION F • **Hide-and-Seek Animals**

- Develop reading skills as the story is reread.
- Gain knowledge of the comprehension skill Compare and Contrast.
- Develop vocabulary by listening to and discussing a selection.
- Develop writing skills by writing about the unit theme.
- Learn about present, past, and future tense of verbs.

Transparencies 3, 18, 33
Decodable Stories and Comprehension Skills, p. 92
Student Reader, pp. 64–67, 68–69
Listening Library Audiocassette/CD
Language Arts, p. T35

Rereading the Selection

Comprehension Skills

Revisiting or rereading a selection allows students to learn and apply skills that give them a more complete understanding of a selection. For today's lesson, reread the selection to students. During the second reading, students will apply the following comprehension skill:

Compare and Contrast: Readers deepen their understanding of what they read by looking for ways in which characters, things, and events in a selection are alike and ways they are different.

After Reading

Reading Reflections

Have students discuss with a partner the Reading Reflections questions on pages 68–69. After partner discussions, have students discuss the answers to the questions as a class.

Independent Reading

- Have students choose books from the *Classroom Library* or other available books to take home and read. Encourage students to read at least one book a week on their own.
- Invite students to sit with partners and talk about the independent reading that they are doing.
- Encourage students to record the titles of the books they are reading on the copy of *Transparency* 3.

TEACHER TIP

Have students listen to the selection recording on the *Listening Library Audiocassette/CD* for a proficient, fluent model of oral reading.

WRITING

Tell students to think about the selections in this unit. Have them write a list of three words that reflect ideas about animal camouflage. For example, students might write *hide, color, safe,* or *tricky.*

SELECTION F • **Hide-and-Seek Animals**

Assessment

Formal

At the conclusion of the lesson, have students complete the assessment Unit 3: Hide-and-Seek Animals. The Lesson Assessments are found in the *Assessment Guide*.

For all the items in this assessment, you should read both the question and answer choices out loud while students follow along silently. Remind students that this is the last lesson in the unit and congratulate them for their hard work.

Ask students to refer to Question 3 of the Unit Assessment. Be sure students know that they should use the information from the story to draw their version of the bat-eared fox. Allow students to create several drafts before creating their final drawing on the assessment page. Have students complete the rest of the Unit Assessment questions. Review the answers as a group activity and give students an opportunity to share the performance items with the rest of the group.

Informal

Read decodable words from the lesson selection "Hide-and-Seek Animals." Ask students to repeat the final consonant sound in the words and think about how it is spelled. Write each word on the board and point out its spelling pattern. Be sure to explain the silent *e* spelling pattern in words such as *safe* and *hide*.

Ending the Lesson

Be sure students have the lesson selection in front of them. Discuss with students how the animals in the story are similar and how they are different. Encourage them to include all the animals in the story, not just the two primary animals.

OBJECTIVES

- Complete lesson and unit assessments.
- Visualize a character.
- Review final consonant sounds.
- Compare and contrast information in a selection.

MATERIALS

Assessment Guide
Student Reader, pp. 64–67

Reading Reflections

Focus on the Characters

- Possible Answer: He wants to be able to watch the opossums play instead of scaring them away or causing them to play dead.
- Possible Answer: Each uses its environment to camouflage itself from other animals. With its stripes, the zebra blends in with the tall grass. The baby deer uses its spots to appear like patches of sunlight on the ground. The rabbit's white fur seems to disappear in the winter snow.
- Possible Answer: They both trick their predators. The walking stick sits still for a long time and appears to be just another stick on the ground. The moth has large spots that look like giant eyes to scare away its enemies.

Focus on the Stories

- "Hide-and-Seek Animals"
- "Night Lights in the Ocean"
- Answers will vary.

Reading Reflections

These questions can help you think about the stories you just read. After you write your responses, discuss them with a partner.

Focus on the Characters

- Why must Steve tiptoe quietly and hide behind a tree in "Opossums"?
- What are some similarities between the zebra, the deer, and the rabbit in "Colors That Hide"?
- How are the walking stick and the moth similar in "Insects Stay Safe"?

Focus on the Stories

- "Colors That Hide" shares different ways that animals hide in order to stay safe from other animals. Name another story in this unit that shares ways that animals use camouflage in order to protect themselves.

68

Look Again

- The spider in "A Tricky Spider" is able to use its camouflage to find food and to stay safe from its enemies. Name another story from this unit that describes a creature that uses its camouflage to find food and to stay safe.
- Using the stories in this unit, what is your favorite way that an animal or insect uses to hide?

Focus on the Theme

- Why is it important that the creatures in this unit learn ways to hide?
- Draw a picture illustrating some of the ways that creatures hide. Test a friend to find your hidden animals and insects.
- Hide-and-seek is a popular children's game. Think about the methods of hiding shared in this unit. How can you use your environment to help you hide better during your next game of Hide-and-seek?

69

Focus on the Theme

- Possible Answer: Without ways to camouflage themselves or to trick their enemies, many animals and insects would be eaten by larger or stronger animals.
- Illustrations will vary.
- Answers will vary.

Pronunciation Key

a as in **at**	**o** as in **ox**	**ou** as in **out**	**ch** as in **chair**
ā as in **late**	**ō** as in **rose**	**u** as in **up**	**hw** as in **which**
â as in **care**	**ô** as in **bought** and **raw**	**ū** as in **use**	**ng** as in **ring**
ä as in **father**		**ûr** as in **turn**; **germ**, **learn**, **firm**, **work**	**sh** as in **shop**
e as in **set**	**oi** as in **coin**		**th** as in **thin**
ē as in **me**	**o͞o** as in **book**	**ə** as in **about**, **chicken**, **pencil**, **cannon**, **circus**	**t͡h** as in **there**
i as in **it**	**o͞o** as in **too**		**zh** as in **treasure**
ī as in **kite**	**or** as in **form**		

The mark (´) is placed after a syllable with a heavy accent, as in chicken (chik´ ən).

The mark (`) after a syllable shows a lighter accent, as in disappear (dis´ ə pēr´).

A

absorb (ab sôrb´) v. To soak up.

afraid (ə frād´) adj. Frightened.

amazement (ə māz´ mənt) n. Overwhelming wonder or surprise.

argue (är´ gū) v. To have a discussion and disagree.

athletic (ath let´ ik) adj. Physically active and strong.

avoid (ə void´) v. To keep away from.

B

baffled (ba´ fəld) A form of the verb **baffle:** To confuse.

bold (bōld) adj. Fearless.

bouquet (bō kā´) n. A bunch of flowers.

bud (bud) n. A small swelling on a plant that will later grow into a flower, stem, leaf, or branch.

bulbs (bulbz) n. Plural form of **bulb:** A usually rounded underground bud from which a plant grows.

C

camouflage (kam´ ə fläzh´) n. A disguise, appearance, or behavior that helps to conceal or deceive.

car lot (kär´ lot´) n. A place where cars are sold.

careless (kâr´ lis) adj. Not paying enough attention.

champion (cham´ pē ən) n. The best in an activity.

chilly (chil´ ē) adj. Cold.

cinch

cinch (sinch) n. A fastening strap.

clever (klev´ ûr) adj. Mentally sharp; quick-witted.

clung (klung) v. Past tense of **cling:** To hold tightly.

codes (kōdz) n. Plural form of **code:** A written symbol that has a special meaning.

contest (kon´ test) n. A competition for a prize.

copper (kop´ ûr) n. A reddish metal.

courage (kûr´ ij) n. Bravery.

crowded (kroud´ ed) A form of the verb **crowd:** To gather closely.

customs (kus´ təmz) n. Plural form of **custom:** A common practice.

D

dashed (dashd) v. Past tense of **dash:** To move with speed.

dawdle (dô´ dəl) v. To waste time.

decades (dek´ ādz) n. Plural form of **decade:** Ten years.

disabled (dis ā´ bəld) adj. Unable to move or act as usual.

disappear (dis´ ə pēr´) v. To pass from sight.

disbelief (dis´ bi lēf´) n. Refusal to believe.

dreary (drēr´ ē) adj. Dull.

drought (drout) n. A long period of dry weather.

E

echoed (ek´ ōd) v. Past tense of **echo:** To repeat.

enemy (en´ ə mē) n. Someone who wishes to do harm to another.

exit (eg´ zit) n. The way out.

extremely (ek strēm´ lē) adv. Very.

F

fancy (fan´ sē) adj. Very decorated.

fascinating (fas´ ə nā´ ting) adj. Very interesting.

ferry (fâr´ ē) n. A boat that carries people across narrow bodies of water.

festivals (fes´ tə vəlz) n. Plural form of **festival:** A feast, holiday, or celebration.

fierce (fērs) adj. Cruel or violent.

finish (fin´ ish) v. To complete.

fir (fûr) n. An evergreen tree that bears cones, such as the pine tree.

flash (flash) n. An instant.

frail (frāl) adj. Fragile; delicate.

future (fū´ chûr) n. The time that is to come.

G

gash (gash) n. A long, deep cut.

gently (jen´ tlē) adv. With care.

glide (glīd) v. To fly without the use of power.

glowed (glōd) v. Past tense of **glow:** To shine.

glowed

Glossary

gnaw   **prairie**

gnaw (nô) v. To bite again and again.

groaned (grōnd) v. Past tense of **groan:** To make a deep, sad sound; to moan.

H

happened (hap´ ənd) v. Past tense of **happen:** To take place.

hazy (hā´ zē) adj. Blurry.

hint (hint) n. A clue or suggestion.

I

illogical (i loj´ i kəl) adj. Showing a lack of good sense or reasoning.

immigrants (im´ i grənts) n. Plural form of **immigrant:** Someone who moves from one country or region to live in another.

incredible (in kred´ ə bəl) adj. Amazing.

innovative (in´ ə vā´ tiv) adj. Creative.

J

journal (jûr´ nəl) n. A record of experiences and thoughts; diary.

judge (juj) v. To decide.

L

laughed (lafd) v. Past tense of **laugh:** To make sounds that show amusement or joy.

layer (lā´ ûr) n. A single thickness of something.

leaning (lē´ ning) A form of the verb **lean:** To bend the body.

lucky (luk´ ē) adj. Having good luck; fortunate.

luring (lûr´ ing) A form of the verb **lure:** To attract greatly.

M

marks (märks) n. Plural form of **mark:** A line or spot made on a surface.

message (mes´ ij) n. Information sent from one person or group to another.

moisture (mois´ chûr) n. Slight wetness.

motionless (mō´ shən lis) adj. Not moving.

mysteries (mis´ tə rēz) n. Plural form of **mystery:** Something that is difficult to explain or understand.

P

petticoat (pet´ ē kōt´) n. A slip or skirt worn as underwear.

phase (fāz) n. A stage in the development of a person or thing.

pillars (pil´ ûrz) n. Plural form of **pillar:** An upright structure that serves as a support for a building or stands alone as a monument.

plucked (plukt) v. Past tense of **pluck:** To pull out.

prairie (prâr´ ē) n. A large, flat grassy area.

predawn   **tangled**

predawn (prē dôn´) n. Before daybreak.

prevented (pri vent´ ed) v. Past tense of **prevent:** To keep from happening.

proclaimed (prō klāmd´) v. Past tense of **proclaim:** To declare publicly.

proposal (prə pō´ zəl) n. A suggestion.

R

reattached (rē ə tachd´) v. Past tense of **reattach:** To connect again.

recall (ri kôl´) v. To remember.

retraced (rē trāsd´) v. Past tense of **retrace:** To go back over.

ridge (rij) n. The long and narrow raised part of something.

riverbank (riv´ ûr bangk) n. The sloped ground along a river.

roaming (rōm´ ing) A form of the verb **roam:** To wander.

S

saddled (sad´ əld) v. Past tense of **saddle:** To put a seat or pad for a rider on a horse.

scene (sēn) n. A view.

scurry (skûr´ ē) v. To move at a quick pace.

secrets (sē´ krits) n. Plural form of **secret:** Private information known by one or a few.

shadows (shad´ ōz) n. Plural form of **shadow:** A dark area that is sometimes made when light shines on a person or thing.

shifted (shift´ ed) v. Past tense of **shift:** To switch or change.

silk (silk) n. Something that looks like the soft, shiny fiber spun by silkworms.

silly (sil´ ē) adj. Funny.

similar (sim´ ə lûr) adj. Alike.

sniffing (snif´ ing) A form of the verb **sniff:** To take short, quick breaths through the nose.

spade (spād) n. A tool with a heavy, flat blade used for digging.

sparkling (spär´ kling) A form of the verb **sparkle:** To shine, as if giving off sparks.

special (spesh´ əl) adj. Not ordinary.

spend (spend) v. To pay out money.

spied (spīd) v. Past tense of **spy:** To notice.

sprouts (sprouts) n. Plural form of **sprout:** A new growth on a plant or flower.

squealed (skwēld) v. Past tense of **squeal:** To make a loud, high-pitched cry.

surroundings (sə roun´ dingz) pl. n. An environment.

T

tangled (tang´ gəld) A form of the verb **tangle:** To catch in something.

182   183

Glossary

tiptoes   **woven**

tiptoes (tip´ tōz´) A form of the verb **tiptoe:** To walk on the tips of one´s toes.

tissue (tish´ ōō) *n.* In animals and plants, a group of alike cells that have the same job.

tomorrow (tə môr´ ō) *n.* The day after today.

trot (trät) *n.* A quick walk.

tumble (tum´ bəl) *v.* To roll about.

U

underneath (un´ dûr nēth´) *prep.* In a lower place.

unusual (un ū´ zhōō əl) *adj.* Not common.

unwise (un wiz´) *adj.* Foolish.

useful (ūs´ fəl) *adj.* Helpful.

V

vanish (van´ ish) *v.* To go out of sight.

village (vil´ ij) *n.* A small community, usually smaller than a town.

W

weary (wēr´ ē) *adj.* Very tired.

weighed (wād) *v.* Past tense of **weigh:** To be of specific weight.

winding (wīn´ ding) *adj.* Full of bends or turns.

wondered (wun´ dûrd) *v.* Past tense of **wonder:** To be curious or doubtful.

woven (wō´ vən) A form of the verb **weave:** To lace together material to make something.

184

Table of Contents

Syllabication

How to Teach Syllabication

- Write the multisyllabic word on the board or chart paper.
- Identify the vowel spellings in the word by placing a *V* under each vowel spelling.
- Identify the consonants between the vowel spellings.
- Identify the vowel and consonant patterns that help mark the syllable breaks. For example, VC/CV in *puppy* or V/CV in *pilot*.
- Identify what the vowel sound should be based upon knowledge of syllable patterns. For example, the vowel in a closed syllable is usually short while the vowel in an open syllable is usually long.
- Pronounce the word.
- Although the vowel-consonant patterns are good predictors for a vowel's correct pronunciation, they do not work all the time. Simply try pronouncing the vowel a different way to see if that makes more sense.

Remember

- Final *-le* acts as if it is spelled *-el*.
- Look for prefixes and suffixes. These are usually separate syllables.
- Divide compound words into smaller words.
- For pronunciation, one syllable in a multisyllabic word usually has more stress or emphasis than the other. In two-syllable words, the stress usually is placed on the first syllable.
- Encourage students to use the generalizations on the following chart when they are reading to decipher the pronunciation of multisyllabic words. Remember that these are generalizations and there are exceptions. If a word does not sound right, then students should be encouraged to use an alternative pronunciation for the vowel spelling.

	Pattern	Division	Example	Generalization
1	VCV	VC/V V/CV	lem/on la/bel	If a word has one consonant after the vowel, the word can be divided before or after the consonant. Dividing after the consonant makes the first syllable closed with a short-vowel sound. Dividing before the consonant makes the syllable open with a long-vowel sound. The only way to know which division is correct is to try one and pronounce the word. If the vowel sound is incorrect, divide the other way.
2	VCCV	VC/CV	kit/ten	If a word has two consonants after the vowel, divide the word between the two consonants. The first syllable is closed, and the vowel in the first syllable is usually short.
3	VV	V/V	cha/os	If a word has two vowels together that make two distinct sounds, divide between the two vowels.
4	VCCCV	VCCCV	hun/dred	Words with three or more consonants in the medial position often contain a blend or a digraph. The blend or digraph should be treated as a single consonant and divided as a VCCV pattern. The first syllable is usually closed, and its vowel sound is short.
5	VCCle VCle	VC/Cle V/Cle	pad/dle ta/ble	Final -le acts like it is spelled -el. If there is a double consonant before the -le, divide between the two consonants as in Number 2 (VC/CV) above. The first syllable is closed, and the vowel is short. If there is a single consonant before the -le, divide before the consonant as in Number 1 (V/CV) above. The first syllable is open, and the vowel is long.
6	Words with Affixes		re/mind/ed un/nam(e)/able	Affixes usually constitute separate syllables. Remove the affixes from a word; syllabify the base word using the consonant/vowel generalizations above. When doing this, the base word should be considered as it was before any spelling changes were made to accommodate the affixes.
7	Compound Words		dump/truck can/dle/stick	Divide the compound into its smaller components. Generally each of the smaller words constitutes a syllable. Sometimes the smaller words contain more than one syllable. The smaller words should be divided using the consonant/vowel generalizations above.

Comprehension Strategy Cards

Duplicate the Comprehension Strategy Cards for each of your students. Use the cards with referenced activities in the *Teacher's Edition.*

Summarizing	**Visualizing**
Asking Questions	**Monitoring and Clarifying**
Making Connections	**Monitoring and Adjusting Reading Speed**
Predicting	

High-Frequency Words

a	color	from	like	of	said	was
again	come	give	look	off	should	what
answer	could	great	many	often	some	where
any	country	have	measure	on	the	who
are	door	heard	mother	once	there	women
become	earth	here	mountain	only	they	would
been	enough	is	move	other	to	
buy	father	learn	never	people	want	

High-Frequency Word Activities

Use the following activities to review sight words. Alternate the activities to avoid tedium.

Make a Word Bank Have each student start his or her word bank. As with a money bank, students can only deposit words they "own" or really know. The purpose of the word bank is to give students a group of words they recognize on sight and with which they are comfortable. Students will find it easier to look for internal features of words when the words are familiar.

Have students review their word-bank words daily. If a student forgets a word and can no longer quickly recognize it, that word should be removed from the word bank until the student is once again fluent with it. Have students continue to accumulate words until they have 200–300 words in their banks.

Word of the Day Each day feature a new sight word for students to think about and learn. Encourage a variety of activities involving the word of the day. Have students

- find the word around the classroom.
- find the word in materials they read.
- create sentences using the word.
- include the word in any word games they play.

Word Sorts When students have accumulated enough words (20 or more), have them use the words in various sorting activities. For example, sort the words by

- part of speech (adjective, adverb, noun, verb).
- vowel sounds.
- initial consonants.
- any structural element you may be working on. Have students look for the element, say the word, point out the target element, and use the word in a sentence.

Familiar Games Have students use their word cards to play a variation of the following games.

- Concentration®
- Bingo®
- Go Fish®

Extending Writing Activities

Various writing activities are suggested throughout the *Teacher's Edition.* Use the following information about the writing process to expand upon these activities.

The Writing Process

Providing a routine or process for students to follow will help them learn a systematic approach to writing. By following the steps of the writing process, students will learn to approach everything they write with purpose and thought. They will learn that although writing takes time and thought, there are steps they can take to make their writing clear, coherent, and appealing to their audience. The writing process consists of the following steps:

Prewriting Prewriting is the phase of the writing process when students contemplate an idea they want to write about. To improve their writing, students should think about and discuss their ideas and plan how they want readers to respond. It is important for students to take time before writing to plan aloud so they can proceed from one phase of the writing process to another without spending unnecessary time making decisions that should have been made earlier. Prewriting is the most time-consuming phase of the writing process, and it may be the most important. The following suggestions can be used as students begin the prewriting phase:

- Circulate around the room as students make notes about writing ideas or work in small groups on prewriting activities.
- Notice which students are having difficulty brainstorming writing ideas. It may help to pair these students with classmates who have many ideas.
- Do not worry if this phase of the process seems noisy and somewhat chaotic. Students must be allowed to let their imaginations roam and to play with words and ideas until they discover an idea they want to explore further. They must be permitted to share ideas and to help each other.

Drafting During the drafting phase of the writing process, students shape their planning notes into main ideas and details. They devote their time and effort to getting words down on paper. Whether students are drafting on scrap paper or on a computer screen, your role is to encourage each writer to put all his or her thoughts on paper. You must also provide a suitable writing environment with the expectation that there will be revision to the original draft.

Sometimes the hardest part of drafting is writing the first sentence. It may help a student to begin in the middle of a story or to write the word *Draft* in big letters at the top of the paper.

- After an initial fifteen or twenty minutes of imposed silence, some students may work better and come up with more ideas if they share as they write.
- You may find that it is difficult to get students to relax as they draft. Remember, most students have been encouraged to be neat and to erase mistakes when they write. It may help to share some of your marked-up manuscripts with students.

Revising The purpose of revising is to make sure a piece of writing expresses the writer's ideas clearly and completely. A major distinction between good writers and poor writers is the amount of time and effort they put into revision.

If your students keep a writing folder, use it to review student progress. Check first drafts against revised versions to see how each student is able to apply revision strategies. If you find that some students are reluctant to revise, you might try the following:

- If a student does not see anything that needs to be changed or does not want to change anything, get him or her to mark the paper in some way—number the details in a description or the steps in a process, circle exact words, or underline the best parts of the paper. Once a paper is marked, the student may not be so reluctant to change it.
- Many students do not like to revise because they think they must recopy everything. This is not always necessary. Sometimes writers can cut and paste selections they want to move. They can use carets and deletion marks to show changes to a piece.
- Give an especially reluctant student a deadline by which she or he must revise a piece or lose the chance to publish it.
- Stress to students the importance of focusing on the intended audience as they revise.

Proofreading After a piece of writing has been revised for content and style, students must read it carefully line by line to make sure it contains no errors. This activity, the fourth phase of the writing process, is called proofreading and is a critical step that must occur before a piece of writing can be published. Students can begin proofreading a piece when they feel it has been sufficiently revised.

- **Proofreading Marks** Student should use standard proofreading marks to indicate the changes they wish to make. Explain to students that these marks are a kind of code used to show which alterations to make without a long explanation. Students may also be interested to know that professional writers, editors, and proofreaders use these same marks. You may want to review these marks one by one, illustrating on the board how to use them.
- Circulate around the room as students are proofreading independently or in pairs.

Publishing Publishing is the process of bringing private writing to the reading public. The purpose of writing is to communicate. Unless students are writing in a journal, they will want to present their writing to the public.

Publishing can be as simple as displaying papers on a bulletin board or as elaborate as creating a class newspaper. Publishing will not and should not always require large blocks of class time. Students may wish to spend more time elaborately presenting their favorite pieces and less time on other work.

- Read the piece, and tell the student if any corrections still need to be made. Also make some suggestions about the best way to publish a piece if a student has difficulty thinking of an idea.
- Make suggestions and give criticism as needed, but remember that students must retain ownership of their publishing. Allow students to make final decisions about form and design.
- Remind students to think about their intended audience when they are choosing the form for their published piece. Will the form they have selected present their ideas effectively to the people they want to reach?

Sound/Spelling Card Stories

Card 1: /a/ Lamb

I'm Pam the Lamb, I am.
This is how I tell my Mommy where
    I am: /a/ /a/ /a/ /a/ /a/.

I'm Pam the Lamb, I am.
This is how I tell my Daddy where
    I am: /a/ /a/ /a/ /a/ /a/.

I'm Pam the Lamb, I am.
That young ram is my brother Sam.
This is how I tell my brother where
    I am: /a/ /a/ /a/ /a/ /a/.

I'm Pam the Lamb; I'm happy where
    I am.

Can you help me tell my family where
    I am? *(Have students respond.)* /a/ /a/ /a/ /a/ /a/.

Card 2: /b/ Ball

Bobby loved to bounce his basketball.
He bounced it all day long.
This is the sound the ball made:
    /b/ /b/ /b/ /b/ /b/.

One day, while Bobby was bouncing
    his basketball,
Bonnie came by on her bike.

Bonnie said, "Hi, Bobby. I have a little
    bitty ball.
May I bounce my ball with you?"

Bobby said, "Sure!" and Bonnie
    bounced her little bitty ball.
What sound do you think Bonnie's ball
    made?
(Encourage a very soft reply.) /b/ /b/ /b/ /b/ /b/

Soon Betsy came by. "Hi, Bobby. Hi, Bonnie," she said.
"I have a great big beach ball. May I bounce my ball with you?"

Bobby and Bonnie said, "Sure!" and Betsy bounced her
    big beach ball.
What sound do you think the beach ball made?
(Encourage a louder, slower reply.) /b/ /b/ /b/ /b/ /b/

(Designate three groups, one for each ball sound.)
Now when Bobby, Bonnie, and Betsy bounce their balls
    together, this is the sound you hear:

(Have all three groups make their sounds in a chorus.)
    /b/ /b/ /b/ /b/ /b/

Card 3: /k/ Camera

Carlos has a new camera. When he
    takes pictures, his camera makes
    a clicking sound like this:
    /k/ /k/ /k/ /k/ /k/.

In the garden, Carlos takes pictures of
    caterpillars crawling on cabbage:
    /k/ /k/ /k/ /k/ /k/.
At the zoo, Carlos takes pictures of a
    camel, a duck, and a kangaroo:
    /k/ /k/ /k/.
In the park, Carlos takes pictures of his
    cousin flying a kite: /k/ /k/ /k/ /k/ /k/.
In his room, Carlos takes pictures of his
    cute kitten, Cozy: /k/ /k/ /k/ /k/ /k/.

Can you help Carlos take pictures with his camera?
(Have students join in.) /k/ /k/ /k/ /k/ /k/ /k/ /k/

Card 4: /d/ Dinosaur

Dinah the Dinosaur loves to dance.
She dances whenever she gets the chance.
Whenever that dinosaur dips and whirls,
This is the sound of her dancing twirls:
/d/ /d/ /d/ /d/ /d/ /d/!

Dinah the Dinosaur dances all day.
From dawn to dark, she dances away.
And when Dinah dances, her dinosaur feet
make a thundering, thudding, extremely
    loud beat:
(loudly, with an exaggerated rhythm)
/d/ /d/ /d/ /d/ /d/ /d/!

Now if you were a dinosaur just like Dinah,
you would certainly dance just as finely as she.
And if you were a Dino, and you had a chance,
what sound would your feet make when you did a dance?
(Have students join in.) /d/ /d/ /d/ /d/ /d/ /d/

Card 5: /e/ Hen

Jem's pet hen likes to peck, peck, peck.
She pecks at a speck on the new red deck.
This is how her pecking sounds:
/e/ /e/ /e/ /e/ /e/.

Jem's pet hen pecks at corn in her pen.
She pecks ten kernels, then pecks again.
This is how her pecking sounds:
/e/ /e/ /e/ /e/ /e/.

Jem's hen pecks at a cracked eggshell.
She's helping a chick get out, alive and well.
This is how her pecking sounds:
/e/ /e/ /e/ /e/ /e/.

Can you help Jem's hen peck?
(Have students say:) /e/ /e/ /e/ /e/ /e/.

Card 6: /f/ Fan

/f/ /f/ /f/ /f/ /f/—What's that funny sound?
It's Franny the Fan going round and round,
and this is the sound that old fan makes:
/f/ /f/ /f/ /f/ /f/.

When it gets too hot, you see,
Franny cools the family: /f/ /f/ /f/ /f/ /f/.
She fans Father's face
and Foxy's fur
and Felicity's feet.
Hear the Fan whir: /f/ /f/ /f/ /f/ /f/.

Can you make Franny the Fan go fast?
(Have students say quickly:)
/f/ /f/ /f/ /f/ /f/.
Faster? /f/ /f/ /f/ /f/ /f/
Fastest? /f/ /f/ /f/ /f/ /f/

Card 7: /g/ Gopher

Gary's a gopher.
He loves to gulp down food.
/g/ /g/ /g/ /g/ /g/, gulps the gopher.

Gary the Gopher gulps down grass
because it tastes so good.
/g/ /g/ /g/ /g/ /g/, gulps the gopher.

Gary the Gopher gulps down grapes—
gobs and gobs of grapes.
/g/ /g/ /g/ /g/ /g/, gulps the gopher.

Gary the Gopher gobbles green beans
and says once more,
/g/ /g/ /g/ /g/ /g/. He's such a hungry gopher!

Gary the Gopher gobbles in the garden
until everything is gone.

What sound does Gary the Gopher make?
(Ask students to join in.) /g/ /g/ /g/ /g/ /g/

Card 8: /h/ Hound

Harry the Hound dog hurries around.
Can you hear Harry's hurrying hound-
    dog sound?
This is the sound Harry's breathing
    makes when he hurries:
/h/ /h/ /h/ /h/ /h/ /h/!

When Harry the Hound dog sees a
    hare hop by,
he tears down the hill, and his four
    feet fly.
Hurry, Harry, hurry! /h/ /h/ /h/ /h/ /h/ /h/!

How Harry the Hound dog loves to hunt
    and chase!
He hurls himself from place to place.
Hurry, Harry, hurry! /h/ /h/ /h/ /h/ /h/ /h/!

When Harry the Hound dog sees a big skunk roam,
He howls for help and heads for home.

What sound does Harry make when he hurries?
(Have students answer.) /h/ /h/ /h/ /h/ /h/ /h/

Appendix

Card 9: /i/ Pig

This is Pickles the Pig.
If you tickle Pickles, she gets the giggles.
This is the sound of her giggling:
/i/ /i/ /i/ /i/ /i/.

Tickle Pickles the Pig under her chin.
Listen! She's giggling: /i/ /i/ /i/ /i/ /i/.
Wiggle a finger in Pickles' ribs.
Listen! She's giggling: /i/ /i/ /i/ /i/ /i/.

Give Pickles the Pig a wink,
and what do you think? First comes a grin.
Then listen!
She's giggling again: /i/ /i/ /i/ /i/ /i/.

Quick! Tickle Pickles the Pig. What will
she say? *(Have students join in.)* /i/ /i/ /i/ /i/ /i/

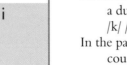

Card 10: /j/ Jump

When Jenny jumps her jump rope,
it sounds like this: /j/ /j/ /j/ /j/ /j/.
When Jackson jumps his jump rope,
it sounds like this: /j/ /j/ /j/ /j/ /j/.

The judges generally agree
that Jenny jumps most rapidly:
(quickly) /j/ /j/ /j/ /j/ /j/.

When Jenny jumps, she jumps to this jingle:
"Jump, jump, jump so quick.
Whenever I jump, I like to kick."
/j/ /j/ /j/ /j/ /j/

The judges generally agree
that Jackson jumps most quietly:
(quietly) /j/ /j/ /j/ /j/ /j/.

When Jackson jumps, he jumps to this jingle:
"Jump, jump, nice and quiet.
See what happens when you try it." /j/ /j/ /j/ /j/ /j/

(to students) Jump rope like Jenny.
(quickly) /j/ /j/ /j/ /j/ /j/
(to students) Jump rope like Jackson.
(quietly) /j/ /j/ /j/ /j/ /j/

Card 11: /k/ Camera

Carlos has a new camera. When he
takes pictures,
His camera makes a clicking sound like this:
/k/ /k/ /k/ /k/ /k/.

In the garden, Carlos takes pictures of
caterpillars crawling on cabbage:
/k/ /k/ /k/ /k/ /k/.
At the zoo, Carlos takes pictures of a camel,
a duck, and a kangaroo:
/k/ /k/ /k/.
In the park, Carlos takes pictures of his
cousin flying a kite: /k/ /k/ /k/ /k/ /k/
In his room, Carlos takes pictures of his
cute kitten, Cozy. /k/ /k/ /k/ /k/ /k/

Can you help Carlos take pictures with his camera?
(Have students join in.) /k/ /k/ /k/ /k/ /k/ /k/ /k/

Card 12: /l/ Lion

Look! It's Leon the Lion.
Leon loves to lap water from lakes,
and this is the sound the lapping lion
makes: /l/ /l/ /l/ /l/ /l/.

Let's join Leon. Quick!
Take a little lick: /l/ /l/ /l/ /l/ /l/.

Are you thirsty lass or lad?
Then lap until you don't feel bad:
/l/ /l/ /l/ /l/ /l/.

What sound do you make when you lap
like Leon the Lion?
(Have students say:) /l/ /l/ /l/ /l/ /l/.

Card 13: /m/ Monkey

For Muzzy the Monkey, bananas
    are yummy.
She munches so many, they fill up
    her tummy.
When she eats, she says:
    /m/ /m/ /m/ /m/ /m/!

Bananas for breakfast, bananas
    for lunch.
Mash them up, mush them up,
Munch, munch, munch, munch!
What does Muzzy the Monkey say?
(Have students say:) /m/ /m/ /m/ /m/ /m/.

Bananas at bedtime? I have a hunch
Muzzy will mash them up, mush them up,
Munch, munch, munch, munch!
Then what does Muzzy the Monkey say?
(Have students say:) /m/ /m/ /m/ /m/ /m/.

Card 14: /n/ Nose

When Norman Newsome has a cold,
    his nose just won't work right.
It makes a noisy, stuffy sound
    through morning, noon, and night.
When Norman has a cold, his nose goes:
    /n/ /n/ /n/ /n/ /n/!

When Norman Newsome has a cold,
    it's hard to just be quiet.
His nose just sniffs and snuffs
    and snarls.
Norman wishes he could hide it!
Instead, his poor, sick noisy nose just goes:
    /n/ /n/ /n/ /n/ /n/!

Norman doesn't hate his nose;
It just does as it pleases!
Even when he sniffs a rose,
he nearly always sneezes.
Then Norman Newsome's nose
again goes *(Have students say:)*
/n/ /n/ /n/ /n/ /n/.

Card 15: /o/ Fox

Bob the Fox did not feel well at all.
He jogged to the doctor's office.
"Say /o/ Mr. Fox! /o/ /o/ /o/."

"My head is hot, and my throat hurts a lot,"
    said the fox.
"Say /o/ Mr. Fox! /o/ /o/ /o/ /o/."

"Yes, you've got a rotten cold," said
    the doctor.
"Say /o/ Mr. Fox! /o/ /o/ /o/."

"Find a spot to sit in the sun," said the doctor.
"Say /o/ Mr. Fox! /o/ /o/ /o/."

He sat on a rock in the sun.
Soon he felt much better.
(with a satisfied sigh) "/o/" said Mr. Fox.
/o/ /o/ /o/

Card 16: /p/ Popcorn

Ping and Pong liked to pop corn. As
    it cooked, it made this sound:
    /p/ /p/ /p/ /p/ /p/ /p/ /p/.
One day Ping poured a whole package of
    popcorn into the pot. It made this sound:
    /p/ /p/ /p/ /p/ /p/ /p/ /p/.

The popcorn popped and popped. Ping filled
    two pots, and still the popcorn popped:
    /p/ /p/ /p/ /p/ /p/ /p/ /p/.
Pong filled three pails with popcorn, and still
    it kept popping: /p/ /p/ /p/ /p/ /p/ /p/ /p/.

"Call all your pals," said their pop. "We'll have
    a party."
And the popcorn kept popping.
(Have students say the /p/ sound very fast.)

Appendix

Card 17: /kw/ Quacking duck

Quincy the Duck couldn't quite quack
   like all the other quacking ducks.
Oh, he could say /kw/ /kw/ /kw/ /kw/,
   but it never seemed just right.

When Quincy tried to quack quietly *(softly)*
   /kw/ /kw/ /kw/ /kw/
   his quack came out loudly *(loudly)*
   /kw/ /kw/ /kw/ /kw/!
When he tried to quack slowly *(slowly)*
   /kw/ . . . /kw/ . . . /kw/ . . . /kw/
   his quack came out quickly *(quickly)*
   /kw/ /kw/ /kw/ /kw/!
Quincy just couldn't quack right!

One day Quincy was practicing quacks.
   His friend Quip quacked along with him.
"Repeat after me," said Quip
   (quietly) /kw/ /kw/ /kw/ /kw/
But Quincy quacked back,
   (in normal voice) /kw/ /kw/ /kw/ /kw/ /kw/!
Quincy still couldn't quack quite right.

But Quincy kept quacking. He said, "I won't quit until I quack
   like the best quackers around."
Can you show Quincy how quacking ducks quack?
(Have students join in.)
/kw/ /kw/ /kw/ /kw/ /kw/ /kw/ /kw/ /kw/

Card 18: /r/ Robot

Little Rosie Robot just runs and runs and runs.
She races round and round to get her chores
   all done.
Here's how Rosie sounds when she's working:
   /r/ /r/ /r/ /r/ /r/!

Rosie can rake around your roses.
Here comes that running robot!
   /r/ /r/ /r/ /r/ /r/!

Rosie can repair your wrecked radio.
Here comes that racing robot!
   (softly) /r/ /r/ /r/ /r/ /r/

Rosie can mend your round red rug.
Here comes that roaring robot!
   (loudly) /r/ /r/ /r/ /r/ /r/!

Rosie rarely does anything wrong.
But there are two things that Rosie can't
   do: rest and relax.
Here comes that roaring robot!
What does she say?
(Have students call out the answer:)
   /r/ /r/ /r/ /r/ /r/.

Card 19: /s/ Sausages

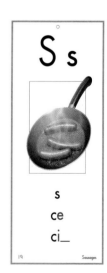

Sue and Sammy had a nice place in
   the city.
On Saturday, Sue and Sammy decided
   to have sausages for supper.
Sammy put seven sausages in
   a skillet. /s/ /s/ /s/ /s/ /s/ /s/ /s/

Soon the smell of sausages filled
   the air.
   /s/ /s/ /s/ /s/ /s/, sizzled the sausages.

"Pull up a seat, Sue," said Sammy.
"The sausages are almost ready to serve."
   /s/ /s/ /s/ /s/ /s/, sizzled the sausages.

Sue and Sammy ate the delicious sausages.
Soon they wanted more, so Sam put six more sausages in the
   frying pan.
   /s/ /s/ /s/ /s/ /s/ /s/, sizzled the sausages.

If you were cooking sausages with Sammy and Sue,
What sound would the sausages make as they sizzled?
(Have students join in:) /s/ /s/ /s/ /s/ /s/ /s/.

Card 20: /t/ Timer

When Tom Tuttle cooks, he uses
 his timer.
Tom Tuttle's timer ticks like this:
/t/ /t/ /t/ /t/ /t/ /t/ /t/

Tonight Tom Tuttle wants tomatoes
 on toast.
Tom turns on the oven.
Tom puts tomatoes on toast in the oven.
Tom sets the timer.
The timer will Ding! when Tom's toast
 and tomatoes are done.
Until the timer dings, it ticks:
/t/ /t/ /t/ /t/ /t/ /t/ /t/.

Tomatoes on toast take ten minutes.
/t/ /t/ /t/ /t/ /t/ /t/ /t/
Tom can hardly wait. /t/ /t/ /t/ /t/ /t/ /t/ /t/
He taps out the time: /t/ /t/ /t/ /t/ /t/ /t/ /t/.

What is the sound of Tom Tuttle's ticking timer?
(Have students join in.) /t/ /t/ /t/ /t/ /t/ /t/ /t/
Ding! Time for dinner, Tom Tuttle!

Card 21: /u/ Tug

Tubby the Tugboat can huff and puff
and push and pull to move big stuff.
 /u/ /u/ /u/ /u/ /u/ /u/ /u/
That's the sound of Tubby the Tug.

If a boat is stuck and will not budge,
Tubby the Tugboat can give it a nudge.
 /u/ /u/ /u/ /u/ /u/ /u/ /u/
It's Tubby the Trusty Tug.

If a ship is caught in mud and muck,
Tubby the Tugboat can get it unstuck.
 /u/ /u/ /u/ /u/ /u/ /u/ /u/
It's Tubby the Trusty Tug.

Can you help Tubby push and pull?
(Have students join in.) /u/ /u/ /u/ /u/ /u/ /u/ /u/

Card 22: /v/ Vacuum

Vinny the Vacuum is cleaning again.
Before visitors visit, he always begins.
This is the sound of his very loud voice:
 /v/ /v/ /v/ /v/ /v/!
If only that Vinny could clean without noise!

Vinny sucks up the crumbs baby Vicki
 dropped.
 /v/ /v/ /v/ /v/ /v/!
He visits nearly everywhere except the
 tabletop.
 /v/ /v/ /v/ /v/ /v/!
Three vine leaves, two vitamins, part of a
 vase—
 all vanish when Vinny goes over the
 place! /v/ /v/ /v/ /v/ /v/

As Vinny vacuums the velvety rug
 a van full of visitors starts to drive up.
But Vinny's not done with the very last room!
Will you help Vinny the Vacuum vacuum?
*(Ask groups of students to say /v/ in a round to make the continuous
sound of a vacuum cleaner.)*

Card 23: /w/ Washer

Willie the Washer washed white clothes all
 week.
When he washed, he went:
 /w/ /w/ /w/ /w/ /w/ /w/ /w/.

All winter, Willie worked well.
 /w/ /w/ /w/ /w/ /w/ /w/ /w/
But last Wednesday, Willie was weak. *(softly)*
 /w/ /w/ /w/ /w/ /w/ /w/ /w/
This week, he got worse. *(slower and slower)*
 /w/ . . . /w/ . . . /w/ . . .
Poor Willie was worn out. *(slowly)* /w/

Then a worker came and fixed Willie's wires.
Willie felt wonderful. *(more loudly)*
 /w/ /w/ /w/ /w/ /w/ /w/ /w/!
Now Willie can wash and wash wildly!
 (quickly) /w/ /w/ /w/ /w/ /w/ /w/ /w/!

How does Willie the Washer sound now when he washes?
(Have students join in.) /w/ /w/ /w/ /w/ /w/ /w/ /w/
Can you wash just like Willie?
(Students together:) /w/ /w/ /w/ /w/ /w/ /w/ /w/.

Appendix

Card 24: /ks/ Exit

Rex is called the Exiting X;
he runs to guard the door.
To get past Rex, make the sound of X:
/ks/ /ks/ /ks/ /ks/.
This is what Rex expects!

The ox knows the sound of X,
so she says /ks/ /ks/ /ks/ /ks/
and gets past Rex.

The fox knows the sound of X,
so he says /ks/ /ks/ /ks/ /ks/
and gets past Rex.

Can you say /ks/ /ks/ /ks/ /ks/
and get past Rex the Exiting X?
(Have students respond:) /ks/ /ks/ /ks/ /ks/!
Did we get past Rex?
(Have students say:) Yes!

Card 25: /y/ Yak

Yolanda and Yoshiko are yaks.
They don't yell.
They don't yelp.
They don't yodel.
They don't yawn.
These young yaks just yak.
Yakety-yak, yakety-yak!
Can you hear the sound they make?
/y/ /y/ /y/ /y/ /y/ /y/ /y/.

Yolanda and Yoshiko yak in the yard.
/y/ /y/ /y/ /y/ /y/ /y/ /y/
They yak on their yellow yacht.
/y/ /y/ /y/ /y/ /y/ /y/ /y/
They yak in the yam patch.
/y/ /y/ /y/ /y/ /y/ /y/ /y/
These yaks yak all year!
/y/ /y/ /y/ /y/ /y/ /y/ /y/

Do you think these yaks like to yak?
(Have students answer:) Yes!
(Ask students to yak like Yolanda and Yoshiko.)

Card 26: /z/ Zipper

Zack's jacket has a big long zipper.
The zipper zips like this: /z/ /z/ /z/ /z/.

When little Zack goes out to play,
he zips the zipper up this way:
/z/ /z/ /z/ /z/.

Later, when he comes back in,
Zack zips the zipper down again:
/z/ /z/ /z/ /z/.

Can you help Zack zip his jacket zipper?
(Have students join in.) /z/ /z/ /z/ /z/

Card 27: /ar/ Armadillo

Arthur Armadillo likes to whistle,
    hum, and sing.
But when he gets a head cold,
    his voice won't do a thing.

To sing and still sound charming—
and not sound so alarming—
Arthur has thought up the thing
of very often gargling.

Then Arthur Armadillo sounds like this:
/ar/ /ar/ /ar/ /ar/ /ar/.

Arthur gargles in the park. /ar/ /ar/ /ar/
    /ar/ /ar/
He gargles in the dark. /ar/ /ar/ /ar/ /ar/ /ar/
He gargles on the farm. /ar/ /ar/ /ar/ /ar/ /ar/
He gargles in the barn. /ar/ /ar/ /ar/ /ar/ /ar/
Arthur is great at gargling! /ar/ /ar/ /ar/ /ar/ /ar/

What does Arthur Armadillo's gargling sound like?
(Have students respond.) /ar/ /ar/ /ar/ /ar/ /ar/

Card 28: /hw/ Whale

Look! It's Whitney the Whispering Whale!
Listen to her whisper: /hw/ /hw/ /hw/ /hw/
/hw/.

When Whitney meets with other whales,
she entertains them, telling tales.
She whispers: /hw/ /hw/ /hw/ /hw/ /hw/.
She's Whitney the Whispering Whale.

What ocean wonders does Whitney relate?
Does she whisper of whirlpools or whales
that are great?
We're the only people, so we'll never guess.
She's Whitney the Whispering Whale!
/hw/ /hw/ /hw/.

Whatever Whitney whispers must be fun.
The other whales whistle when she's done.
They whoop and whack the white-capped waves.
They love Whitney the Whispering Whale! /hw/ /hw/ /hw/.

If you were Whitney, what sounds would you whisper
to your whale friends as they gathered to listen?
(Have students whisper:) /hw/ /hw/ /hw/ /hw/ /hw/.

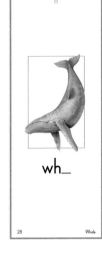

Card 29: /er/ Bird

Bertie the Bird is the oddest bird
    that anyone has ever heard.
He doesn't caw like a crow or a gull,
    or tweet like a robin or a wren.
Instead, he makes a chirping sound—
    over and over again!
/er/ /er/ /er/ /er/ /er/ /er/!

Bert can't fly, since his wings are too short.
He arranges his feathers in curls.
He admits, "I've short wings and I don't really
    sing,
But I still am an interesting bird!"
/er/ /er/ /er/ /er/ /er/ /er/

Can you chirp like Bertie the Bird?
(Have students say:) /er/ /er/ /er/, /er/ /er/ /er/!

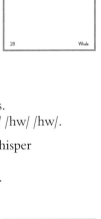

Card 30: /sh/ Shell

Sheila and Sharon went to the seashore.
They saw lots of shells.
Sheila rushed from shell to shell.
Sharon held a shell to Sheila's ear.

"Do you hear anything?" asked Sharon.
"Yes, it sounds like the ocean crashing on
    the shore," shouted Sheila,
"/sh/ /sh/ /sh/ /sh/ /sh/."

"Let's try different shaped shells," said Sharon.
She found a big shell. It made a loud /sh/
    /sh/ /sh/ /sh/.
Sheila found a small shell. It made a soft
    /sh/ /sh/ /sh/ /sh/.
They found a thin shell. It made a high
    /sh/ /sh/ /sh/ /sh/.
They found a fat shell. It made a deep /sh/ /sh/ /sh/ /sh/.

Sheila and Sharon listened to lots of shells. But no matter
What the size and shape, what do you think Sheila and Sharon
Heard in every shell?
(Have students join in.) /sh/ /sh/ /sh/ /sh/

Card 31: /th/ Thimble

Theodore Thimble is a thinker.
Theodore thinks and thinks and thinks.
And when he thinks, he rubs his head.
/th/ /th/ /th/ /th/ /th/ /th/ /th/ /th/ /th/

Theodore thinks of thumbs—
Thin thumbs
Thick thumbs
All different kinds of thumbs.
/th/ /th/ /th/ /th/ /th/ /th/ /th/ /th/ /th/

Theodore thinks of thread—
Red thread
Blue thread
All different color thread.
/th/ /th/ /th/ /th/ /th/ /th/ /th/ /th/ /th/

Thread and thumb
Thumb and thread
These are the thoughts
In Theodore's head.
/th/ /th/ /th/ /th/ /th/ /th/ /th/ /th/ /th/

Appendix

Card 32: /ch/ Chipmunk

Chipper the Chipmunk is cheerful and chubby.
He chats and he chatters all day.
/ch/ /ch/ /ch/ /ch/ /ch/ /ch/
He sits on a chimney.
Can you hear him chat?
He chats and he chatters this way:
/ch/ /ch/ /ch/ /ch/ /ch/ /ch/.

Chipper stuffs cherries into his cheek.
Then he chatters /ch/ /ch/ /ch/ /ch/ /ch/ /ch/.
Chipper likes chestnuts and acorns to eat.
Then he chatters /ch/ /ch/ /ch/ /ch/ /ch/ /ch/.

Can you children chatter like Chipper?
(Have students answer.)
/ch/ /ch/ /ch/ /ch/ /ch/ /ch/

Now chat with the chipmunk child beside you.
(Ask partners to have chipmunk conversations.)
/ch/ /ch/ /ch/ /ch/ /ch/ /ch/

Note: Cards 33 through 37 are long vowel cards and do not have corresponding stories.

Card 38: /ng/ Gong

The young king has slept much
    too long.
Let's go and awaken the king with
    a gong.

A pinging gong? It makes a quiet song:
(softly) /ng/ /ng/ /ng/ /ng/ /ng/.

That gong is wrong.
(softly) /ng/ /ng/ /ng/ /ng/ /ng/.
We need a louder gong!

A dinging gong? It makes this song:
(a bit louder) /ng/ /ng/ /ng/ /ng/ /ng/ /ng/.

That, too, is wrong.
(as before) /ng/ /ng/ /ng/ /ng/
We need an even louder gong!

A clanging gong?
It makes this song: *(loudly)* /ng/ /ng/ /ng/ /ng/ /ng/!

That's just the thing! /ng/ /ng/ /ng/ /ng/ /ng/!
That's the gong we needed all along!

Now, which gong should we bring to awaken the King?
(Have students make the /ng/ sound loud enough to wake the king.) /ng/ /ng/ /ng/ /ng/ /ng/

Card 39: /ow/ Cow

Wow! Can you see poor Brownie
    the Cow?
She got stung by a bee and look at
    her now!
She jumps up and down with an
    /ow/ /ow/ /ow/ /ow/.

Poor Brownie found that a big buzzing sound
meant bees all around—in the air, on the
ground.
Just one little bee gave Brownie a sting.
Now you can hear poor Brownie sing:
    /ow/ /ow/ /ow/ /ow/.

Now if you were a cow and a bee found you
You'd probably jump and shout out too!
(Have students join in.) /ow/ /ow/ /ow/ /ow/

Card 40: /aw/ Hawk

Hazel the Hawk never cooks her food;
Instead, she eats it raw.
And when she thinks of dinnertime
She caws: /aw/ /aw/ /aw/ /aw/.

Hazel the Hawk likes rabbits and mice
and catches them with her claws.
In August, she flies high above the fields
and spies them below, in the straw.
Sometimes she even snatches a snake!
And when she's caught one, she caws:
    /aw/ /aw/ /aw/ /aw/.

If you were a hawk thinking of dinnertime,
    what do you think you'd say?
(Have students answer.) /aw/ /aw/ /aw/ /aw/

Card 41: /o͞o/ Goo

/o͞o/ /o͞o/ /o͞o/ /o͞o/
What can be making that sound?
Could it be a new flute playing a tune?
No. It's goo!
/o͞o/ /o͞o/ /o͞o/ /o͞o/

The goo is oozing all over my hand.
/o͞o/ /o͞o/ /o͞o/ /o͞o/

The goo is oozing on my boots.
/o͞o/ /o͞o/ /o͞o/ /o͞o/

The goo is oozing off the roof.
The goo is oozing everywhere!
/o͞o/ /o͞o/ /o͞o/ /o͞o/

The goo is as sticky as glue.
It is as thick as stew.
/o͞o/ /o͞o/ /o͞o/ /o͞o/

Soon the goo will fill the school!
/o͞o/ /o͞o/ /o͞o/ /o͞o/

Soon the goo will reach the moon!
/o͞o/ /o͞o/ /o͞o/ /o͞o/

What sound does the oozing goo make?
(Have students join in.) /o͞o/ /o͞o/ /o͞o/ /o͞o/

Card 42: /o͝o/ Foot

Mr. Hood took off his shoes and socks
    And went out walking in the wood.
He kicked a rock and hurt his foot.
    /o͝o/ /o͝o/ /o͝o/ /o͝o/

"Look, look!" said Mr. Hood. "There's a
    babbling, bubbling brook. I'll walk
    in the brook, so I won't hurt my foot."
So he stepped in the water, and guess what?
    /o͝o/ /o͝o/ /o͝o/ /o͝o/

Mr. Hood stepped on a hook!
    /o͝o/ /o͝o/ /o͝o/ /o͝o/
Mr. Hood stood. He shook his foot.
    /o͝o/ /o͝o/ /o͝o/ /o͝o/

"This isn't good," said Mr. Hood.
"I think I'll go home and read a book.
At least that won't hurt my foot."
(Have students join in.) /o͝o/ /o͝o/ /o͝o/ /o͝o/

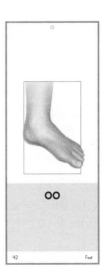

Card 43: /oi/ Coil

Boing! Boing! Boing! Boing!
Roy the Coil is a bouncing toy,
and this is the sound of his bounce:
    /oi/ /oi/ /oi/ /oi/ /oi/.

Doing! Doing! Doing! Doing!
Roy the Coil just dances for joy.
This is the sound of his dance:
    /oi/ /oi/ /oi/ /oi/ /oi/.

Ke-boing! Ke-boing!
Roy the Coil springs over a boy.
What springing sound does he make?
(Have students join in.)
    /oi/ /oi/ /oi/ /oi/ /oi/

Index

A

About the Words and Sentences, Unit 1: 2H–2I, 3C, 4G, 7C, 8G, 11C, 12G, 13C, 14G, 17C, 18G, 19C; **Unit 2:** 22H, 25C, 26F, 29C, 30F, 31C, 32F, 35C, 36F, 37C, 38F, 41C; **Unit 3:** 44H, 47C, 48F, 51C, 52F, 57C, 58F, 59C, 60F, 63C, 64F, 67C; **Unit 4:** 70H, 75C, 76F, 81C, 82F, 89C, 90F, 95C, 96F, 101C, 102F, 105C; **Unit 5:** 108H, 113A, 114F, 117A, 118F, 123A, 124F, 127A, 128F, 133A, 134F, 137A; **Unit 6:** 140F, 145A, 146D, 153A, 154D, 159A, 160D, 165A, 166D, 171A, 172D, 177A

Activate Prior Knowledge, Unit 1: 2K, 4I, 8I, 12I, 14I, 18I; **Unit 2:** 22K, 26I, 30I, 32I, 36I, 38I; **Unit 3:** 44K, 48I, 52I, 58I, 60I, 64I; **Unit 4:** 70K, 76I, 82I, 90I, 96I, 102I; **Unit 5:** 108K, 114I, 118I, 124I, 128I, 134I; **Unit 6:** 140I, 146G, 154G, 160G, 166G, 172G

Alliterative Word Game, Unit 2: 29A

Answering Questions, Unit 1: 14; **Unit 2:** 38; **Unit 4:** 74, 98; **Unit 5:** 114, *see also* Asking Questions

Apposition, Unit 2: 22K–22L, 26I–26J, 30I, 32I–32J, 36I–36J, 38I–38J; **Unit 3:** 48I–48J, 58I–58J, 64I–64J; **Unit 4:** 82I–82J, 96I–96J, 102I–102J; **Unit 5:** 114I–114J, 128I–128J; **Unit 6:** 140I–140J, 172G–172H

Asking Questions, Unit 1: 2L, 2, 14J, 14; **Unit 2:** 30J, 30, 38J, 38; **Unit 3:** 44L, 44, 46, 58J, 58, 64J, 64; **Unit 4:** 70L, 70, 72, 96J, 96, 102J, 104; **Unit 5:** 114J, 114, 116; **Unit 6:** 140J, 142, 144, 154H, 156, 158, 166H, 166, 168, 170

Assessment, Unit 1: 3F, 7F, 11F, 13F, 17F, 19F; **Unit 2:** 25F, 29F, 31F, 35F, 37F, 41F; **Unit 3:** 47F, 51F, 57F, 59F, 63F, 67F; **Unit 4:** 75F, 81F, 89F, 95F, 101F, 105F; **Unit 5:** 113D, 117D, 123D, 127D, 133D, 137D; **Unit 6:** 145D, 153D, 159D, 165D, 171D, 177D

Audiocassettes, *see* Listening Library Audiocassettes/CDs

Author's Point of View, Unit 6: 173, 175, 177, 177C

Author's Purpose, Unit 1: 5, 7, 7E; **Unit 3:** 59, 59E; **Unit 4:** 97, 99, 101, 101E; **Unit 5:** 125, 127, 127C; **Unit 6:** 161, 163, 165, 165C

B

Background Information, Unit 1: 2K, 4I, 8I, 12I, 14I, 18I; **Unit 2:** 22K, 26I, 30I, 32I, 36I, 38I; **Unit 3:** 44K, 48I, 52I, 58I, 60I, 64I; **Unit 4:** 70K, 76I, 82I, 90I, 96I, 102I; **Unit 5:** 108K, 114I, 118I, 124I, 128I, 134I; **Unit 6:** 140I, 146G, 154G, 160G, 166G, 172G

Blending Exercise, Unit 1: 2H, 3B, 4F, 7B, 8F, 11B, 12F, 13B, 14F, 17B, 18F, 19B; **Unit 2:** 22H, 25B, 26F, 29B, 30F, 31B, 32F, 35B, 36F, 37B, 38F, 41B; **Unit 3:** 44H, 47B, 48F, 51B, 52F, 57B, 58F, 59B, 60F, 63B, 64F, 67B; **Unit 4:** 70H, 75B, 76F, 81B, 82F, 89B, 90F, 95B, 96F, 101B, 102F, 105B; **Unit 5:** 108H, 113A, 114F, 117A, 118F, 123A, 124F, 127A, 128F, 133A, 134F, 137A; **Unit 6:** 140F, 145A, 146D, 153A, 154D, 159A, 160D, 165A, 166D, 171A, 172D, 177A

Building Fluency, Unit 1: 2J, 3D, 4H, 7D, 8H, 11D, 12H, 13D, 14H, 17D, 18H, 19D; **Unit 2:** 22J, 25D, 26H, 29D, 30H, 31D, 32H, 35D, 36H, 37D, 38H, 41D; **Unit 3:** 44J, 47D, 48H, 51D, 52H, 57D, 58H, 59D, 60H, 63D, 64H, 67D; **Unit 4:** 70J, 75D, 76H, 81D, 82H, 89D, 90H, 95D, 96H, 101D, 102H, 105D; **Unit 5:** 108J, 113B, 114H, 117B, 118H, 123B, 124H, 127B, 128H, 133B, 134H, 137B; **Unit 6:** 140H, 145B, 146F, 153B, 154F, 159B, 160F, 165B, 166F, 171B, 172F, 177B

C

Cause and Effect, Unit 1: 13, 13E; **Unit 2:** 37, 37E; **Unit 3:** 49, 51, 51E

CDs, *see* Listening Library Audiocassettes/CDs

Clarifying, *see* Monitoring and Clarifying

Classifying and Categorizing, Unit 3: 53, 55, 57, 57E; **Unit 4:** 103, 105, 105E; **Unit 6:** 167, 169, 171, 171C

Classroom Library, Unit 1: 2B; **Unit 2:** 22B; **Unit 3:** 44B; **Unit 4:** 70B; **Unit 5:** 108B; **Unit 6:** 140B

Compare and Contrast, Unit 2: 31, 31E; **Unit 3:** 65, 67, 67E; **Unit 4:** 91, 93, 95, 95E; **Unit 5:** 129, 131, 133, 133C

Comparing Word Length, Unit 1: 11A

Comprehension Skills, *see* Author's Point of View; Author's Purpose; Cause and Effect; Classifying and Categorizing; Compare and Contrast; Drawing Conclusions;

Fact and Opinion; Main Idea and Details; Making Inferences; Reality and Fantasy; Sequence

Comprehension Strategies, *see* Asking Questions; Making Connections; Monitoring and Adjusting Reading Speed; Monitoring and Clarifying; Predicting; Summarizing; Visualizing

Confirming Predictions, *see* Predicting

Context Clues, Unit 1: 2K–2L, 4I–4J, 8I–8J, 12I–12J, 14I–14J, 18I–18J; **Unit 3:** 52I–52J, 60I–60J; **Unit 4:** 70K–70L, 76I–76J, 90I; **Unit 5:** 118I–118J, 134I–134J; **Unit 6:** 146G–146H, 154G–154H, 160G–160H

D

Decodable Stories, Unit 1: 2J, 3D, 4H, 7D, 8H, 11D, 12H, 13D, 14H, 17D, 18H, 19D; **Unit 2:** 22J, 25D, 26H, 29D, 30H, 31D, 32H, 35D, 36H, 37D, 38H, 41D; **Unit 3:** 44J, 47D, 48H, 51D, 52H, 57D, 58H, 59D, 60H, 63D, 64H, 67D; **Unit 4:** 70J, 75D, 76H, 81D, 82H, 89D, 90H, 95D, 96H, 101D, 102H, 105D; **Unit 5:** 108J, 113B, 114H, 117B, 118H, 123B, 124H, 127B, 128H, 133B, 134H, 137B; **Unit 6:** 140H, 145B, 146F, 153B, 154F, 159B, 160F, 165B, 166F, 171B, 172F, 177B

Dictation, Unit 1: 2I, 3C, 4G, 7C, 8G, 11C, 12G, 13C, 14G, 17C, 18G, 19C; **Unit 2:** 22I, 25C, 26G, 29C, 30G, 31C, 32G, 35C, 36G, 37C, 38G, 41C; **Unit 3:** 44I, 47C, 48G, 51C, 52C, 57C, 58G, 59C, 60G, 63C, 64G, 67C; **Unit 4:** 70I, 75C, 76G, 81C, 82G, 89C, 90G, 95C, 96G, 101C, 102G, 105C; **Unit 5:** 108I, 113B, 114G, 117B, 118G, 123B, 124G, 127B, 128G, 133B, 134G, 137B; **Unit 6:** 140G, 145B, 146E, 153B, 154E, 159B, 160E, 165B, 166E, 171B, 172E, 177B

Discussing the Selection, Unit 1: 3, 7, 11, 13, 17, 19; **Unit 2:** 25, 29, 31, 35, 37, 41; **Unit 3:** 47, 51, 57, 59, 63, 67; **Unit 4:** 75, 81, 89, 95, 101, 105; **Unit 5:** 113, 117, 123, 127, 133, 137; **Unit 6:** 145, 153, 159, 165, 171, 177

Drawing Conclusions, Unit 1: 19, 19E; **Unit 2:** 39, 41, 41E; **Unit 3:** 61, 63, 63E; **Unit 5:** 109, 111, 113, 113C

E

Ending the Lesson, Unit 1: 3F, 7F, 11F, 13F, 17F, 19F; **Unit 2:** 25F, 29F, 31F, 35F, 37F, 41F; **Unit 3:** 47F, 51F, 57F, 59F, 63F, 67F; **Unit 4:** 75F, 81F, 89F, 95F, 101F, 105F; **Unit 5:** 113D, 117D, 123D, 127D, 133D, 137D; **Unit 6:** 145D, 153D, 159D, 165D, 171D, 177D

F

Fact and Opinion, Unit 4: 83, 85, 87, 89, 89E; **Unit 6:** 155, 157, 159, 159C

Fantasy and Reality, *see* Reality and Fantasy

Fluency, *see* Building Fluency

G

Grammar

Abbreviations, **Unit 5:** 125

Action Verbs, **Unit 3:** 59; **Unit 4:** 73, 85, 103; **Unit 6:** 167

Adjectives, **Unit 4:** 93, 103; **Unit 6:** 175

Adverbs, **Unit 4:** 97, 103; **Unit 6:** 175

Capitalization, **Unit 1:** 9; **Unit 6:** 141

Commas in a Series, **Unit 5:** 115, 131; **Unit 6:** 141

Common Nouns, **Unit 2:** 23, 39; **Unit 4:** 103; **Unit 6:** 157

Compound Sentences, **Unit 5:** 111

Conjunctions, **Unit 5:** 111

Dialogue, **Unit 5:** 119, 135

End Marks, **Unit 1:** 5, 19; **Unit 6:** 141

Incomplete Sentences, **Unit 1:** 15

Irregular Plural Nouns, **Unit 2:** 33, 39; **Unit 6:** 157

Kinds of Sentences, **Unit 1:** 3, 19; **Unit 6:** 141

Linking Verbs, **Unit 3:** 61; **Unit 4:** 85, 103; **Unit 6:** 167

Nouns, **Unit 2:** 23, 27, 31, 33, 37, 39; **Unit 4:** 103; **Unit 6:** 157

Plural Nouns, **Unit 2:** 31, 39; **Unit 6:** 157

Possessive Nouns, **Unit 2:** 37, 39; **Unit 6:** 157

Possessive Pronouns, **Unit 3:** 49; **Unit 6:** 163

Pronoun-Antecedent Agreement, **Unit 3:** 55

Pronouns, **Unit 3:** 45; **Unit 4:** 103; **Unit 6:** 163

Proper Nouns, **Unit 2:** 27, 39; **Unit 4:** 103; **Unit 6:** 157

Quotation Marks, **Unit 5:** 119, 135

Subject/Verb Agreement, **Unit 4:** 77

Subjects and Predicates, **Unit 1:** 13; **Unit 6:** 149

Verbs, **Unit 3:** 59, 61, 65; **Unit 4:** 73, 85, 103; **Unit 6:** 167

Verb Tenses, **Unit 3:** 65; **Unit 4:** 85; **Unit 6:** 167

Appendix

Unit 5: 108H, 113B, 114F, 117B, 118F, 123B, 124F, 127B, 128F, 133B, 134F, 137B; Unit 6: 140F, 145B, 146D, 153B, 154D, 159B, 160D, 165B, 166D, 171B, 172D, 177B

Overview of Selection, Unit 1: 2B; **Unit 2:** 22B; **Unit 3:** 44B; **Unit 4:** 70B; **Unit 5:** 108B; **Unit 6:** 140B

P

Phonemic Awareness, Unit 1: 2E–2F, 3A, 4C–4D, 7A, 8C–8D, 11A, 12C–12D, 13A, 14C–14D, 17A, 18C–18D, 19A; **Unit 2:** 22E–22F, 25A, 26C–26D, 29A, 30C–30D, 31A, 32C–32D, 35A, 36C–36D, 37A, 38C–38D, 41A; **Unit 3:** 44E–44F, 47A, 48C–48D, 51A, 52C–52D, 57A, 58C–58D, 59A, 60C–60D, 63A, 64C–64D, 67A; **Unit 4:** 70E–70F, 75A, 76C–76D, 81A, 82C–82D, 89A, 90C–90D, 95A, 96C–96D, 101A, 102C–102D, 105A; **Unit 5:** 108E–108F, 114C–114D, 118C–118D, 124C–124D, 128C–128D, 134C–134D, *see also* Listening Game; Segmentation

Phonics

/a/, **Unit 1:** 2G–2J, 19B–19D; **Unit 6:** 159A–159B

/ā/, **Unit 2:** 22G–22J, 31B–31D, 32E–32H, 41B–41D; **Unit 4:** 76E–76H, 82E–82H; **Unit 5:** 137A–137B; **Unit 6:** 172C–172F

/ar/, **Unit 1:** 18E–18H, 19B–19D; **Unit 4:** 81B–81D; **Unit 5:** 124E–124H; **Unit 6:** 140E–140H, 177A–177B

/aw/, **Unit 3:** 58E–58H, 59B–59D, 63B–63D, 67B–67D; **Unit 4:** 89B–89D; **Unit 5:** 117A–117B, 137A–137B; **Unit 6:** 171A–171B

/b/, **Unit 1:** 7B–7D, 19B–19D; **Unit 5:** 123A–123B

/ch/, **Unit 2:** 29B–29D, 31B–31D; **Unit 4:** 102E–102H; **Unit 5:** 113A–113B, 133A–133B; **Unit 6:** 159A–159B, 165A–165B

/d/, **Unit 1:** 4E–4H, 19B–19D; **Unit 4:** 70G–70J; **Unit 5:** 108G–108J

/e/, **Unit 1:** 8E–8H, 19B–19D; **Unit 4:** 101B–101D; **Unit 5:** 124E–124H; **Unit 6:** 171A–171B

/ē/, **Unit 2:** 22G–22J, 31B–31D, 35B–35D, 41B–41D; **Unit 5:** 108G–108J, 133A–133B; **Unit 6:** 166C–166F

/er/, **Unit 1:** 17B–17D, 18E–18H, 19B–19D; **Unit 4:** 75B–75D, 101B–101D; **Unit 5:** 114E–114H, 127A–127B; **Unit 6:** 160C–160F

/f/, **Unit 1:** 7B–7D, 19B–19D; **Unit 2:** 26E–26H, 31B–31D, 41B–41D; **Unit 4:** 90E–90H, 96E–96H

/g/, **Unit 1:** 8E–8H, 19B–19D; **Unit 4:** 70G–70J; **Unit 5:** 127A–127B; **Unit 6:** 154C–154F

/h/, **Unit 1:** 2G–2J, 3B–3D, 19B–19D; **Unit 5:** 128E–128H

/hw/, **Unit 2:** 22G–22J, 31B–31D; **Unit 4:** 75B–75D; **Unit 6:** 153A–153B

/i/, **Unit 1:** 3B–3D, 19B–19D; **Unit 6:** 153A–153B

/ī/, **Unit 2:** 22G–22J, 31B–31D, 36E–36H, 41B–41D; **Unit 4:** 90E-90H, 96E–96H; **Unit 6:** 146C–146F, 154C–154F

-ion, -tion, **Unit 3:** 44G–44J, 57B–57D

/j/, **Unit 1:** 8E–8H, 13B–13D, 14E–14H, 19B–19D; **Unit 4:** 82E–82H, 105B–105D; **Unit 5:** 124E–124H, 134E–134H; **Unit 6:** 177A–177B

/k/, **Unit 1:** 7B–7D, 12E–12H, 19B–19D; **Unit 4:** 81B–81D, 82E–82H; **Unit 5:** 118E–118H; **Unit 6:** 146C–146F, 160C–160F

/ks/, **Unit 1:** 11B–11D, 19B–19D; **Unit 6:** 145A–145B

/kw/, **Unit 1:** 14E–14H, 19B–19D; **Unit 4:** 90E–90H; **Unit 6:** 154C–154F

/l/, **Unit 1:** 7B–7D, 19B–19D; **Unit 4:** 89B–89D

/m/, **Unit 1:** 4E–4H, 19B–19D; **Unit 5:** 123B–123B; **Unit 6:** 146C–146F

/n/, **Unit 1:** 4E–4H, 19B–19D; **Unit 2:** 30E–30H, 41B–41D **Unit 5:** 123A–123B; **Unit 6:** 166C–166F

/ng/, **Unit 2:** 25B–25D; **Unit 5:** 108G–108J, 133A–133B

/o/, **Unit 1:** 11B–11D, 19B–19D

/ō/, **Unit 2:** 25B–25D, 31B–31D, 37B–37D, 41B–41D; **Unit 4:** 70G–70J; **Unit 5:** 118E–118H; **Unit 6:** 165A–165B

/oi/, **Unit 3:** 60E–60H, 67B–67D; **Unit 5:** 117A–118B

/o͞o/, **Unit 3:** 48E–48H, 51B–51D, 57B–57D, 64E–64H; **Unit 4:** 105B–105D; **Unit 5:** 128E–128H; **Unit 6:** 159A–159B, 160C–160F

/o͝o/, **Unit 3:** 47B–47D, 57B–57D, 64E–64H; **Unit 5:** 113A–113B; **Unit 6:** 140E–140H

/or/, **Unit 1:** 17B–17D, 19B–19D; **Unit 4:** 96E–96H; **Unit 6:** 154C–154F

/ow/, **Unit 3:** 52E–52H, 57B–57D, 64E–64H, **Unit 4:** 95B–95D; **Unit 5:** 123A–123B; **Unit 6:** 145A–145B, 165A–165B

/p/, **Unit 1:** 2G–2J, 3B–3D, 19B–19D; **Unit 5:** 118E–118H

/r/, **Unit 1:** 8E–8H, 19B–19D; **Unit 2:** 30E–30H; **Unit 5:** 124E–124H; **Unit 6:** 146C–146F

/s/, **Unit 1:** 2G–2J, 3B–3D, 12E–12H, 19B–19D; **Unit 4:** 75B–75D; **Unit 5:** 128E–128H, 134E–134H

/sh/, **Unit 2:** 26E–26H, 31B–31D; **Unit 4:** 89B–89D; **Unit 6:** 153A–153B, 172C–172F

/t/, **Unit 1:** 2G–2J, 3B–3D, 19B–19D; **Unit 4:** 95B–95D

/th/, **Unit 2:** 26E–26H, 31B–31D; **Unit 5:** 113A–113B; **Unit 6:** 145A–145B, 177A–177B

-tion, -ion, **Unit 3:** 44G–44J, 57B–57D

/u/, **Unit 1:** 14E–14H, 19B–19D; **Unit 5:** 134E–134H

/ū/, **Unit 2:** 25B–25D, 31B–31D, 38E–38H, 41B–41D; **Unit 4:** 102E–102H; **Unit 5:** 114E–114H

/v/, **Unit 1:** 11B–11D, 19B–19D; **Unit 4:** 81B–81D; **Unit 6:** 166C–166F

/w/, **Unit 1:** 8E–8H, 19B–19D; **Unit 5:** 127A–127B

/y/, **Unit 1:** 11B–11D, 19B–19D; **Unit 5:** 117A–117B

/z/, **Unit 1:** 4E–4H, 11B–11D, 19B–19D; **Unit 4:** 95B–95D, 102E–102H; **Unit 6:** 140E–140H, 177A–177B

Phonics—Blending: Set 1, *see* Blending Exercise, Phonics

Phonics—Blending: Set 2, *see* Blending Exercise, Phonics

Predicting, Unit 1: 4J, 4, 6; **Unit 2:** 26J, 26, 28, 30J, 30, 36J, 36; **Unit 4:** 82J, 84, 86, 88; **Unit 5:** 134J, 134, 136; **Unit 6:** 172H, 174, 176

Prefixes

bi-, **Unit 3:** 60, 64

dec-, **Unit 3:** 60, 64

dis-, **Unit 3:** 48, 64; **Unit 6:** 142

il-, **Unit 3:** 58, 64; **Unit 6:** 158

mis-, **Unit 3:** 58, 64; **Unit 6:** 158

multi-, **Unit 3:** 60, 64

poly-, **Unit 3:** 60, 64

pre-, **Unit 3:** 54, 64; **Unit 6:** 150

re-, **Unit 3:** 44, 64; **Unit 6:** 142

tri-, **Unit 3:** 60, 64

un-, **Unit 3:** 54, 64; **Unit 6:** 150

Preview and Prepare, Unit 1: 2L, 4J, 8J, 12J, 14J, 18J; **Unit 2:** 22L, 26J, 30J, 32J, 36J, 38J; **Unit 3:** 44L, 48J, 52J, 58J, 60J, 64J; **Unit 4:** 70L, 76J, 82J, 90J, 96J, 102J; **Unit 5:** 108L, 114J, 118J, 124J, 128J, 134J; **Unit 6:** 140J, 146H, 154H, 160H, 166H, 172H

R

Read Aloud, Unit 1: 2L, 4J, 8J, 12J, 14J, 18J; **Unit 2:** 22L, 26J, 30J, 32J, 36J, 38J; **Unit 3:** 44L, 48J, 52J, 58J, 60J, 64J

Reading Reflections, Unit 1: 19E, 20–21; **Unit 2:** 41E, 42–43; **Unit 3:** 67E, 68–69; **Unit 4:** 105E, 106–107; **Unit 5:** 137C, 138–139; **Unit 6:** 177C, 178–179

Reality and Fantasy, Unit 1: 9, 11, 11E; **Unit 2:** 27, 29, 29E; **Unit 5:** 115, 117, 117C

Rereading the Selection, Unit 1: 3E, 7E, 11E, 13E, 17E, 19E; **Unit 2:** 25E, 29E, 31E, 35E, 37E, 41E; **Unit 3:** 47E, 51E, 57E, 59E, 63E, 67E; **Unit 4:** 75E, 81E, 89E, 95E, 101E, 105E; **Unit 5:** 113C, 117C, 123C, 127C, 133C, 137C; **Unit 6:** 145C, 153C, 159C, 165C, 171C, 177C

S

Segmentation

Clapping Syllables in Names, **Unit 1:** 3A, 7A

Initial Blends, **Unit 4:** 95A, 101A, 105A

Initial Consonant Sounds, **Unit 2:** 31A, 37A, 41A

Repeating Final Consonants, **Unit 3:** 67A; **Unit 4:** 75A, 81A

Repeating Word Parts, **Unit 1:** 13A, 17A

Restoring Final Consonants, **Unit 3:** 47A, 51A, 57A, 59A

Restoring Initial Phonemes, **Unit 1:** 19A; **Unit 2:** 25A

Selections

Aloha! Hello and Good-bye, **Unit 6:** 166–171

Ann, **Unit 5:** 128–133

Benny's Flag, **Unit 6:** 140–145

A Bike Race, **Unit 5:** 134–137

Colors That Hide, **Unit 3:** 52–57

An Elephant Story, **Unit 1:** 8–11

The Fall, **Unit 5:** 118–123

From Rocks to Books, **Unit 1:** 2–3

A Grand Fourth, **Unit 6:** 172–177

Helen Keller: A Woman of Courage, **Unit 5:** 124–127

Helping Others, **Unit 2:** 30–31

Hide-and-Seek Animals, **Unit 3:** 64–67

How Do Seeds Travel?, **Unit 4:** 90–95

How Do You Read Rings?, **Unit 4:** 102–105

Insects Stay Safe, **Unit 3:** 60–63

Keeping Secrets, **Unit 1:** 12–13

Appendix